The History Of
Marine Corps Recruit Depot
San Diego

Marine Corps Recruit Depot
Museum Historical Society
and
Meredith R. Vezina

Published by:
MCRD Museum Historical Society
&
Heritage Press & Productions
Escondido, California

© 1997
MCRD Museum Historical Society
All Rights Reserved

Acknowledgements

Ellen B. Holzman, journalist, designed this book, wrote the chapters on the MCRD Command Museum and Historical Society, and on the base commanders, and was the first in a long line of editors.

Dr. John Hancock, professor of urban design and planning at the University of Washington, unselfishly provided expertise and resources from his research for his unpublished book on the Marine Corps Recruit Depot, San Diego.

Allan J. Rappoport, former District Director, U.S. Customs and member of the MCRD Museum Historical Society Board, provided wise direction and counsel in the contractual and financial arrangements for this book.

Victor H. Krulak, Jr., executive director of the MCRD Museum Historical Society, provided expert knowledge on the Marine Corps, the Depot, and in editing.

The following also contributed substantially to this book: San Diego military historian James W. Hinds, Maj. Gen. Marc Moore, USMC (Ret.), and Maj. Jack Buck, USMC (Ret.).

Many active duty Marines and civilian employees at the Depot were generous with their time in chasing down resource material, including:

Chief of Staff Col. James M. Guerin and his staff; Capt. Brendan Cook, operations officer for the assistant chief of staff G-3; Public Affairs Officer Maj. Katie Haddock and her staff, particularly Lt. Cliff Gilmore, and Staff Sgt. Charlotte Crouch; Maj. Stan Packard, director of the Drill Instructor School; Lt. Col. Bob Foley, director of the Recruiters School; Personnel from the Training And Audio Visual Support Center; Sharon Smith, supervisory general engineer, Facilities Division, Public Works Branch; Mary Guerin, assistant to the executive director of the MCRD Museum Historical Society; and Ellen Guillemette, archivist for the MCRD Command Museum.

The Historical Division, Headquarters, Marine Corps, Washington, D.C., also provided research time and material.

ISBN 0-9657139-0-3

About The Authors

The Marine Corps Recruit Depot Museum Historical Society and Meredith R. Vezina are the authors of this book commemorating the 75th anniversary of the continuing U.S. Marine Corps presence in San Diego.

MCRD Museum Historical Society's primary purpose is to provide material and personnel support to the MCRD Command Museum. The mission of the Command Museum is to serve as a recruiting and training facility for MCRD by establishing exhibits that dramatize the past, present and future roles of the Marine Corps to Marine recruits, their families and the general public. The Historical Society also seeks, through public education programs, to promote personal responsibility, self-discipline, patriotism and attention to duty. The Society places special emphasis on the motivation of young people.

Meredith R. Vezina has a MA and a BA in history from San Diego State University. She has taught history and writing at San Diego City College and San Diego State University. Her articles on military history have been published in national magazines and newspapers. Since May 1994, she has been the owner and publisher of *Traditions: San Diego's Military Heritage* magazine. In January 1996, she produced a one hour documentary video on the history of MCRD, San Diego. Her 1997 video project documented Steel Knight, the annual Marine Corps live fire exercise at Marine Corps Air and Ground Combat Base at Twenty-nine Palms, Calif.

The majority of photographs contained in this book are official U.S. Marine Corps photographs.
Some photographs were contributed by: Traditions Magazine; the San Diego Hall of Champions; Maj. Jack Buck, USMC, Ret; and Maj. Gen. Marc Moore, USMC, Ret.
The photograph of the MCRD Museum Historical Society Board of Directors was taken by Photography by Aldo of Spring Valley, Calif. The photograph of Commandant, Gen. Charles C. Krulak on the back cover was taken by Marine LCpl. Brian D. Hafenstiner. The opening photograph for Chapter 13, The Crucible, was taken by Cpl. Jason Collier.

Copyright © 1997
Marine Corps Recruit Depot
Museum Historical Society

No part of this publication may be reproduced or transmitted by any means without the written consent of the Historical Society.

10 Aug 1996

      Since 1775 the Marine Corps has done two things for this nation. It has won battles and it has made Marines. The Corps' reputation for winning battles is legendary and for the past seventy-five years the Recruit Depot in San Diego has been making Marines that won those battles. Over a million men have been forged in the crucible of recruit training here. From the "Banana Wars" in the twenties and thirties to Desert Storm, the Marines made here have fought in every clime and place -- their exploits recorded in our history books -- the stuff of legend.

      A transformation begins when young Americans accept the challenge of becoming United States Marines. After they arrive at Marine Corps Recruit Depot, San Diego and they place their feet on those yellow footprints, from that day forward their lives are irrevocably changed. After 12 weeks of the toughest training in the world, the transformation is complete. These young Americans are now Marines, and with the title they join one of the most elite and respected fighting organizations known to man, the United States Marine Corps. The Marine Corps Recruit Depot, San Diego is where this transformation takes place, and this book tells its story.

      Marines created here have not only gone out and fought and won our country's battles, they have also served their communities. Whether after one enlistment or a long career, these Marines have returned to their communities to become national assets, instilled with values such as honor, courage and commitment. Armed with these values these Marines have served as role models for our future generations. Once a Marine, always a Marine. Semper Fidelis -- always faithful -- is not just a slogan, it is a way of life for all those transformed at this recruit depot.

Semper Fidelis,

C. C. KRULAK
General, U.S. Marine Corps
Commandant of the Marine Corps

Contents

Acknowledgements
Preface

Chapter 1
San Diego's Own — 1

Chapter 2
From The Ground Up — 13

Chapter 3
**The Old Corps: Marine Expeditionary Force
To Fleet Marine Force** — 25

Chapter 4
World War II — 41

Chapter 5
The New Corps: Korea, Vietnam and Beyond — 51

Chapter 6
Making Marines — 71

Chapter 7
Riflemen All — 82

Chapter 8
The Drill Instructor — 97

Chapter 9
The Schools — 106

Chapter 10
Sports Legends — 123

Chapter 11
Base Commanders — 136

Chapter 12
Preserving History: The MCRD Command Museum — 150

Chapter 13
The Crucible — 157

Epilog
The Tradition Continues — 162

Corporate Sponsors, Patrons and Sponsors — 166

Index — 170

Selected Bibliography — 172

San Diego's Own

As Brig. Gen. Joseph H. Pendleton raised Old Glory for the first time on Dec. 1, 1921, at Marine Corps Base, San Diego, he might have been recalling less auspicious beginnings. Six years earlier as a colonel, he had commanded the 4th Marine

In March 1911, Col. Charles Doyen brought the 4th Provisional Marine Regiment to North Island, San Diego, establishing Camp Thomas, which was praised for its efficiency and sanitation.

Regiment at a small wind-swept base of operations called Camp Howard. Not much more than a glorified bivouac on North Island in San Diego Bay, Camp Howard operated for a mere six months. Nevertheless, it served as an important footnote on the way to the establishment of a permanent Marine Corps Base, which evolved into Marine Corps Recruit Depot, San Diego.

But even Col. Pendleton's Marines were not breaking entirely new ground when they secured their North Island site.

Camp Howard was built on the same location as that of an earlier base established by the 4th Provisional Marine Regiment on March 20, 1911. Even more short-lived than Camp Howard, Camp Thomas is also important because it marks the beginning of an enduring relationship between the Corps and the City of San Diego.

And what about the regiment that came and left, and then came again? Under the skillful command of "Uncle Joe" Pendleton, the 4th Marines won the admiration of the local population, and eventually earned the unofficial title of "San Diego's own."

It was trouble with Mexico that brought them to San Diego in 1911. Not since the end of the Mexican-American War in 1848 had the Marines been in the region in such force. In 1900, a revolution plunged Mexico into a civil war that engulfed the entire country. This established the dictatorship of Porfirio Diaz, who cultivated American investments in Mexico's railroads and heavy industry. The dictator's hold on the country ended when President William Howard Taft, viewing Diaz as a threat to American economic interests in Mexico, dispatched Army and Marine Corps units to the border as a show of strength.

On the East Coast, the 1st Provisional Marine Brigade held training exercises at Guantanamo Bay, Cuba. Out West, a provisional regiment began to assemble at the Navy Yard at Mare Island, in the San Francisco Bay Area.

On March 6, 1911, the Commandant, Maj. Gen. William P. Biddle, received the Navy Department order to activate the regiment. The following day, Marine Headquarters relayed the orders to all posts and stations on the West Coast.

Col. Charles A. Doyen, in command of Marine Barracks, Puget Sound Navy Yard, was ordered to report immediately to San Francisco to assume command of the regiment. In the company of four officers and 215 enlisted men slated for the new regiment, Col. Doyen boarded a Seattle train bound for San Francisco.

At Mare Island, the rest of the regiment was forming — eight officers and 244 enlisted men. These Marines boarded the naval transport USS *Buffalo* on March 9. Equipped with three months rations, they also stowed on board two of the Corps' latest weapons: Colt heavy machine guns and Springfield Model 1903 rifles, issued to West Coast Marines for the first time.

On March 10, *Buffalo* stopped at Vallejo Junction to embark the Marines arriving from Puget Sound, and then she steamed out the Golden Gate bound for San Diego.

Reaching San Diego Bay two days later, the Marines immediately transferred aboard five armored cruisers — *California*, *Maryland*, *Pennsylvania*, *South Dakota* and *West Virginia* — in anticipation of making a dash for Mexico. But no orders came; and after a week aboard the fighting ships, the men disembarked on March 20, 1911, to bivouac on North Island.

The Marines cleared the sagebrush from their encampment, named in honor of Rear Adm. Chauncey Thomas, who was then the Commander in Chief of the Pacific Fleet. They immediately transformed it into what on March 20 *The San Diego Union* newspaper called a model of efficiency: "If one would search the entire country it would be impossible to find a camp which compares with that of the Marines with regards to sanitary arrangement and sanitary conditions." One month later, on April 20, the unit was officially designated the 4th Provisional Regiment, U.S. Marines.

For nearly three months, the 4th Marine Regiment occupied North Island, spending all its time training. Close order drill and marches under full pack were a daily routine. Lt. Holland M. Smith, who would gain fame during World War II as Lt. Gen. "Howling Mad" Smith, was given the task of overseeing the construction of a rifle range on the island.

Col. Doyen was determined to take advantage of the North Island stay to train what he called "the mob" into an efficient fighting unit. In many ways, the training paid off. Organized into two battalions of two rifle companies each, the men received high marks from Adm. Thomas. After inspecting the North Island Marines on May 5, he wrote to the Commandant, "The discipline of the force, and their steadiness and perfection in drill merits the highest praise."

But the glowing report failed to address a growing morale problem in the regiment. By the end of May, accounts of numerous desertions were reaching Washington. Col. Rufus H. Lane, the assistant Adjutant and Inspector, came out to investigate. When he arrived at Camp Thomas on June 1, he found the regiment listed 90 deserters, approximately 20 percent of the regiment. Most of the missing Marines, disillusioned with the rigors of

Col. Joseph H. Pendleton, below, shipped out with the re-established 4th Provisional Marine Regiment bound for Mexico aboard several ships, including the collier *Jupiter*, above. Later, *Jupiter* would become the United States' first aircraft carrier, *Langley*. The regiment pitched tents at Camp Howard, bottom, on July 14, 1914, on North Island.

Maj. Gen. George Barnett, left, was convinced Mare Island Naval Station in Vallejo, Calif., below, was a far superior site to one in San Diego for a West Coast Marine base.

life at Camp Thomas, were young recruits with less than three months in the Corps.

Little action was taken to solve the regiment's problem because the Mexican Revolution ended on May 25 with the resignation of Diaz, and the regiment was ordered to disband. One month later, part of the 4th Marine Regiment was disbanded and by the end of July, the remaining officers and men at Camp Thomas returned to their previous stations.

But the incidents of desertion at Camp Thomas were not forgotten. The Marine Corps, as always, learned from adversity. It addressed the problems of young, inexperienced recruits later that year by instituting the recruit depot system for the basic training of all Marines.

A few years later, new trouble on the border brought the Marines back to San Diego.

Peace in Mexico was short-lived. Francisco Madero was unable to deliver the reforms he promised. On February 19, 1913, Madero was forced to resign by Mexican Gen. Victoriano Huerta, who placed himself at the head of a conservative counter-revolutionary government. U.S.-Mexican relations became strained when, on April 9, 1914, Mexico seized the American ship, USS *Dolphin*. The officers and crew were released unharmed, but Gen. Huerta failed to make the formal apology demanded by the United States. President Woodrow Wilson countered with a show of force by ordering a concentration of ships and Marines off both coasts of Mexico.

At Puget Sound and Mare Island, Marines prepared for "temporary foreign tropical shore service beyond the seas."

Col. Joseph H. Pendleton, commanding officer of Marine Barracks, Navy Yard, Puget Sound, was ordered to Mare Island to organize the 4th Marines. On April 18, the 25th, 26th, and 27th Companies left Puget Sound aboard the armored cruiser USS *South Dakota* to link up at Mare Island with the 31st, 32nd, 34th, and 35th Companies. While the 31st and 32nd Companies joined the Marines from Puget Sound aboard the USS *South Dakota*, the 34th and 35th Companies were assigned to the collier USS *Jupiter*, which had also taken on a full load of coal, artillery, small arms ammunition, and supplies.

The 4th Marines left San Francisco aboard the two ships on April 21 with orders to proceed immediately to Mazatlan and stand ready to invade Mexico's West Coast. En route, USS *South Dakota* was directed to proceed "with all possible speed" more than 300 miles further south to Acapulco. As *South Dakota* entered Acapulco's gleaming harbor on April 28, the Marines prepared for what they thought would be a march overland toward Mexico City.

Instead, during the next two weeks, "San Diego's Own" passed the time fishing, swimming, and enjoying fresh vegetables and fruits that were brought to the ship by enterprising Mexicans.

On May 14, the regiment was ordered to Mazatlan, where it was reinforced by the 28th and 36th Companies arriving aboard *West Virginia*. For two months the ships anchored at several Mexican ports without incident. On June 25, tension relaxed when the United States and Mexico, meeting at Niagara Falls, N.Y., agreed to settle their differences peacefully. The 4th Marines were ordered home. At La Paz, the two companies on board *Jupiter* transferred to the cruisers. On July 5, *South Dakota* arrived in San Diego. Two days later, *West Virginia* arrived, and on July 10 the 4th Marines went into camp once again on North Island.

A San Diego company lent the Marines a mule-drawn mowing machine to clear the area. The men pitched tents, dug latrines, laid a camp road, and secured the southwest end of the island for a rifle range. The camp was named in honor of Rear Adm. Thomas Benton Howard, Commander of the Pacific Fleet.

The Marines initially built bonfires to light up the camp at night, and a barge anchored near the camp provided the men with fresh water. During the ensuing weeks, electric lights were installed and water was piped in, giving the camp some appearance of garrison life.

On July 31, 1914, the regiment's strength was 19 officers and 874 enlisted men, and consisted of two infantry battalions, a light field artillery company, and a small regimental headquarters. Each infantry battalion included three rifle companies. Attached to regimental headquarters was a machine gun company. The regiment also had four three-inch naval landing guns, which the gun-crews had to pull across the beach with long ropes into firing position. Called "manning the drag," the operation was onerous.

Although the regiment was small — approximately one third of present-day strength — the fact that it was still together was unprecedented. The normal procedure would have been to disband the regiment, but San Diego was under consideration as a Marine Corps advance base station on the West Coast. This concept gained momentum in April 1914, when Assistant Secretary of the Navy Franklin D. Roosevelt came to San Diego on a fact-finding trip. He was so impressed with the area that he recommended San Diego as a possible site. But not everyone agreed.

Marine Corps Commandant, Maj. Gen. George Barnett, argued that San Diego had only one thing going for it — the weather.

During hearings in Washington before the House Naval Affairs Committee on Dec. 7, 1914, Gen. Barnett argued vehemently against stationing the Marines permanently in San Diego. "We must have a place near the center of the recruiting district (in San Francisco) because it would cost too much money to send the recruits down there (to San Diego) and bring them back when we want them." Gen. Barnett made sense, reasoning that the base would have to be started from scratch and he posed the obvious question: Why spend the money to build a new base when the recruiting district for the West Coast and major naval bases were already in San Francisco?

But conventional wisdom ran counter to the vision of two persuasive and steadfast allies: Congressmen William Kettner and Col. Pendleton.

Soon after he was elected to office in 1912, Kettner began the work that would earn him the title "the father of San Diego's Navy." During his first two-year term, Kettner secured $249,000 in federal funds to deepen San

Diego's harbor, $95,000 for the completion of a coal wharf and fuel oil station on the east side of Point Loma, and $300,000 for a Navy radio station.

According to Kettner, Col. Pendleton first approached the congressman in spring 1915 to make a case for a permanent Marine advance base on North Island. "This sounded rather amusing," wrote Kettner, "but I listened at-

Congressman William Kettner, top, had his own ideas about where to locate a Marine Corps Base in San Diego — Dutch Flats, shown above on Jan. 24, 1919.

In 1915 before a Brazilian display at San Diego's Panama-California Exposition are from left: a Marine orderly; George Burnham; banker G. Aubrey Davidson; Dr. Eugenio Dahne, who donated his collection for the exhibit; President Theodore Roosevelt; unknown person; Marine Capt. Charles Lyman; Exposition Director-General David C. Collier; and Col. Pendleton.

tentively to what he had to say and even took up the question of location with him." Kettner preferred an area known as Dutch Flats, which was nothing more than a low-lying tidal marsh that was covered with water at high tide. But Kettner had a clear view of the flats from his house on Horton's Hill. His dream — transform it into a beautiful place.

Wrote Kettner, "We discussed this question for some two or three weeks, and the General finally agreed that, if I were to take the matter up in Washington, he would support me and he surely did."

Col. Pendleton had already been spreading the gospel in San Diego. Taking keen interest in civic affairs, he became a regular speaker at luncheons held throughout the city. On Sept. 16, 1914, he spoke at a banquet celebrating the launching two weeks earlier of armored cruiser No. 6, USS *San Diego* (previously named *California*). The colonel's agenda: enlighten the guests on the merits of building a Marine advance base in San Diego.

In an effort to win the hearts and minds of San Diegans,

he held open house at Camp Howard twice a week. He paraded the entire regiment accompanied by the band, and drum and bugle corps. The parades became so popular that a boat service was started to ferry visitors across the harbor. All the colorful pageantry inspired chief trumpeter George V. Rowbottom, leader of the drum and bugle corps, to compose a special march entitled "Hail Sunny California." The piece was finished in time for the Panama-California Exposition, which opened in Balboa Park at midnight Jan. 1, 1915.

The 4th Marine Regiment was assigned to exposition duty on Dec. 10, 1914.

Split in two, the 1st Battalion was ordered to the exposition in San Francisco, and the 2nd Battalion was stationed at the San Diego exposition in a model Marine Corps camp. Col. Pendleton and his staff also moved to Balboa Park, setting up his regimental headquarters at the exposition's Science and Education Building.

Because it had been consigned to caretaker status, Camp Howard rated just two corporals and 27 privates. They manned the rifle range, where Marines from Balboa Park and sailors from San Diego-based ships periodically came for rifle practice.

The Marines' exposition duties included the usual drills and inspections. In addition, the band gave concerts at the Spreckels music pavilion, and the Marines battled civilian teams on the baseball diamond.

One important by-product of exposition duty was the introduction of the first mechanical artillery movers. Capt. Ellis B. Miller, in command of the 25th Company, borrowed a track-laying tractor from one of the industrial exhibitors. His men successfully employed the tractor to tow their 3-inch naval landing guns, proving the superiority of machines over Marines in "manning the drag."

With the Marines seemingly entrenched at the exposition, San Diego's boosters, with help from Col. Pendleton, made sure Kettner understood their high priority on getting the 4th Marine Regiment permanently stationed in San Diego. On Jan. 7, 1915, the Balboa Park Board of Park Commissioners sent a letter to Kettner in Washington.

"As you know we are very anxious to have a regiment each of Cavalry and Marines permanently stationed in San Diego," the board wrote. "And in order to encourage the Army and Navy Department to do this, we have offered them the use of their present locations (in Balboa Park) for a period of five years free of charge."

But after only six months on exposition duty, the bulk of the regiment was called on again to respond to trouble in Mexico. This time, it was to protect American citizens and property from marauding bands of Yaqui Indians. Aboard the cruiser USS *Colorado*, the Marines arrived in the Mexican port of Guaymas on June 20, 1915, to find the situation defused. The regiment returned to exposition duty in August only to be called back to Mexican waters in November to protect American interests once again.

Meanwhile, a culmination of political pressure and economic carrots cajoled a reluctant Gen. Barnett to visit San Diego in the summer of 1915 to consider the possibility of an advance base. According to Kettner, Col. Pendleton's unabashed enthusiasm along with his "persuasive powers" induced Gen. Barnett to write in his report to Congress on Aug. 26, 1915:

Marines provided security along the route of the 1915 Point Loma Road Race. The race committee requested 200 Marines be assigned to the event. Col. Pendleton agreed, provided the committee took care of transportation to the guard points and instructed the Marines on their duties during the race. The opportunity for the Marines to participate in a civic event undoubtedly helped the colonel's lobbying efforts to establish a permanent base in San Diego.

To: Maj. John Marston, U.S.M.C.
Commanding Marine Detachment,
American Legation,
Managua, Nicaragua
From: Headquarters Fifth Brigade
San Diego, California
January 12, 1923

My dear Major:
The monkey, Charley, which the Marines of your command have presented to the zoo at San Diego was received in fine shape, and promptly presented to the management of the zoo, who very much appreciated him, and he is a general favorite. ... I can assure you that your interest in our institution is very much appreciated by the good citizens of San Diego, and I thank you very much for your kindness and promptness.
With my very best regards,
Sincerely yours,
Joseph H. Pendleton
Brigadier General, U.S.M.C.

Above is one of a series of letters from and to Gen. Pendleton regarding animals provided by Marston and others to the San Diego Zoological Society.
On July 28, 1923, Maj. Marston wrote to Gen. Pendleton that he had persuaded a Nicaraguan general to provide specimens of every variety of animal on his properties for the zoo.
On Aug. 12, 1923, the society's T.N. Faulconer wrote to Gen. Pendleton, praising Maj. Marston's efforts and noting that almost every section of the zoo now had birds, animals or reptiles that had been donated by the Marines stationed in Nicaragua.

Above, Balboa Park is a parade and staging ground for Marines during and after the 1915 Panama-California Exposition. Below and right, the 4th Marines occupied a model camp during the two-year exposition. The exposition also proved to be an excellent site for showing the Marines to good advantage to visiting congressmen.

Headquarters U.S. Marine Corps
Commandant's Office
Washington
January 11, 1916

My dear Mr. Kettner:
Your note has just reached me, with which you enclose a snapshot picture taken at San Diego, which is a very nice souvenir of our wonderful visit there, where you all did so much to make our stay pleasant.

I know you will be interested to hear that a plan of keeping the Fourth Regiment at San Diego after their return from the west coast of Mexico has been approved, and the necessary orders have been issued. I hope that it has been so fixed that it will be possible for the officers to get commutation of quarters, for, as I told you before, I could conscientiously only approve of the scheme if that were possible. I hope this is only the beginning, and that the future will see necessary and proper arrangements made there for housing and quartering the officers and men.

I have written this information to Colonel Pendleton, and hope you will communicate it to your friends in San Diego. It is impossible, of course, to tell when the regiment will return from southern Mexico, but I hope it will be in the near future, as things on that coast seem to be quieting down.

Mrs. Barnett has been quite ill lately, and is still confined to the bed with a nurse, having had the grippe, and being threatened with pneumonia, which danger has now passed, I think.

With kindest regards and best wishes for you and Mrs. Kettner.

Very sincerely yours,
George Barnett

The 4th Marines march west on the Cabrillo Bridge, leaving Balboa Park in 1915.

"Climatic conditions in San Diego are particularly suitable for an advance base or expeditionary regiment or brigade to work outdoors the year round." The general concluded by stating, "San Diego, being the southern most harbor in the United States on the Pacific Coast, is particularly well suited for such a post."

In the fall of 1915, San Diegans voted overwhelmingly — 40,288 to 305 — to transfer 500 acres of tide lands to the Navy. On Jan. 5, 1916, Kettner authored a bill to provide $250,000 for the purchase of . Two weeks later, the commissioners updated Kettner on their proposal to keep the Marines in Balboa Park after the exposition ended: "I am glad to inform you that we are already completing arrangements with the Marines, and the contract is in their hands for signature."

Kettner continued his work in Washington. By the time the bill came up for an important hearing in March, Kettner had managed to get 107 senators and congressmen to visit San Diego. He enlisted William Stephens, who would become California's governor in 1917, to help lobby congressional committee members, along with D.C. Collier (former director-general of the Panama-California Exposition Co.), George Burnham (a San Diego developer) and Sen. Warren G. Harding. Together, they won over 19 of the 21 congressmen on the Naval Affairs Committee.

That was apparently enough to sway the Secretary of the Navy, Josephus Daniels, and Rear Adm. Frederic R. Harris, chief of the Bureau of Yards and Docks. Testifying before the Committee on Naval Affairs, Daniels said, "It would be a very desirable piece of property for the Navy to own, because we ought to have a Marine base at San Diego."

On Feb. 3, Col. Pendleton, who had returned to San Diego, relieved Maj. William McKelvy as the commanding officer at Balboa Park. On Feb. 18, the entire regiment was reunited in San Diego. During the preceding two years, the regiment made three cruises into Mexican waters, and had nothing to show for it but a commendation for speedy embarkation. But the forays off the coast of Mexico provided Kettner with persuasive ammunition, and he capitalized on the strategic significance of San Diego as a base for launching expeditions to Mexico and

Latin America.

On March 31, 1916, *The San Diego Union* described a crucial hearing for Kettner's bill: "Mr. Kettner began by explaining the need of a base 'necessary near the territory (Mexico and South America) where there is possibility of trouble'... . He further showed that 'the Navy Department has recognized San Diego as a strategical base' as evidenced by the fact that since trouble has been pending in Mexico a force of Marines has been kept in tents at points in and near San Diego and several times has been sent to points of disturbance along the western coast of Mexico."

Lt. Ernest Swanson, left, presents San Diego Securities Co. President George Burnham with a check to buy Dutch Flats and adjoining tide lands in 1917.

The newspaper noted that if Kettner's bill were approved, it would add a payroll of up to 2,000 to the city's economy. "It would also mean improvements that would render very sightly a part of the bay front that is not at present especially attractive."

On June 16, the 4th Marine Regiment was ordered to Santo Domingo to help the Navy cope with a revolution, leaving three officers and 50 enlisted men behind in San Diego. Although the 4th would get an opportunity to test its mettle in the tropics, Col. Pendleton would not be in San Diego for the final assault to secure a permanent base.

Nearly a year to the day after Gen. Barnett changed his testimony in favor of the San Diego Marine base, Kettner's bill passed and its provisions were incorporated into the 1916 Naval Appropriations Act.

The city of San Diego deeded 500 acres of tidal land to the government on Dec. 1, and six months later, on May 15, 1917, the front page of *The San Diego Union* trumpeted: "Money for site of Marine post provided by Uncle Sam. $250,000 set aside to be paid San Diego concern for 232 acres abutting on Dutch Flats; land will be improved with building for sea soldiers; deal near close."

Navy spokesman Lt. Ernest Swanson told the newspaper that as soon as all formalities were cleared, "It will not be necessary to take this matter up any more with Washington. As soon as everything is ready I will send word to the Army engineer in charge of the Southern California district that he can start dredging operations at once." The newspaper reported that $225,000 had been appropriated by Congress for dredging at Dutch Flats.

"From that time on," Lt. Swanson said, "I expect that things will move rapidly."

The government issued a check for Dutch Flats on June 15, 1917.

Even so, the lieutenant's prediction of fast action was premature. Construction did not begin for another two years. The initial reclamation work alone took a year and World War I delayed further advancements.

Throughout this period, the Marines remained in Balboa Park. Since the close of the exposition Jan. 1, 1917, the Marines, under the command of Capt. E.C. Long, requested leases on several of the vacant buildings. These buildings were known by the names of the states and counties that used them during the exposition. The men were tired of living in tents and barracks would surely boost morale.

Initially, the plan ran into problems. In a letter to Capt. Long, the park commission board pointed out that the Kansas building had been sold to the Theosophical Society, the New Mexico Commission wanted to wreck its building for salvage value, and three other buildings the Marines wanted — Alameda, Utah, and Montana — would not come under park control until April.

More important, strict interpretation of state and city law did not allow the park commissioners to grant permanent occupancy of buildings for purposes other than to conserve the landscape or contribute to its use as a park.

Nevertheless, the board stretched the law and offered the Washington, Utah, and Montana buildings to the Marines. The board even offered to buy the Kansas building so the Marines could use it, but the board did not feel it could grant a lease.

On April 9, the commissioners gave the Marines a permit to use Kern-Tulare, along with Alameda County, San Joaquin Valley, and Salt Lake.

On June 25, the board granted permission to make alterations to several buildings. The Utah building became a hospital, the Montana building a supply depot, the Kansas building was revamped for offices, the Alameda building was used as a guard house, the Kern-Tulare and San Joaquin Valley buildings were turned into barracks, and the Salt Lake building — which is now The Museum of Man — became the commanding officer's headquarters.

The park also profited from the relationship. The Marines reroofed and painted several of the buildings and other repairs were done "to conform with the present ar-

11

Highlights of Maj. Gen. Joseph H. Pendleton's career

Joseph Pendleton's San Diego career started when he was a colonel in 1914 with his advocacy for a permanent Marine base. He left San Diego with the 4th Marines for the Dominican Republic in 1916. He returned in October 1919 as a brigadier general and took command of the 2nd Advanced Base Force, overseeing construction of the Marine Base. He was assigned as commanding officer of the 5th Marine Brigade on Oct. 4, 1921, when that organization was established. In December, he raised the flag at the new base. He was promoted to major general on Dec. 10, 1923. He retired June 2, 1924, at the statutory age of 64. But once a Marine, always a Marine. Uncle Joe was at the docks to greet "San Diego's Own," the 4th Marine Regiment, when it returned from the Dominican Republic just two months after his retirement.

While he was on active duty, he also took part in veterans and civic affairs. He joined the local chapter of the United Spanish War Veterans, and in 1920 was commander of the Coronado Camp. In 1923 he served as a special aide de camp to the department commander of the United Spanish War Veterans, and the following year was a special aide de camp to the national commander in chief. He was also a commander of San Diego Post 6 of the American Legion. The general joined the Sons of the American Revolution and served a term as president of the local chapter. After his retirement, he served on the Coronado School Board for 14 years, and spent several years on the City Council. He was mayor of Coronado from 1928 to 1930. He was an honorary member of the San Diego Rotary Club.

It is fitting that his civic activities brought him full circle from his first involvement in San Diego during the 1915 Panama-California Exposition. Two decades later, he served as director of the San Diego Centennial Exposition of 1934-35.

Following are some highlights of "Uncle Joe" Pendleton's career:
- Born June 2, 1860, at Rochester, Pa.
- Graduated July 1882 from U.S. Naval Academy. Served two years as a cadet engineer in the Navy before transferring to the Marine Corps.
- Married in August 1882 to Mary Helen Fay of Annapolis, Md. Daughter, Helen Fay, was born at Annapolis July 26, 1885. Son, Edgar Bache, was born at Sitka, Alaska, on Aug. 2, 1892.
- Commissioned a second lieutenant July 1, 1884.
- Took command in 1891 of the Marine Barracks at Sitka, Alaska.
- Assigned in April 1898 to USS *Yankee* for Cuban blockade at outbreak of Spanish-American War.
- Promoted to captain April 4, 1899, and ordered to the Marine Barracks at Sitka on Oct. 9, staying until March 1904. While there, the Tlingit Alaskan Indian tribe adopted him. The commandant of the Marine Corps gave Maj. Pendleton special recognition in his 1903 Annual Report for the quality of his work.
- Joined the 1st Brigade of Marines in the Philippine Islands May 1904 and took command of the 1st Marine Regiment at Cavite and later the 2nd Marine Regiment at Olongapo.
- Took command as colonel Aug. 23, 1912, of the 1st Provisional Regiment for service in Nicaragua and is credited with assault and capture of Coyotepe, which crushed the revolution and restored peace to Nicaragua. Organized and led a mounted mapping expedition to Matagalpa in the northern district, proving that American units could move peacefully and freely anywhere in the country.
- Organized and commanded in 1914 the reactivated 4th Marines as an expeditionary force headed for Mexico.
- Ordered to the Dominican Republic with the 4th Marine Regiment on June 4, 1916. Placed in command of all naval forces ashore. Issued orders to troops as occupying force to restore peace and order, protect life and property, and support the constituted government. They were not to confiscate property, fire unless fired upon, or do anything to create antagonism among the civilian population. Successfully led troops against hostile fire to capture the capital, Santiago. As Dominican Secretary of War and Navy and Secretary of Interior and Police, disarmed population and set up a national guard to serve as basis for impartial police force. Twice served as military governor.
- Promoted to brigadier general Aug. 29, 1916.
- Awarded the Navy Cross in 1920 for service in the Dominican Republic.
- Oct. 1, 1921 to Nov. 7, 1921, and from May 1922 to September 1922 in command of the Department of the Pacific in San Francisco.
- Promoted to major general Dec. 10, 1923.
- Died Feb. 2, 1942. Camp Pendleton named in his honor Sept. 25, 1942.

---

chitecture."

With the entry of the United States into World War I on April 6, 1917, there was increased interest in preparedness. The Marines wanted to simulate war conditions as "nearly as possible," so the board granted permission on Oct. 30 for the 4th Marine Regiment to dig a "modern military trench" south of the Montana building.

The trench was used to train Marines for fire-communication and cover and "in the instruction of field work as now employed at the Front."

On May 24, 1918, the park commissioners agreed to grant the Marines a long-term lease. By then, however, the handwriting was on the wall. Congress had already appropriated funds for the new Marine Corps Base on Dutch Flats.

On March 2, 1919, the House of Representatives Naval Affairs Committee visited the Marine Barracks at Balboa Park and the site for the new base at . A crowd was on hand to witness the ceremony, marked with numerous speeches by civic leaders and Navy and Marine Corps officers. When Kettner's turn came, the audience applauded the congressman for his efforts to bring the base to San Diego. Rising to the occasion, Kettner said, "This (base) is my baby, and I want it to stand as a monument of my works in Congress for the City of San Diego."

Parts of Chapters 1 and 2 appeared in the December 1996 edition of *Leatherneck* magazine without the authors' consent.

The center of the arcade exemplifies the architecture of Bertram Goodhue, who designed the new base.

From The Ground Up

hree quarters of a century ago, *The San Diego Union* proclaimed Marine Corps Base, San Diego "the finest Marine brigade post in the United

Architect Bertram Goodhue's concept of the base, as seen from the air, conveys a sense of stateliness.

States." Since then, a parade of military and civilian authorities have echoed those words.

When the base officially opened on Dec. 1, 1921, everyone, including visiting dignitaries, marveled at the Spanish colonial-revival architecture, the symmetry of the connecting arcades, the red-tiled stucco roofs and the seemingly endless corridors of cream-colored tinted walls. And the Marine Corps emblem — cast with a five-foot heroic eagle — capped the 1,000-foot arcade that faced the bay from which the base was spawned.

The newest Marine Corps base was an architectural achievement, well worth the $3 million already spent by the Navy.

Despite the lavish praise, the base was far from complete and prospects for finishing the post as originally designed were bleak.

Chief Architect Bertram Goodhue's original 1919 plans called for one of the largest projects ever authorized by the Marine Corps. The proposed project included: a three-story administration building with a tall central clock tower, six two-story barracks to accommodate 1,200 Marines, gymnasium, expeditionary storehouse, power plant, laundry, bakery, officers quarters, guardhouse — 45 permanent Spanish-styled buildings in all.

The buildings would be placed in a horseshoe formation facing the bay and grouped in an area of approximately 50 acres. The remaining 682 acres were reserved for a parade ground, athletic fields and a proposed aviation field.

The estimated cost — $5 million.

World War I delayed full-scale construction. Then the post-war downturn in military expenditures under Presidents Harding, Coolidge and Hoover curtailed the scope of the original plans. Cost overruns of $1.5 million on the first six barracks led the Navy to postpone any construction that was not deemed essential to base operations and to economize whenever possible.

But Gen. Pendleton fought to maintain the integrity of the base as originally designed, waging war against Navy planners who wanted to streamline the layout. He corresponded regularly with Marine Corps authorities in Washington, D.C., and San Francisco for five years, lobbying for additional funds to finance the completion of the base as originally envisioned.

By the time the officers quarters were finished in 1925, expenditures on buildings totaled more than $4 million. Even so, only 60 percent of the original plan was complete. The slow pace of construction was a problem from the beginning. The Marines gained clear title to Dutch Flats on June 15, 1917, but the entry of the United States into World War I two months earlier delayed construction. Dredging in the bay and filling the tidelands continued throughout and after the war. The dredge USS *Oakland* performed most of the work, throwing an estimated 2 million cubic yards of fill behind the dikes by April 1919. Approximately 732 acres of land were reclaimed at a cost of $300,000.

Groundbreaking ceremonies were held March 15, 1919. Congressman Lemuel P. Padgett, head of the Naval Affairs Committee, was allowed the honor of turning the first shovel of dirt, and he passed the shovel to Congressman William Kettner.

The Dawson Construction Company of Washington won the contract over eight other companies to construct the barracks with a low bid of $1,096,156 for six buildings. The first phase of construction called for two-story barracks buildings with concrete foundations and floors. Three of the barracks were classified as type-A, central units that were 319 feet long by 42 feet wide with smaller one-story dormitory and kitchen wings. The remaining barracks were type-C buildings, L-shaped 181 feet long by 153 feet wide with a dormitory wing. The barracks would be connected by an arcade 14 feet wide.

Carleton M. Winslow of Los Angeles, who had worked previously with Goodhue on other large projects, served as supervising architect and Chester W. Hansen of the Dawson Company was in charge of construction.

The city granted the contractor a permit to build a railroad spur through public property to the base for transporting building materials.

The Bureau of Yards and Docks awarded contracts for a U-shaped industrial complex, quartermaster storehouse, sewer and water mains, and underground electric and steam power lines.

Meanwhile, the Navy Department ordered Gen. Pendleton back to San Diego to activate Headquarters, 2nd Advanced Base Force, the nucleus of the brigade that would eventually occupy the base. Gen. Pendleton arrived Oct. 1, 1919, and soon became immersed in plans for the base.

The Spanish-style courtyard at Marine Corps Recruit Depot, San Diego carries out Bertram Goodhue's vision.

A view to the west from across Barnett Avenue toward Point Loma, showing the base under construction.

He toured the new base with architect Goodhue during the summer of 1920. Goodhue's original plans for the base were being re-evaluated by Navy planners, and the architect wanted the general to understand fully the significance of the original layout and design of the buildings. Goodhue knew he did not have final authority over the construction and sought Gen. Pendleton's help to protect the integrity of his plans. But Gen. Pendleton needed little in the way of persuasion. He was already on the record in favor of Goodhue's plan.

Gen. Pendleton had demonstrated his enthusiasm for Goodhue's work two months earlier in a letter to Maj. Gen. Littleton W.T. Waller, HQ, 1st Advanced Base Force, Philidelphia, PA. On April 22, 1920, Gen. Pendleton wrote that he believed the base would be the "most beautiful and picturesque military post in the United States."

Gen. Pendleton and Goodhue became allies. During the first phase of construction, Gen. Pendleton kept Goodhue informed of any changes Navy planners were considering to the original scheme.

Goodhue's site plans contained four important elements:

Architect built his reputation in San Diego

Bertram Grosvenor Goodhue, artist, architect and designer, was born in Connecticut in 1869 and educated at Russell's Collegiate and Military Institute through the age of 14.

He worked his way up from office boy to renowned architect. In 1891, he joined the firm of Cram and Wentworth, whose principal architect, Ralph Adams Cram, was a well-known designer of gothic churches. Goodhue soon became a partner in the firm, and by 1914 had established his own architectural firm.

His association with San Diego began in 1910, when he learned of the planning for the Panama-California Exposition. Goodhue convinced the exposition planners to adopt Spanish colonial revival style architecture over the mission-style they had favored earlier. He had written a book about this style of architecture titled "Mexican Memories" in 1892.

His work in designing the site and buildings at Balboa Park convinced Congressman Kettner and others to recommend Goodhue to the Navy Department as the designer for the new Marine expeditionary base.

Bertram Grosvenor Goodhue

Another strong point in favor of hiring Goodhue: his work in designing major groups of structures as well as individual buildings.

Between 1903 and 1914, Goodhue helped bring the firm he was working with into national prominence, designing the U.S. Military Academy at West Point, Rice University, and in New York, St. Thomas's Church and the Chapel of the Intercession.

His work on the Panama-California Exposition brought him more work in the Western United States until his death in 1924 at the age of 55. Among other major projects, he designed the California Institute of Technology in Pasadena and the Los Angeles Public Library.

The first six barracks are shown on July 30, 1920. Gen. Pendleton used one of these structures for an all-purpose building, including an armory.

- The barracks would be linked by a great arcade facing the parade grounds.
- Secondary structures, such as the dispensary and administration buildings, would form a long axis behind the arcade, creating a series of courtyards.
- Less important structures, such as the laundry and the bakery, would be arranged informally behind the secondary structures.
- And married officers' quarters would be located away from the parade grounds in a meandering park-like setting.

During the next two years, Gen. Pendleton focused intensely on every detail pertaining to the construction of the base. He petitioned the Commandant, Maj. Gen. John Archer Lejeune, to intercede when Navy planners attempted to make changes to the drawings. He also appealed repeatedly to his old friend Gen. George Barnett, who in October 1920 became the first Commanding General of the Department of the Pacific. And he called upon his civilian ally, Congressman Kettner, to prevent cuts in appropriations and to secure additional funds for the base.

Gen. Pendleton's obsession with the base eventually led him to believe there was a conspiracy by the Navy to undermine his authority and to acquire part of the Marine base.

"There is a good deal of quiet but persistent opposition to our ever getting this post finished, and a good many delays have been unnecessary and to my mind unforgivable," Gen. Pendleton wrote Gen. Lejeune on Oct. 5, 1921. "When this post was first planned in a general way, about the fall of 1916, some of the Navy personnel, who were in San Diego when the (House) Naval committee ... were visiting the city, were aroused to a spasm of jealousy to think the Marine Corps should have such a beautiful post."

When Navy planners at the Bureau of Yards and Docks tinkered with the plans by suggesting that the administration building be located more centrally on the base, Gen. Pendleton became outraged, accusing the chief of the Bureau of being behind the plot to "ruin" the post.

Corresponding with Goodhue on Jan. 17, 1922, Gen. Pendleton called Rear Adm. C.W. Parks a "stuffed toad."

Even after learning of the admiral's retirement, Gen. Pendleton confided to Goodhue, "I hope that the change will be a helpful one to us, though I suppose (Parks) inoculated a good many of them in the Bureau with his fool fat-headed ideas."

Gen. Pendleton found enemies closer to home, too. As the senior brigadier general of the Marine Corps, Gen. Pendleton worried in January 1920 that Rear Adm. Roger Wells, who was commander of the 11th Naval District (now Naval Base, San Diego) had "improperly" included the Marine Corps base within the admiral's jurisdiction. In a letter to Brig. Gen. Charles H. Long, at Headquarters, Marine Corps, Gen. Pendleton ar-

Workers huddle in the shade of a platform south of Building 9, the power house.

gued that Adm. Wells should be "subservient" to him because a general was equal to an admiral and Gen. Pendleton had received his commission earlier than Adm. Wells. Soon after, Gen. Pendleton was disappointed to receive word from Gen. Long that General Order No. 514 did indeed place the Marine Corps Base under Navy jurisdiction.

By October 1920, the barracks were nearly complete, and the general was pushing the public works officer in charge of the project "to get the roads and walks laid out, at least in order that we can do what we can towards planting." Built on landfill, the barracks stood 14 feet above high tide. Gen. Pendleton concluded that was "plenty sufficient" to withstand any waves that might come over the proposed sea wall. But the general was concerned that the composition of the landfill, primarily sand and silt, would blow into the barracks when winter winds swept through the base.

Gen. Pendleton looked forward to planting local grasses and flowers to hold the soil in place. In anticipation, he sent work details to nearby Mission Beach to collect wild morning glory and verbena seeds. He also planned to use cuttings of ice plant to cover the ground "right to the shore." In time, he hoped to cover the massive parade ground and all the drill fields with Bermuda grass. Top soil would be used in areas where trees and shrubs were to be planted.

Gen. Pendleton was particularly enthusiastic about a plan he devised to bring fresh water to the base. In an Oct. 29, 1920, letter to Marine Corps Headquarters, Washington, D.C., Gen. Pendleton wrote, "I have been working up a scheme with (quartermaster) Maj. (Edward W.) Banker and Cmdr. Smith (public works officer), together with the San Diego Water Commission and the City Council, whereby we hope to have turned over to us the old wells in the Mission Valley."

The wells had been abandoned years before. Although the well-house buildings were still there, the pumps and machinery were long gone. Nevertheless, Gen. Pendleton believed the wells could be resurrected to meet the irrigation needs of the base. The general even envisioned providing water to the Naval Training Station, which was being constructed just west of the Marine Base.

The city could still supply the base with water for drink-

Gen. Pendleton felt construction of the base was being deliberately slowed down by naval officers.

Above, the newly completed quarters of the Commanding General. The architect wanted this and other officers' quarters set aside from the main base in a parklike setting. Left, the CG's quarters in a photo taken during the 1990s.

Recruit Depot moves to San Diego

The Marine Corps Recruit Depot for the western half of the United States moved from Mare Island, San Francisco, to San Diego in August 1923, after a nine-month delay.

The Mare Island facility was one of two original recruit depots established on the West Coast in 1911. Puget Sound Navy Yard in Washington was the other installation. In 1912, Headquarters Marine Corps closed Puget Sound and increased the size of the Mare Island facility.

Marine Commandant, Maj. Gen. John A. Lejeune envisioned moving the depot to San Diego in December 1922, but delayed implementation because he did not want to cause any "dissatisfaction" among the officers and men at Mare Island.

The first draft of recruits — 250 men under the command of Lt. G.L. Gloeckner — arrived in San Diego aboard the transport USS *Sirius* on Aug. 12, 1923.

Recruit training actually began a week earlier under the command of Maj. (later Maj. Gen.) Emil P. Moses. He had earlier commanded the recruit depot at Mare Island.

By Aug. 15, there were five platoons of 65 men each in training. Recruits were called "applicants" during the first two days. They watched training procedures and, after that, they could join if they still wanted to. Training lasted eight to 10 weeks and included daily parades at 4 p.m. on the sand-covered parade deck.

Reveille was at 5 a.m., followed by physical training, area cleanup, and breakfast. After morning colors, the days were filled with close order drill and extended order drill, with a break for the noon meal. All recruits also learned signal drills.

Col. Emil P. Moses in 1932, first Recruit Depot commander.

ing and cooking, but Gen. Pendleton pushed hard for "an independent water supply." In part, he was afraid that the lack of water for landscaping would delay the opening of the base. "It is unquestionable that as (Brig. Gen. Charles L.) McCawley (at HQ) says, the buildings would be uninhabitable or a least extremely uncomfortable, if something is not done to prevent the blowing of sand and dust."

Gen. Pendleton's plan was never put into action and nothing was done officially to landscape the base until 1923, when the landfill had had an opportunity to leech its high level of salt. As a short-term measure, the Bureau of Yards and Docks graded the base, installed sprinklers and planted salt grass to control blowing sand.

A formal landscape plan was drawn up for the arcade areas, courtyard and industrial sectors with the help of Superintendent of City Parks John Morley. A landscape expert, Morley greatly expanded the city's park system during the 25 years he was superintendent.

On June 15, 1923, the Bureau of Yards and Docks put a landscape contract out for bid. The selection of trees and plants was governed by four factors:

• They had to be species that would flourish in San Diego's semi-arid climate.
• They had to tolerate sandy soil.
• Their tap roots could not extend beyond five to seven feet, where they would encounter the salt water table.
• And only plants and trees requiring a minimum amount of water could be used.

The requirements posed no problems for local landscapers who had kept pace with the city's changing regional tastes. From 1905 to 1920, the city went through a remarkable transformation from a western version of an East Coast town to a re-creation of a Mediterranean community. Between those years, San Diego neighborhoods became more Hispanic in architecture and landscape. Streets were planted with rows of slender palms, and exotic plants such as bougainvillea gained wide acceptance.

Milton P. Sessions won the contract to plant the trees and shrubs on the base. A nephew of famed horticulturist Kate O. Sessions, he operated the family nursery in Old Town San Diego.

Originally, major roads were planted exclusively with black acacias. But the acacias' shallow root system buckled curbs and roads, and eventually most were replaced by palm trees. A few acacias can still be seen on the base today.

During October 1920, Gen. Pendleton reported to Headquarters, Marine Corps that the barracks and power plant were nearly complete, and the "kitchen equipment" for the barracks had arrived and was about to be installed.

Gen. Pendleton knew it would be some time before the next phase of construction would be completed, so he devised a plan that would allow early occupation of the base. "I figured on using C-1 building, which is capable of holding comfortably 250 men, for a storehouse, sick bay, guardhouse, post exchange, officer of the day's office and, in fact, everything not accommodated in company buildings.

"The last of the contracts at present is figured to be finished January 7th (1921)," wrote Gen. Pendleton. But ever pessimistic, the general concluded, "This, however, will not be carried out, and I suppose it will probably (be) the middle of February before they are all done, or possibly a little later, although we hope not."

His fears were well-founded. The Marines didn't move from Balboa Park onto the new base until Dec. 1, 1921. Several days later, Gen. Pendleton wrote, "We are very comfortably situated in our new offices, and after we get them fixed up I think we will like it very much. We hoisted the flag over here on the first day of December and made a little event of it, although not very much because we only had a handful of men."

Several developments early in 1922 gave Gen. Pendleton reason for concern.

First — in March, the Navy announced plans to relocate training from Goat Island in San Francisco to the new Naval Training Station, San Diego, by July 1.

Gen. Pendleton reacted to the news by requesting that the Marine Corps send as many men as possible to fill up the Marine barracks in San Diego, or the Navy "will make some kind of excuse to borrow any barracks building we have empty at the time." In conclusion Gen. Pendleton stated, "I am opposed to letting the Navy get hold of any of our post here in San Diego."

Second — once again Navy planners insisted on making changes to the original plans in an attempt to economize.

During this period, the Bureau of Yards and Docks stopped communicating with Goodhue, so the architect asked Gen. Pendleton to keep him posted on any changes to his design. He wrote, "I wish I knew what was the status of the two groups of government buildings at San Diego that I have fathered. The last I heard of the Marine Base is that certain changes were being made that thoroughly displeased me."

Six major support buildings, including the medical dispensary and post exchange, plus several small utility structures were constructed during 1922. Both the dispensary and exchange were built according to Goodhue's original design, but the Navy decided to erect only part of each of the structures.

On April 3, 1922, Gen. Pendleton wrote Kettner in Washington, D.C., asking the congressman to speak with the new chief of the Bureau of Yards and Docks "to talk him out of making these changes."

One of the last events during Gen. Pendleton's watch must have been a bitter one. After fighting long and hard to keep the Navy's mitts off the base, on March 1, 1924, it was officially designated Marine Corps Base, Naval Operating Base, San Diego. There could be no doubt of who was in charge.

Gen. Pendleton retired at the mandatory age of 64 on June 2, 1924, to his home in Coronado, Calif. The retired general never lost his interest in the progress of his base,

Still unfinished during the 1930s, Marine Corps Base, San Diego was nonetheless impressive to visitors. To the left of the building in the foreground is an outdoor boxing ring. White lines in the foreground held up laundry on a tall pole.

Above, Spanish-style arches mirror the design used for the Panama-California Exposition in Balboa Park. Below, as World War II approached, Marine Corps Base, San Diego was finally completed, and several of the buildings, like this one, used the original design that Bertram Goodhue conceived in 1918. In the background are some of the original structures.

Brig. Gen. Joseph H. Pendleton was sent to San Diego in 1919 to organize the 2nd Advanced Base Force.

visiting often until his death on Feb. 4, 1942.

During the fall of 1924, the Commandant issued an alert for the Marines at San Diego to prepare for expeditionary service in China. The base expanded as several new areas were developed for training in bayonet, entrenchment practice and weapons drill.

The buildup for China resulted in a flurry of construction activity in 1925. The Bureau of Yards and Docks was under orders to "complete the Marine (base)" to meet the present needs of the Corps.

W.E. Kier Construction Company of San Diego received contracts to build a seventh barracks building, a second storehouse, and five sets of officers quarters using Goodhue's designs.

But the base remained almost unchanged physically from 1925 until 1939 when President Franklin D. Roosevelt declared a limited national emergency following the outbreak of war in Europe.

Many of the structures called for in the original plans were finally built and, in some cases, modified.

So, while World War I delayed construction, World War II gave it renewed impetus, and Gen. Pendleton got to see the completion of his dream.

But the buildup for World War II brought many changes never envisioned by Goodhue or Gen. Pendleton.

Communications, motor transport, and drill instructors schools were added and 27 new warehouses were built. The Navy Department authorized additional barracks, and hundreds of 16-man Quonset huts were erected to accommodate the thousands of recruits pouring into the base.

More buildings were added during the Korean and Vietnam wars. MCRD, San Diego, had more than 110 permanent buildings by the early 1970s. The 1980s saw a veritable building boom. According to the Chief of Staff's office, the 210 buildings on the base today are valued at $750 million.

The original plans for the base that Gen. Pendleton fought so hard to preserve were finally given their due.

Twenty-five buildings built in those first years were

New construction occurred on the base in the 1970s and 1980s. Left, a recruit processing center is under construction in the 1980s. In 1997, the base was valued at more than $750 million.

2nd Advanced Base Force takes shape

The Navy Department in 1919 took the first step to organize an expeditionary force to occupy the new Marine base, appointing probably the most appropriate officer to oversee the work: Brig. Gen. Joseph H. Pendleton.

Pendleton had returned to the United States in October 1918, after three years with "San Diego's Own" — the 4th Marines — in Santo Domingo, and assumed command of Marine Barracks, Parris Island, S.C.

Adm. R.E. Coontz, Chief of Naval Operations, told Gen. Pendleton he was the proper man to start the work in San Diego and that Coontz knew Gen. Pendleton was held in high esteem in the region. On Sept. 25, 1919, Headquarters ordered him back to San Diego to activate Headquarters, 2nd Advanced Base Force. He arrived Oct. 1, 1919.

The post at San Diego was still at Balboa Park. During Gen. Pendleton's absence, the barracks detachment left by the 4th Marines grew from a platoon to 10 officers and 300 men. Following the end of World War I, on Nov. 11, 1918, there was some reduction in manpower, but a senior officer remained in charge.

When Gen. Pendleton arrived, Col. John F. McGill was in command of the post. Two skeleton companies, the 152nd and 209th, were attached to the post. On Nov. 1, 1919, manpower totaled 235 Marines, including 11 officers: the barracks had seven officers and 183 enlisted men; the 152nd Company had one officer and 20 enlisted men; the 209th had one officer and 17 enlisted men; Headquarters, 2nd Advanced Base Force had two officers and four enlisted men.

Gen. Pendleton was frustrated, however, because the 4th Marines would not be placed under his command until the troops occupied the base. Gen. Pendleton worked hard to speed up the process, trying to nail down as many details in advance as he could.

On Nov. 8, 1919, the Commandant denied Gen. Pendleton's request for a Brigade Quartermaster because there was a shortage of senior officers, and there would be "nothing for him (the quartermaster) to do in San Diego."

Nevertheless, Gen. Pendleton received a letter from Maj. Edward W. Banker, Post Quartermaster of the Marine Barracks, Parris Island, six days later saying the Commandant had approved the idea of the major serving as Brigade Quartermaster in San Diego in the spring "when there would be a need for one."

Gen. Pendleton didn't just tussle with officials back at Headquarters, Washington, D.C. He was sure that various naval officers were out to get him.

Early in the new year, he let Congressman Kettner know that he wanted to keep the Advanced Base Force completely independent of the Navy. Gen. Pendleton confided that the only obstacle to independence was "the intense obsession that Naval officers have that the Marine Corps should always be subservient to them — not to the Navy Department I mean, alone, but to them."

Gen. Pendleton did not get along with Rear Adm. Roger Wells, the senior naval officer in San Diego and the Commander of the 11th Naval District (today Naval Base, San Diego). On Feb. 1, 1920, Adm. Wells embarrassed Gen. Pendleton when he told the general about a "certain slackness on the part of Marines" while on liberty in downtown San Diego "about rendering salutes, particularly to Army officers."

When Gen. Pendleton was told that the base was under the jurisdiction of the Navy in early 1920, he found a silver lining in the fact that the order said nothing specifically about jurisdiction over the 2nd Advanced Base Force.

But in February, he was notified by Marine Corps HQ that the Advanced Base Force was also under Navy command. "The news you give me is a bitter pill to swallow," wrote Gen. Pendleton to Brig. Gen H.C. Haines in the Adjutant and Inspectors office in Washington, D.C. "I wish the decision on the question of the subordination of the Second Advanced Base Force had been put up to the Secretary (of the Navy) instead of (the Chief of Naval) Operations. Anyone who had known (CNO Adm. R.E.) Coontz as I had for forty years would know that he is a worshiper of the Line-of-the-Navy fetish — so of course he would go as far as he could in making any Marine interests subservient to the Navy."

Haines must have feared that Gen. Pendleton's tirade against high-ranking Navy officers might have repercussions in Washington, where the Marines were fighting a Congress that wanted to slash manpower. So he told Gen. Pendleton to suffer the present indignities for the good of the Marine Corps. "I am not going to start anything that would injure the prospects of the Corps at this time, when you tell me that the question of the permanent increase of the Corps is at stake," wrote Gen. Pendleton on Feb. 19, adding: "But it is hard to sit tight and suffer unwarrantedly to such unnecessary, and to my mind illegal, subordination to such a person as Wells. As (author Rudyard) Kipling would say 'it's a damn tough bullet to chew.' However, you need not be afraid of my spilling the beans when the interests of the Corps are at stake."

Despite the jurisdiction issue, the size of Gen. Pendleton's 2nd Advanced Base Force grew. On April 1, 1921, the 1st Battalion, 7th Marine Regiment came to San Diego. The regiment was organized during World War I and disbanded in 1919. The Marine Corps reactivated the unit to increase the manpower levels of the 2nd Advanced Base Force.

During November 1921, the 2nd Advanced Base Force under Gen. Pendleton was redesignated the 5th Marine Brigade, and the 1st Battalion, 7th Marines became the 1st Separate Battalion, 5th Brigade. About 400 of these Marines left San Diego at about this time for mail guard duty on trucks that were being subjected to a rash of robberies, leaving Gen. Pendleton feeling somewhat shorthanded when the Marines finally took up residence at their new base on Dec. 1, 1921.

recognized as historically significant in 1991 and listed on the National Register of Historic Places. The buildings form an historic district of 110 acres bounded on the west by married officers quarters, on the north by Montezuma and Tripoli Avenues, on the east by Vera Cruz Avenue and on the south by the parade ground.

Even his contemporaries gave the general the credit for the Marine Base. Congressman Kettner, who was known to be protective of his own role in the development of the base, wrote, "Too much credit cannot be given to our dear friend General Joe. His love of the Marines and San Diego is truly unlimited."

Members of the 2nd Marine Brigade, Fleet Marine Force practice an amphibious assault Feb. 16, 1937. The brigade was based at Marine Corps Base, San Diego.

The Old Corps

During the years spanning the two world wars, Marine Corps Base, San Diego welcomed back the 4th Marine Regiment from its eight-year campaign in the West Indies, and the post became a staging area for two

The main gate (Gate 3) of the San Diego Marine Corps Base in the late 1920s as seen on a postcard.

expeditions to the Far East. San Diego Marines also provided security for the U.S. Post Office as the Western Mail Guard in 1926, and their flawless performance won the admiration of the entire country. In addition, the base played a pivotal role during the mid-1930s as the Corps cultivated a new mission for itself as an amphibious assault force. The base became headquarters to the Fleet Marine Force, and San Diego became a testing ground for new tactics that would eventually lead the Marines across the islands of the Pacific to victory against Japan during World War II.

Despite these momentous times for the Marines in San Diego, the events were closely shadowed by fiscally lean budgets for the Corps as a whole. The Corps' budget was devastated by reductions in military expenditures during the years following World War I, when the San Diego base experienced a severe shortage in manpower. Understrength battalions and regiments were the rule rather than the exception.

Even so, these were also carefree days for Marines stationed in San Diego. While close-order drill, long conditioning hikes and field exercises still ruled the work days, parades and social events filled the weekend calendar. The country was slowly emerging from the ravaging national Depression, and the next great war was beyond the horizon.

On Aug. 25, 1924, the 4th Marines returned to San Diego from expeditionary duty in Santo Domingo. The men stood jubilantly on the crowded decks of the transport ship USS *Henderson* as she docked in San Diego, according to a report in the *Los Angeles Times*.

San Diego's welcome matched the regiment's enthusiasm at its homecoming. As the men marched up Broadway, they were probably gratified to see their former commanding officer, retired Maj. Gen. Joseph H. Pendleton, in the reviewing stand. Grateful citizens presented the Marines with baskets of fresh fruit at the gate of the new base. "San Diego's Own" was home once again.

The 4th Marines soon absorbed the other infantry units stationed at the base. The regiment consisted of 26 officers and 653 men, well below full strength.

These were austere times for the Marine Corps. The "war to end all wars" had concluded six years earlier, and the federal government was intent on reducing military expenditures. But the 4th Marine Regiment was saved temporarily from budget cuts by a civil war in China and a perceived threat to American interests in that region. The Marines were put on alert for expeditionary duty by Commandant, Maj. Gen. John A. Lejeune, who ordered the regiment's size increased to 42 officers and 1,000 enlisted men.

By October 1924, Col. Alexander S. Williams, the regiment's commanding officer, reported that the regiment was at its authorized strength, in a "high state of efficiency" and set to go. But before the month ended, the orders were rescinded; the regiment returned to its previous manpower levels and resumed garrison duty.

Gen. Lejeune, who wanted the Corps to be known and respected throughout the country, jumped at an opportunity for Marine participation in a joint Army-Navy exercise in Hawaii during the spring of 1925. The plan called for an amphibious assault by the Marines, and Gen. Lejeune wanted to prove his Leathernecks could handle a large-scale operation. The Commandant ordered the 4th Marines raised to 750 men by March 1, 1925, and authorized the activation of a provisional company of communications specialists.

Gen. Lejeune also ordered the 1st Provisional Battalion, 10th Marines (artillery) from Quantico, Va., to join the 4th Marines in San Diego. The units spent a week training together, which culminated in a full-dress attack in Mission Valley, several miles east of the Marine base.

The Marines departed San Diego aboard the USS *Henderson* on April 10, and joined the Fleet in San Francisco. Bound for Hawaii, the Fleet included USS *Langley*, the nation's first and then only aircraft carrier.

The exercise commenced April 25. A Marine landing force stormed ashore on Molokai Island to seize it for an air base. Two days later, Marines assaulted the Oahu beaches.

This exercise taught the Marines an important lesson. Although they proved their ability to establish a beachhead, the real problem was getting on the beach safely. The landing craft — boats with high brows and deep drafts— were at the mercy of the waves. Some boats were tossed onto the shore, while other were smashed into coral reefs.

By the end of April, the exercise was over and the 4th Marines returned to San Diego on May 8.

In 1926, Congress approved enough money for only 18,000 Marines, a reduction of 1,500 from the previous year, and the 4th Marine Regiment's numbers dwindled again as men were transferred to other Marine Corps posts.

This cutback probably didn't help morale at the base, and the new commanding general was soon embroiled in problems that embarrassed the Marines in San Diego.

Brig. Gen. Smedley D. Butler took over command of the San Diego base in February 1926. Several months later, harassed by the press, he persuaded Lt. Col. (later Commandant) Alexander A. Vandegrift to come to San Diego as the base operations officer.

"General Butler wanted me primarily for moral support," Gen. Vandegrift wrote in his memoirs, *Once A Marine*.

Gen. Butler — a staunch Prohibitionist — had found "open bootlegging and other questionable activities" on the base and he clamped down hard, according to Gen. Vandegrift. "By depriving certain influential citizens of their illegal income, he soon became a popular press target," wrote Gen. Vandegrift, who believed Gen. Butler was not suited for civilian political infighting.

Shortly before then-Lt. Col. Vandegrift arrived in the spring, an incident in San Diego brought the local and national press down on Gen. Butler in full force.

Col. Alexander Williams, a 25-year veteran of the

Members of the 4th Marine Regiment, "San Diego's Own," disembark at the San Diego waterfront Aug. 25, 1924, after eight years of expeditionary duty in Santo Domingo.

Above, the 2nd Advanced Base Force Band at Balboa Park in the late 1920s or early '30s. Below, Marines guard the mail in 1926.

"Our mission was to furnish armed guards both in mail cars hauling large money shipments and in certain post offices concerned with handling large sums of money."
Lt. Col. (later Gen.) A.A. Vandegrift

Corps, hosted a dinner at his home and a dance at the Hotel Del Coronado. Col. Williams served drinks at his home and even tried to press one on Gen. Butler, although he knew the general's feelings about drinking.

According to Gen. Vandegrift, "Later at the dance, when the host (Col. Williams), now very intoxicated, disgraced his uniform, Butler ordered him escorted from the premises." The upshot was a court-martial for Col. Williams, who was reduced in rank and sent to San Francisco. Gen. Vandegrift faulted the press for telling a "lopsided anti-Butler version" of the event.

The story was revived when Col. Williams was killed six months later in a car accident, and many called it a suicide.

In his memoirs, Gen. Vandegrift also concluded that Gen. Butler — twice decorated with the Medal of Honor for courage under fire — was bored with his job. "Trouble also stemmed from his commanding a brigade that consisted of the understrength 4th Marine Regiment, altogether a force of only some 600 men quite adequately commanded by the regimental colonel." Wrote Gen. Vandegrift, "A man of action, Smedley Butler was miserable without it."

But events in the summer and fall of 1926 gave Gen. Butler an outlet for his energy. Wrote Gen. Vandegrift, "We got some action — and it proved the necessary anodyne for my old friend."

A recurrence of mail robberies was climaxed by a particularly brutal attack on postal employees in Elizabeth, N.J., on Oct. 14. President Calvin Coolidge ordered 2,500 Marines to provide security for the U.S. mail. Gen. Butler was put at the head of what was known as the Western Mail Guards, and 15 officers and 679 men of the 4th Marines were dispersed to states throughout the West. The general established headquarters in San Francisco.

"Our mission was to furnish armed guards both in mail cars hauling large money shipments and in certain post offices concerned with handling large sums of money," wrote Gen. Vandegrift.

The crisis subsided in January 1927, and Lt. Col. Vandegrift was recalled to San Diego to assume command of the newly organized 3rd Battalion, 4th Marines and prepare for expeditionary duty in Nicaragua. "We had stacked seabags under the arcade at San Diego and we were waiting to board ship when new orders canceled the move. Instead of Nicaragua, we sailed for China."

The 4th Marines left San Diego on the naval transport USS *Chaumont* on Feb. 3, 1927, under the command of Col. Charles S. Hill. No one suspected that the officers and men of the 4th Marines would never return as a unit to San Diego.

On April 7, the 4th Marine Regiment was bolstered with elements of the 6th and 10th regiments and a Marine aviation squadron, which embarked from San Diego aboard the *Henderson*. The SS *President Grant*, a commercial vessel, transported additional units. More than 4,000 Marines staged at and embarked from Marine Corps Base, San Diego — the largest operation of its kind prior

Hollywood Marines

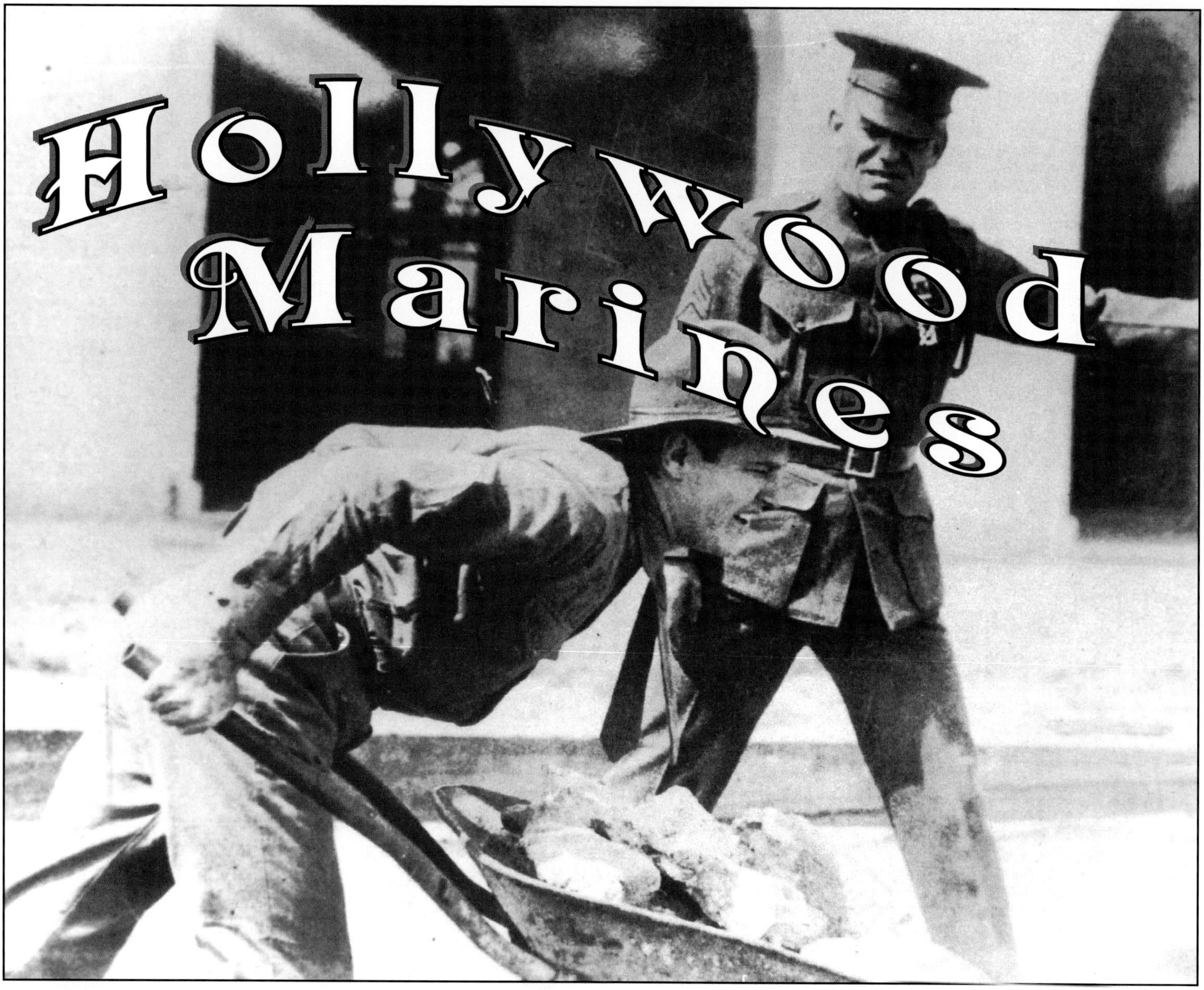

In the 1926 silent film "Tell It To The Marines," Lon Chaney Sr. as a sergeant keeps Marine William Haines moving, top, and coaches him in a boxing match above. It was one of Chaney's few roles in a non-horror movie, and was made at Marine Corps Base, San Diego.

All the base is a stage

Many film makers have used MCRD. San Diego as a background, including:
- "Moran Of The Marines," 1928, about Marines in China with Richard Dix;
- "Gung Ho," 1943, dramatizing the history of Carlson's Raiders at Makin Island with Randolph Scott and Robert Mitchum.
- "Marine Raiders," 1944, a World War II drama focusing on jungle fighting and amphibious warfare with Pat O'Brien.
- "The D.I.," 1957, about drill instructors and recruits with Jack Webb.
- "The Outsider," 1961, about Pima Indian Ira Hayes, a Marine who helped raise the U.S. flag on Iwo Jima with Tony Curtis and James Franciscus.

Photographs during filming on the base show, clockwise from top left: Charles Bickford and Florence Rice in "Pride of the Marines" in 1936; Pat O'Brien in 1935 during filming of "Devil Dogs of the Air" and a scene from that movie; and the San Diego Marine Band visiting a Hollywood set in 1938.

Top, Marines in the galley in 1931, and above, the post exchange in the 1930s. According to a 1931 Marine Corps publication, some civilians had criticized the San Diego base, complaining that "in building for beauty certain conveniences were overlooked (and) that an unduly large enlisted force would be required to maintain such an extensive establishment." The booklet responds that only 150 men were needed in the Base Service Company, and: "Their song runs something like this: We have carpenters, plumbers and painters, chauffeurs, mechanics and bakers, and we tote you around in our cars. We build you a house, and launder your blouse, then find time to look at the stars. When you turn out for drill, we too get that thrill, and march to the tune of the band. We shoot all the guns, and cook all your buns, for we're good 'Marines,' understand."

The base band leads Marines marching down Broadway in San Diego during the 1930s.

to World War II.

The expedition to China left the base short of personnel. When the 3rd Brigade was disbanded in China in September 1928, all units except the 4th Marines were pulled out.

The 6th Battery, 10th Marines was ordered to San Diego and arrived New Year's day in San Diego. The battery was under the command of Capt. Jimmy Wyat and consisted of four gun companies with eight in reserve. Its authorized strength was four officers and 130 enlisted men.

In 1931, the total strength of the base was 50 officers and approximately 1,000 enlisted men, with Marine detachments at the rifle range in La Jolla, the Destroyer Base (now Naval Station, San Diego) in the southern part of the county, and at the Marine Corps Aviation Force stationed across San Diego Bay at North Island.

The Recruit Depot had a staff of 33 Marines authorized to train a maximum of 270 recruits.

Formation of the new 6th Marines, Fleet Marine Force (FMF), with the 2nd Battalion, 10th Marines (Artillery) effectively replaced the 4th Marine Regiment.

On Sept. 1, 1934, the 6th Marine Regiment was reactivated in San Diego. Lt. Col. Andrew B. Drum took command of the two-battalion regiment. The 2nd Battalion,

Two base commanders

Left, Brig. Gen. Robert H. Dunlap listens to Col. Harry R. "Daddy" Lay at Marine Corps Base, San Diego in the 1930s. Col. Lay was base commander in 1929, and then resumed duties as Chief of Staff in 1930 when Gen. Dunlap became Commanding General. The next year, Gen. Dunlap was killed rescuing a landslide victim (see Page 137). Col. Lay, appointed a second lieutenant in 1900, was a veteran of the Boxer Rebellion in China in 1900 and the Samar Campaign in 1901. During World War I, he earned the Navy Cross, participating with the 5th Marines in the St. Mihiel Offensive, and the Meuse-Argonne offensives at Champagne and the Argonne Forest. Col. Lay died July 26, 1930, at age 52 while on active duty as Chief of Staff at Marine Corps Base, San Diego.

Aircraft squadrons are headquartered at base

The pioneer Marine aviation unit on the West Coast was organized in San Diego in 1924 with headquarters at Marine Corps Base, San Diego. Planes were stationed across the bay at North Island Naval Air Station at Coronado, Calif.

Observation Squadron One (VO-1M), the first organized air unit in the Corps, had six DeHavilland-4 observation planes. It was transferred from Santo Domingo to San Diego and arrived Aug. 16 aboard the collier USS *Jason*.

Commanding officer Maj. Ross E. Rowell established the Observation Squadron of the West Coast Expeditionary Force. The planes were equipped with machine guns and bomb racks, and crews started training in practical observation and ground attack.

When Fighter Squadron Three, equipped with Vought single-seater planes, was established at Naval Air Station on Sept. 1, 1925, the organization was redesignated Aircraft Squadrons, West Coast Expeditionary Force. The squadron was later known as the Red Devil Squadron.

By 1926, there were four Marine air squadrons in San Diego consisting of three observation squadrons and one fighter squadron.

Marines of VO-1M again broke ground in February 1927 when they accompanied troops to Nicaragua, becoming the first Marine aviators to join a Marine expedition. VO-1M performed reconnaissance duties over the Nicaraguan war fronts and was "shot up" on a number of occasions. Twice, planes of the squadron went into action for their own defense.

The squadron returned to San Diego in June, carrying 23 bullet holes in the planes as souvenirs of the expedition.

In the meantime, VF-3M was ordered to accompany a Marine expedition to China, sailing for the Orient in April 1927 under Brig. Gen. Smedley Butler. The Red Devils provided aerial photography and reconnaissance.

In 1931, the squadrons had 43 pilots, and 18 observation and fighter planes. The organization's total strength was 267 Marines, including 33 officers. Although the organization was essentially an expeditionary operating unit, a large portion of its activities was devoted to the final training of new pilots and reserve officers. Their activities included bombing, gunnery, ground attack tactics, radio and visual communications, visual and photographic reconnaissance, aerial sketching, infantry liaison and the maintenance and overhaul of aircraft, engines, motor transport, armament, and parachutes.

Left, Aircraft Squadrons commander Maj. Ross E. Rowell in 1931. Below, an airman with his Curtiss F6C Fighter at North Island Naval Air Station in the 1930s.

A machine gun company of the 6th Marines passes in review at Marine Corps Base, San Diego during the early 1930s. Such parades were held regularly on Friday afternoons, followed by a parade tea for officers and their ladies.

10th Marines (Artillery) joined with smaller units from Quantico, and the whole organization was given brigade status in 1935, though it was severely understrength for that designation.

The 2nd Brigade formed the West Coast segment of the FMF in 1935. The FMF was a specially trained, highly mobile unit capable of rapid expansion in time of war.

The strength of the base in 1935 grew to approximately 100 officers and 2,000 enlisted men. The increase in numbers was due mostly to the organization of the 10th and the 6th Marines as part of the FMF.

The 2nd Battalion, 10th Marines transfered to San Diego, while its counterpart — the 1st Battalion — remained on the East Coast. It would be four years before the two battalions became a true regiment under a single command. During the winter of 1939, regimental headquarters and service battery was organized in San Diego under the command of Col. Thomas E. Bourke.

Between 1935 and 1939, the two battalions operated independently of one another without a regimental headquarters or commander. Nevertheless, the battalions were brought together to participate in Pacific Fleet exercises on Midway Island in mid-1935.

Gen. Charles Lyman, then in command of the FMF, was transferred to San Diego in time to oversee the exercise. Gen. Lyman had been one of "San Diego's Own," having served with Gen. Pendleton and the 4th Marines in Santo Domingo. As a colonel, he was also commanding officer of the San Diego Marine Corps Base during the late 1920s.

From Jan. 6-30, 1936, the 1st Battalion, 10th Marines conducted firing practice east of San Diego out in the Borrego Desert. On June 1, Maj. William H. Harrison took command of the battalion. On Sept. 29, 1937, the battalion's new commander, Lt. Col. Lloyd L. Leech, led the men for two weeks of artillery practice a few miles north of the San Diego Marine base to what was once a World War I Army base called Camp Kearny.

During the summer of 1937, Marines from the 4th Marine Regiment stationed at the International Settlement in Shanghai, China, were caught in a crossfire between Japanese and Chinese troops. As a result, San Diego became a staging area for the 2nd Marine Brigade under the command of Brig. Gen. John C. Beaumont.

The Marines were rushed to Shanghai in August with orders to help the 4th Marine Regiment keep the warring factions out of the International Settlement. By February 1938, the fighting had passed west of Shanghai, and the brigade returned to San Diego, where in the spring of 1939 it helped build Camp Nimitz on San Clemente Island, off the coast of Southern California.

Another component attached to the San Diego base at that time was the 2nd Signal Company, which was organized Dec. 1, 1931. After boot camp, men with an aptitude for electronics were given 21 weeks of intensive training in subjects such as code, basic electricity, radio and field equip-

Left, Fleet Marine Force Medical Unit circa 1935. Below, a 155 mm howitzer on the base, circa 1930s.

ment. The mission of the company was to maintain serviceable equipment and to provide trained personnel as replacements for the West Coast and stations in the Pacific.

The primary function of units attached to the San Diego base throughout the 1920s and 1930s was to prepare for expeditionary duty. The histories of regiments stationed in Haiti and Nicaragua, for example, are those of occupying forces. But during the latter half of the 1930s, the role of the Marine Corps changed significantly. Marine Corps Base, San Diego played an important part in the evolution of the Marine Corps from a land-based expeditionary force to an amphibious assault force.

Maj. Gen. John Henry Russell Jr. believed the Marine Corps should have a striking force available and ready as part of the Fleet. Gen. Russell, as acting Commandant, sent a letter on Aug. 17, 1933, to the Chief of Naval Operations, outlining his concepts and suggesting that the most important mission of the Marine Corps in time of war was to "advance with the fleet" and provide for the establishment of a land base.

"Following this line of thought," Gen. Russell argued, "it appears that the present title, expeditionary force, is a misnomer. A more appropriate title would be 'Fleet Base Defense Force or Fleet Marine Force.'"

The letter made its way up the chain of command and was eventually forwarded to Adm. David F. Sellers, Commander-in-Chief, U.S. Fleet. The admiral was the first base commander of San Diego's Naval Training Station. Adm. Sellers endorsed the concept Sept. 2. "When the Fleet Marine Force is attached to the U.S. Fleet, the Commander-in-Chief will establish close contact with its commander and utilize such elements as are available during Fleet Tactical Exercises and Fleet Problems." In essence, a new relationship between the Navy and the Marine Corps was formally instituted.

The withdrawal by 1933 of the last of the Marines from Nicaragua meant that enough officers and enlisted men were available for a reorganization of the Corps with respect to its new relationship with the Navy. On Dec. 7, 1933, Navy Department General Order No. 241 inaugurated the FMF. Its establishment meant the Corps had committed itself to a new wartime role — to serve the Fleet by seizing bases for naval operations.

Capt. (later Lt. Gen.) Edward A. Craig stands in front of his troops, 'A' Company, 1st Battalion, 6th Marines, at Marine Corps Base, San Diego in 1934. The company was one of the first Fleet Marine Force units.

Below, troops parade at Marine Corps Base, San Diego in the 1930s. Bottom, an air-cooled machine gun on display.

"I believe that the first Fleet Marine Force combat unit was the 5th Battalion, Fleet Marine Force, which was organized under the command of Lt. Col. Keller Rockey in January 1934 at MCB, San Diego, Cal.," wrote Lt. Gen. Edward A. Craig in his description of the origins of the FMF on the West Coast in his unpublished memoirs. "I was assigned command of Company 'A' of this battalion. Attached to the battalion was a battery of 75 mm Pack Howitzers." According to Gen. Craig, the "life of this battalion was short-lived. It was organized to participate in Fleet Tactical Exercises."

In September 1934, Gen. Craig received new orders to command "A" Company, 1st Battalion, 6th Marines, FMF. In June 1935, he was relieved from his duties with the FMF and assigned as an instructor with the Western Platoon Leaders Class on the San Diego base to train college students as officer candidates. "Maj. Herbert Hardy commanded and Capt. F.M. Wulbern and myself were instructors .... This was the first class of its kind and the only one on the West Coast."

Gen. Craig was transferred back to the FMF in the fall of 1935 — this time as commanding officer of Headquarters Company, FMF.

Early in its development, headquarters for the FMF was located on the East Coast in Washington. But Gen. Russell, who was then Commandant, believed the FMF should be located near the bulk of the U.S. Fleet, which was on the West Coast. Gen. Russell spent much of his career on the West Coast and served as Commanding General at Marine Corps Base, San Diego from December 1930 to November 1931.

Below, Building 131, the boathouse, at MCRD in April 1970. It was built in 1936 for the base CG, Maj. Gen. Douglas C. McDougal, pictured bottom, seated fourth from left. Gen. McDougal was also in command of the Fleet Marine Force. Others in the 1936 photo of the Commanding General and staff FMF are, seated from left: Lt. Col T.E. Watson, supply; Cmdr. J.T. Boone, FMF surgeon; Lt. Col. (later Maj. Gen.) W.H. Rupertus, chief of staff; Gen. McDougal; Col. B. Puryear Jr., FMF quartermaster; Lt. Col. H.K. Pickett, FMF artillery officer; and Lt. Col. C.I. Murray, personnel. Standing from left: Capt. G.A. Williams, intelligence; Maj. R.H. Schubert, FMF communications; Maj. H.D. Campbell, air liaison officer; Lt. Col. J.W. Webb, operations; Maj. J.T. Smith, assistant operations officer; and 1st Lt. E.B. Games, aide.

In September 1935, Headquarters, FMF was transferred to the Marine Corps Base in San Diego.

When the West Coast component of the FMF was given brigade status, Marine Corps Base, San Diego was assigned the 2nd Brigade. As of June 30, 1935, the 2nd Brigade consisted of the 6th Marine Regiment less the 3rd Battalion, the 2nd Battalion less Battery F of the 10th Marines, and Aircraft Squadron Two. As World War II approached, the 2nd Brigade would be redesignated the 2nd Marine Division in February 1941.

In April 1939, a combined East and West Coast FMF maneuver took place on San Clemente Island off the coast of Southern California. "This was the first big maneuver of the 1st and 2nd Brigades of the Fleet Marine Force," Gen. Craig wrote. "It did much to promote amphibious thinking among those who participated and brought out many problems."

Life at the base, however, was not totally focused on the new Marine Corps mission.

"Take, for example, the case of Building 131," wrote retired Lt. Gen. Victor H. Krulak in his book *First To Fight: An Inside Look At The U.S. Marine Corps*.

Gen. Krulak was serving on the base in the 2nd Engineer Company in 1936 when Brig. Gen. Douglas C. McDougal, the Commanding General, wanted a boathouse. "Being a Commanding General, he wanted it right away and told me to 'see what I could do,'" wrote Gen. Krulak. "Our small engineer unit had no materials and no

Members of the 1st Battalion, 6th Marines load up in trucks in San Diego during 1935 for maneuvers on Midway Island.

way of getting any. We did, however, have Wolkovitz, which turned out to be quite enough."

Sgt. Peter Paul Wolkovitz, a carpenter and a veteran of Nicaragua, Haiti, China and Alaska was — according to Gen. Krulak — a man who knew the "art of midnight entrepreneurship" and was capable of "almost miraculous feats of procurement."

Using a Marine Corps truck and with the help of two privates, Sgt. Wolkovitz liberated materials from Consolidated-Vultee Aircraft, which was building its plant next door to the base. Gen. McDougal also wanted a marine railway for his tiny fleet of boats, so Wolkovitz secured rails from the San Diego Railway Company, which was installing track near the base.

"The Commanding General never asked me where the materials came from or how it all happened. I had a feeling he already knew," wrote Gen. Krulak.

Shortly after the 30-foot by 90-foot boathouse was completed, a representative of the Adjutant and Inspector of the Marine Corps came to the base for an annual inspection. Assuming that the boathouse must be part of a public works program, the inspector asked Gen. McDougal why there was no official number on the building as required by the Marine Corps. Gen. McDougal claimed it was an oversight, assigned the number 131 arbitrarily and had it painted on the structure.

Marine Corps Base, San Diego was considered a good duty station during the 1930s. The weather was glorious, and when the Fleet was out the Marines were "top dogs" in downtown San Diego, wrote Lt. Gen. William K. Jones in *A Brief History Of The 6th Marines*.

"Morning colors started the day. The units formed on the parade ground facing the flagpole shortly before 0800," he recalled.

While still in college during the late 1930s, Gen. Jones attended summer training courses in Platoon Leaders Class at the base. He later joined the 6th Marines in San Diego. Wrote Gen. Jones, "Young officers had to report at 0730 to polish their riding boots or leather puttees, shine their San Browne belts, check their swords and plan their day."

The area between the parade ground and San Diego Bay was a sandy expanse and used for most activities — gun drills, bayonet practice, and field meets. The battalion or separate company commanders often led their men off the base on conditioning hikes through the foothills surrounding San Diego. "Water discipline as it was known," noted Gen. Jones, "consisted of trying to make these grueling hikes on one canteen of water, carrying a pack, weapons and wearing a World War I type of helmet."

The routine of drills and marches were capped every Friday afternoon with a parade that kicked off the weekend.

"The entire Brigade fell in on the parade grounds in front of the barracks," wrote Gen. Jones. Reviewing stands were set up for the local spectators. After the review, officers with

A car is pulled off the road leading to the base during the winter of 1939-40.

Marines from the 2nd Brigade, Fleet Marine Force practice landing on a beach Feb. 17, 1937. The formation of the FMF signaled a significant change in the mission of the Corps.

their ladies moved to the mess hall for the Parade Tea. Saturday was dance night, and on special occasions variety shows and costume parties were organized. "These were hilarious affairs," noted Gen. Jones. "One such was the night when one of the lieutenants, dressed as a floradora girl, insisted on putting two grapefruits in his dress to portray breasts. Slightly inebriated, after the show he sat on Major General Upshur's lap and one of the grapefruit fell out. The startled general, who had a front row table since he was Commanding General, was nonplused."

Married officers and NCOs lived off base in civilian housing. The staff NCOs and officers each had their own clubs on the base.

Life for enlisted Marines was also agreeable. The Spanish-styled barracks were comfortable. Offices and mess halls occupied the first floor. Squad bays for enlisted men on the second floor were outfitted with double-decked iron cots. Each man had a locker box and shared a common shower. The men kept their rifles in racks in the squad bay. Enlisted Marines found their entertainment in downtown San Diego, particularly on weekends when the bars, tattoo parlors, and burlesque houses along lower Broadway were in full swing.

"In downtown San Diego, (Marines) were always under the suspicious eye of the shore patrol," wrote Gen. Jones. "If a Marine did get into trouble, the San Diego police would lock him up for the night." The next morning the police would release the offender into the hands of his platoon leader.

The six-story Army-Navy YMCA opened on Broadway in 1924. There, Marines could rent a locker and clean, inexpensive rooms, eat home-style meals, and attend dances and sporting events known as smokers (boxing matches). The Armed Services YMCA counted 1,269,124 servicemen coming through its front doors in 1935. By 1945, that figure would jump to nearly 8 million.

From the commanders to the junior enlisted men stationed in San Diego, "live, love, and be happy" was the prevailing mood, Gen. Jones wrote. The Depression was slowly giving way to better economic times, and few recognized that the good life was about to end abruptly.

World War II

Marines parade at Marine Corps Base, San Diego on April 21, 1941, and motor transport Pvt. Anne Laurenzi, a member of the Women Reserves, pumps gas at the base in 1944.

Predictably, the beginning of World War II taxed the resources of Marine Corps Base, San Diego. Until then, the base

Camouflaged buildings were the first things recruits saw when they arrived at Marine Corps Base, San Diego during 1943.

"In those days, three weeks after Pearl Harbor, the base was spreading like an unruly forest fire. More than 18,000 boots arrived for training in one month. Every officer was handling from two to four full-time jobs, and had to until new officers reported in."

Capt. Robert P. White, Public Relations Officer,
Marine Corps Base, San Diego 1943

Recruits drill at Marine Corps Base, San Diego during World War II. In the background is the base theater built during February 1943. It replaced the outdoor theater built shortly after the war began.

A *Leatherneck* magazine cartoon shows a Marine on base in San Diego in 1941 picking up a cigar butt. It was part of a series of 12 postcards illustrated by Clair Des Voignes of San Diego.

had been understaffed and the units attached to it were usually understrength. Even with war preparations that began during the late 1930s, the base was still not equipped to handle the thousands of men who poured in after the war began on Dec. 7, 1941. New Marine Corps camps were quickly opened to make room for the expansion of the Recruit Depot.

Early on, Marines found ways to adjust to the wartime influx — ways to boost morale, ways to feed so many. By 1944, the base was functioning smoothly with the help of approximately 700 Women Reserves, who took over jobs from men so they could be sent to the battlefields. Then new challenges emerged when thousands of battle-hardened Marines from the South Pacific returned to the base for processing as the war wound down.

Marine Corps Base, San Diego, played an important role in the war — a conflict that would forever change the mission of the base.

Despite all the new construction that began in 1939, the facilities at Marine Corps Base, San Diego were still inadequate for its dual role as a Fleet Marine Force (FMF) base and a recruit depot.

There was little room for any real expansion. The base was bordered on the east and north by the City of San Diego, on the south by the municipal airport and the bay, and on the immediate west by the Naval Training Station.

During the 1920s, the rifle range — eventually called Camp Matthews — had to be located on a small tract of land a few miles northeast of La Jolla. And land that was once part of Camp Kearny, a World War I Army base about 12 miles from downtown San Diego, was leased from the city in 1934 for artillery and machine gun practice six to eight months of the year.

To accommodate wartime expansion, the Marine Corps began in mid-1940 to construct buildings in the Kearny Mesa area, referring to them unofficially as Camp Holcomb in honor of Marine Commandant, Maj. Gen. Thomas Holcomb. But Gen. Holcomb believed that no Marine base should honor a living person and quashed the name.

Even before the Japanese attack on Pearl Harbor, President Franklin D. Roosevelt had declared an unlimited national emergency, and by the middle of 1941 volunteers began pouring into the Depot. The 2nd Marine Division of the FMF — upgraded from a brigade with the addition of more troops — had already moved from the Marine Corps Base to the sprawling Kearny Mesa facility, officially named in June 1941 in honor of Maj. Gen. George F. Elliott, the 10th Commandant of the Marine Corps. But Camp Elliott was too close to residential areas for the Marines to conduct large-scale tactical maneuvers and war games.

Few cities in the United States experienced greater changes because of the war than San Diego. As a result of an unprecedented boom in defense spending, the city's population expanded from 200,000 to more than 300,000 in the year before the war started. There were more than 90,000 civilian defense workers by 1941.

Housing for these people became critical. Nearby Mission Valley, where the Marines had maneuvered just a few years earlier, became a sea of auto trailers, sitting on empty lots and connected by temporary gas meters. The federal government began construction of the Linda Vista housing project in March 1941. The 5,400-unit project was on the south portion of Kearny Mesa, directly west of Camp Elliott.

The housing mushrooming around the camp made large-scale exercises prohibitive. So, on Feb. 27, 1942, Gen. Holcomb asked the Navy to buy a huge tract of land near Oceanside, about 40 miles north of San Diego.

A tent city at Marine Corps Base, San Diego in 1943 helped to house thousands of new recruits pouring into the base.

Named in honor of Gen. Joseph H. Pendleton, the 125,000-acre camp gave the Marines plenty of room for tactical training for the three divisions that would eventually form there. And Camp Elliott became the FMF training center for individual replacements for combat units overseas.

All this expansion took place outside the property limits of Marine Base, San Diego. Other bases — Camp Gillespie in San Diego for Marine paratroopers, Camp Dunlap near the Salton Sea for artillery training, and Camp C.J. Miller in Del Mar for specialized conditioning — sprang up to further lighten the burden on the San Diego base.

The first few months of the war brought little to cheer about. The Marines took a beating in the Pacific as the Japanese overran Guam, Wake Island and the Philippines. And locally, Marines and civilians mourned the death of Gen. Pendleton, who died at his Coronado, Calif., home on Feb. 4, 1942. The 81-year-old general, known affectionately as "Uncle Joe," served 46 years in the Marines Corps, and was instrumental in bringing the Marines to San Diego.

One likely morale booster for the troops occurred in the fall, when President Franklin D. Roosevelt made a secret trip to tour military bases and defense plants on the West Coast.

The President arrived at Marine Corps Base, San Diego on Sept. 25, 1942, at 5:10 p.m., his fifth stop in San Diego County after touring the Naval Training Station. The President was accorded full honors— with the exception of a gun salute — including a full guard and band as well as a drum and bugle corps standing in formation.

Roosevelt was greeted by the Commanding General, Brig. Gen. James L. Underhill, who joined the president in his car for a tour of the base. After starting his inspection, the President paused to witness a demonstration of a number of amphibious craft on the bay. His route then took him through the main parade ground, where approximately 30 battalions of 500 Marines each had fallen in for review. The President left the base at 5:25 p.m., driving on to Consolidated-Vultee Aircraft next door.

Three officers, who were well-known on the San Diego base, share a drink. From left are Col. Gilder D. Jackson, Col. Leo D. Hermle and Col. Elmer Hall. Col. Jackson commanded the base for seven months in 1946, prior to Gen. Hermle's assuming command. Gen. Hall led the base's sports program in the mid-1920s, and the football field was later named in his honor.

New recruits in San Diego wait to get their gear in 1943.

During his visit, Roosevelt was probably informed that the primary mission of the base had become recruit training. But other operations continued to function: Sea School, Motor Transport School, Signal School, First Sergeants' School, and a Military Police School were among the many training programs that utilized the base.

The base also boasted a new outdoor theater. In January 1942, Col. William H. Rupertus, the base commander, ordered construction of the theater, a move that boosted morale and earned the colonel the affection of the men under his command.

Building the theater was probably one of Col. Rupertus' first acts after taking command of the base the day after Pearl Harbor was attacked. He assumed command from Maj. Gen. William P. Upshur, who was transferred to command the Department of the Pacific.

On Feb. 11, 1942, the new outdoor theater opened on the southeast end of the parade ground. "The new theater is the result of (Col.) Rupertus' single-handed fight for entertainment facilities for the men of his command," base newspaper, the *Chevron,* reported.

With money tight, Col. Rupertus solicited and received $7,000 worth of movie equipment from the Fox-West Coast Theater Corp. The equipment was lent to the base by the company for the duration of the war. "It gives me great pleasure to be of service to the U.S. Marines," said Charles P. Skouras, president of the nationwide theater corporation. Previously, movies had been shown in the base auditorium, which had very limited seating capacity. With base expansion, movies were discontinued because the auditorium was reserved for "lectures, instructions and special schools." The new outdoor theater accommodated 5,000 Marines.

The first show opened to a full house on Feb. 14. Movie star Jeanette McDonald led the Marines in the national anthem. "Standing before those men and singing the greatest song in the World — the Star Spangled Banner — I realized, as I looked out at the sea of faces before me, that our country was in safe hands," McDonald told the *Chevron*. "There is something about United States Marines that says, 'We don't give up!'"

The presentation that evening featured a "March of Time" newsreel about the Marines' heroic defense of Wake Island.

On Feb. 25, Kay Kayser and his "Kollege of Musical Knowledge" broadcast his nationally aired show from the San Diego base. The enthusiasm shown by the Marines in the audience prompted the sponsor, the American Tobacco Company, to endorse the base as the "finest place for air (radio) shows."

The word soon reached Hollywood. First, Jack Benny made arrangements to broadcast live from the base. Then Bob Hope brought his show to San Diego, prompting the *Chevron* to announce in bold headlines, "Marines Get Nation's Finest Entertainment."

Col. Rupertus was also responsible for beginning the base newspaper in January 1942. In one year, the *Chevron* grew from a four-page weekly of 8,000 copies to a 20-page newspaper of 50,000 copies delivered to Marines around the world. Col. Rupertus insisted that the paper focus on what enlisted men were doing, and act as a line of communications between those stateside and those overseas. "It (the *Chevron*) must not be a propaganda sheet," announced Col. Rupertus. "The less we have in it about officers the better."

Col. Rupertus was reassigned to the East Coast in March 1942. "During his short tour of duty, he endeared himself to his men as a fearless, fighting (Marine) who got things done with the traditional Marine Corps expediency," proclaimed the *Chevron*.

Col. Matthew H. Kingman was placed in command

Above, bakers on base in 1946 package loaves of bread. Food preparation was a major operation during World War II. By the end of 1942, the bakery was putting out 12,000 loaves of bread a day. Below, a Marine buys war bonds on the base in 1943.

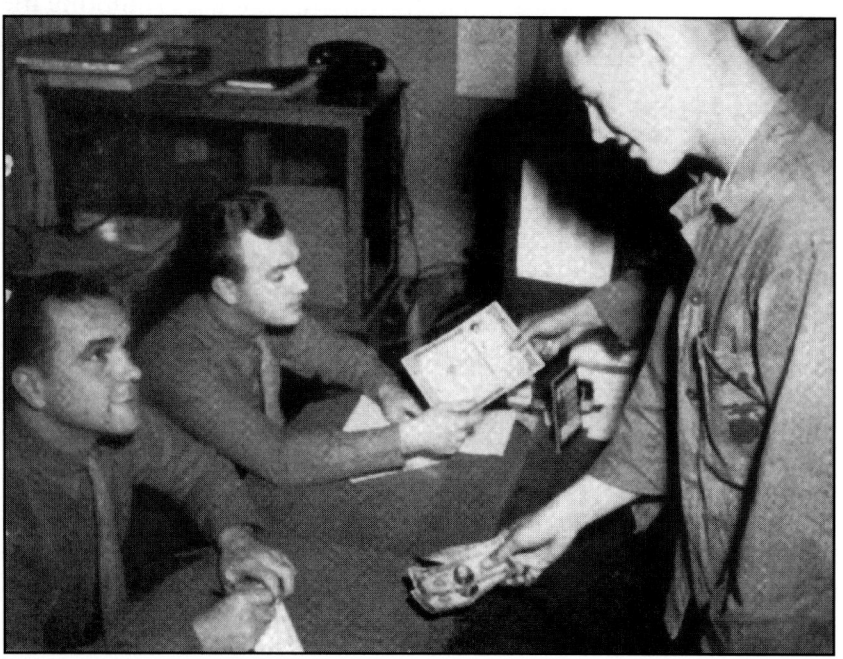

temporarily until Gen. Underhill assumed permanent command in early April, just in time to welcome a unique group of recruits.

A much-publicized platoon of Navajo Indians arrived at the processing center May 5. As the first "all Indian" platoon in the history of the Marine Corps, the 29 men were part of a secret experiment to use them on the battlefield as "code talkers." Their job would be to confuse the enemy during battles by communicating with each other in an unbreakable code based on the Navajo language.

They received close scrutiny during their seven-week training period. Early on, their drill instructors reported the Navajos were "far above the average in military adeptness." Gen. Underhill sent a letter to Washington, calling the group one of the most outstanding platoons in Marine Corps history. "You obey orders like seasoned and disciplined soldiers," Gen. Underhill announced before the Navajos were transferred to Camp Elliott for special training. "You have maintained rugged health. You have been anxious to learn your new duties, and you learn quickly. As a group, you have made one of the highest scores on the rifle range."

By May 1942, the 16-man crew at the receiving barracks was being overwhelmed by new recruits. The record, according to the newspaper, was "918 men in a single day."

The *Chevron* in bold headlines on Oct. 3, 1942, announced "Largest Payroll In History Of Recruit Depot Is Distributed." All activities at the base pay office came to an abrupt halt when Marine guards walked in with a large sack and dumped the contents on a table. "The office personnel stared at the bundle of currency as more than $400,000 slid onto the table," said the *Chevron*. "Twenty-four hours later, the currency had been distributed to Recruit Depot personnel and recruits, and had been tucked away safely into pockets, lockers, and seabags for future use when the boots will have their first liberty."

Some local citizens took too much "liberty" with the young recruits on liberty. In December, the barbershop at 638 West Broadway was placed off limits for overcharging sailors and Marines. The average price for a haircut was about $1. But these entrepreneurial barbers were charging $3.75, claiming that a "special tonic" accounted for the exorbitant price.

While some San Diego businesses were off-limits to Marines, the entire city of Tijuana,

Below, the administration building is camouflaged during World War II. Part of the original plans for the base, it wasn't constructed until January 1943. The chapel was built next door. Bottom, Catholic chaplain Cmdr. Walter Mahler celebrates Mass in 1944.

Mexico, was out-of-bounds for Leathernecks in 1942. Military police were posted at the border with orders to stop all sailors and Marines from crossing into Mexico. "We've heard some pretty good stories" from Marines trying to cross the border, confided Sgt. Joe L. Moulton to the *Chevron*. The sergeant said it was often difficult to keep a straight face. "One Marine said his commanding officer told him that he could go there due to the fact that Mexico was our ally, now that she had declared war on Germany."

The rapid expansion of the base created a housing shortage for recruits. Although more barracks had been built in 1939, new recruits had to be quartered first in tents and then in the hundreds of Quonset huts that were quickly erected during the war.

Feeding the ever-expanding number of Marines put a mounting strain on services such as the base bakery. Before the war, the bakery supplemented the Marines' daily ration of bread with pies and fancy pastries. But by December 1942, the 24-hour operation was turning out 12,000 loaves of bread a day, leaving the 30 bakers no time to produce anything else.

A new swimming pool opened in September 1942, accommodating approximately 7,000 Marines every week. In January 1943, the new administration building opened, consolidating the Commanding General's office with numerous administration offices under one roof. The administration building also housed a vault for the intelligence department's decoding machines, and several lecture halls. A new 2,506-seat indoor theater opened in February 1943. The theater, equipped with a radio studio, broadcast a weekly show over the airwaves called the "Halls of Montezuma."

The close proximity of the base to military and civilian airfields resulted in several accidents on the base. During March 1943 two Army P-38 interceptors collided in mid-air over the base. Both pilots bailed out, but one was killed when his parachute failed to open. Falling airplane parts crashed through base windows, and recruits on the parade ground

47

Below, NCOs prepare for barracks inspection during 1944; and below left, a WR checks her uniform and unpacks.

scattered to escape pieces from the tail assembly.

On May 10, 1943, three Marines were killed and 63 injured when an experimental aircraft jumped the runway at Lindbergh Field and plowed into the barracks. The XB-32, nicknamed "The Terminator," was a prototype for a heavy bomber being built by the Consolidated-Vultee factory in San Diego. The plane never made it off the ground as it raced into the barracks at 135 mph.

The spring of that year also witnessed two milestones in base history: In April, the first all-black unit arrived, and the following month the first Women Reserves made their appearance.

On April 5, the *Chevron* reported the arrival of the 1st Marine Depot Company, an all-black unit that had trained at Montford Point, N.C. "After spending their first few hours squaring their gear," the *Chevron* reported, "the men put on a warmup demonstration of close order drill that left observers gaping" in admiration. But they didn't stay long. On April 16, the company boarded the destroyer USS *Hunt* and two days later sailed for Noumea, New Caledonia.

The women, however, were on the base for the duration. In May, Maj. Ruth Streeter and two female junior officers arrived to inspect the base. As head of the Women Reserves (WRs), Maj. Streeter was on a tour of all Marine posts in the San Diego area to make sure they were preparing to absorb the hundreds of women Marines who would soon arrive.

In August, the women's area on the base was nearly complete with two barracks to accommodate 700 WRs. Located on an old athletic field, the women's area was completely self-sufficient with its own mess hall, officers quarters, dispensary, PX, and basketball and softball fields. Women's quarters at the rifle range were also near completion.

The first WRs arrived in November. By the end of the month, 80 were on the base. Many worked as secretaries and office clerks, but 10 WRs were immediately assigned to Motor Transport, where they worked as gas station attendants, grease rack operators, and drivers for staff cars and light trucks.

A Women's Reserve Battalion, under the command of Maj. Troy A. Nubson, formed in December 1943. Second Lt. Margaret E. Myers was appointed battalion executive officer and 2nd Lt. Maxine E. Coats served as the battalion's adjutant.

The Marine Corps in 1944 was immense — 390,000 men and women, with four divisions on the battlefields and a fifth shaping up at Camp Pendleton. Thousands of wounded Marines — veterans of campaigns such as Guadalcanal and Tarawa — were recuperating in military hospitals around the country. Many of these veterans had come home with malaria and were later reassigned to Marine bases. Lt. Cmdr. Ralph J. Metcalf was in charge

Below, artist Pfc. Thompson in 1944 silk screens a poster to be used for training male boots. Right, motor transport Cpl. Margo Hirt works on an engine that year. And bottom, Brig. Gen. Matthew Kingman and Capt. Dorothy Miller review a WR trick drill platoon in 1944. Barracks 337 is in the background.

Below, a World War II transport brings troops to the Broadway Pier in San Diego. Bottom, Marines have their photo taken with a newspaper on V-J day in San Diego.

"Peace is near. Peace— for which we fought and bled and saw our buddies die — is close at hand. You want to cheer, but there is a lump in your throat that stops it; you would like to cry — but hold it back. Thoughts of the future are already crowding the realities of the moment."

Chevron editorial, Aug. 11, 1945

pieces of their civilian lives. All of them needed processing and Marine Corps Base, San Diego became a major separation center. The arrival nearly every week of Navy transports crowded with hundreds of war-weary men strained the resources of the base. By the end of 1945, Base Separation Company had processed nearly 20,000 Marines.

The primary function of the base as a recruit training center was officially recognized in 1948 when its designation was changed to Marine Corps Recruit Depot, San Diego. That same year, the Depot also gave birth to a reserve tank battalion. Nearly 300 reservists trained at MCRD until they were called to active duty in 1950 for the Korean War.

The war placed a burden on the Depot to supply the manpower needs for replacement drafts. And once again, the Depot served as a separation center when Marines rotated home.

The Vietnam War created many of these same challenges at the base. In addition, the social and political upheaval of the 1960s and early 1970s reverberated throughout the Marine Corps, leaving its mark on Marine bases around the country.

The 1980s and early 1990s at MCRD were most notable for a flurry of new buildings valued at more than $51 million, and ranging from a 96-square-foot chlorinating building to a 137,950-square-foot bachelor enlisted quarters. These projects were the biggest boom in building to hit the base since World War II.

Much had changed during the 50 years from the end of World War II to the mid-1990s. Leathernecks of the new Corps and the old Corps would hardly recognize the same base or the way the Marine Corps operated.

It was the immediate future, however, that weighed heavily on the minds of veterans returning from World War II. On Aug. 10, 1945, news of Japan's imminent defeat reached Marine Corps Base, San Diego, and the question "I wonder what I'll do now?" seemed to be on everybody's mind.

According to the base newspaper, the *Chevron*, the mood was subdued throughout the day. "The various activities of the Base moved on without interruption Friday morning (Aug. 11) despite a general murmur of optimism and relief that spread through barracks and office buildings," reported the newspaper. "There was no general outburst of cheering or other displays of emotions among the many overseas veterans stationed here." The paper noted that the streets in downtown San Diego were also quiet, "more quiet than usual."

The restraint was short-lived, however, as civilians and servicemen and women poured out onto Broadway four days later to celebrate V-J Day. Like other cities across the nation, San Diego had its share of wild celebrations. But on the base, the mood remained subdued throughout the day.

"There were no screams or shouts and nothing in the way of open demonstration," the *Chevron* proclaimed. That evening, however, a dance was held on the base basketball courts. "The affair started slowly, and most of the Base personnel seemed to look upon V-J Day as 'just another day,' but the celebration gradually gained momentum and by 2100 the courts were packed with Marines celebrating their eventual liberation."

World War II was finally over, and for many Marines, both at home and abroad, the big question was demobilization — when would it begin and how would it affect them? Consequently, the air of victory that swept over the base in August 1945 gave way to the challenge of separating tens of thousands of Leathernecks for eventual re-entry into civilian life..

Marines soon found out they would be separated from the service by a point system adopted from the Army. The system initially required 85 points for men and 25 points for women. One point was awarded for every month of service since Sept. 15, 1940, another point for each month overseas or afloat since that date, five points for each decoration and 12 points for each child under 18, up to three children. The system did not apply to men currently serving a four-year enlistment.

Col. John Groff

The Marine Corps promptly declared a plan to return approximately 75 percent of Leathernecks back to civilian life, some 350,000 men and women. By Sept. 15, 1945, the base announced that it would step up the discharges to 200 Marines every day. "Our primary mission," said Chief of Staff Col. John Groff, "is to help get people out of the service."

The colonel must have understood the expectations of many Marines as they made the transition back to civilian life because he would be leaving the service himself in two months.

Col. Groff came to San Diego in 1937 to serve as communications officer of the Fleet Marine Force. Two years later, he was appointed commanding officer of the Recruit Depot. Col. Groff served at nearby Camp Elliott from 1942 to 1944 as chief of staff to Brig. Gen. Matthew Kingman. He resumed command of the Recruit Depot in June 1944 and seven months later was appointed chief of staff for the entire base. The colonel went on inactive duty in November 1945, and was replaced by Col. William W. Davies.

Base Separation Company was expanded just as Wash-

Troops from the 1st Marine Division, Fleet Marine Force, Pacific get ready to leave for Korea from a dock at Naval Station, San Diego on July 13, 1950.

ington announced in the fall of 1945 that it was reducing the number of points needed for discharge from 85 to 70 for men. Women would still need 25 points.

On Oct. 12, 1945, more than 900 men of the 4th Marine Division arrived in San Diego aboard the aircraft carrier USS *Attu*. They were the vanguard of thousands more Marines and sailors who were on their way to San Diego for processing.

The 1st Separation Company, organized at Marine Corps Base, San Diego in late 1944, announced that by the end of 1945 its personnel had processed 19,712 Marines.

Early in the new year, plans to disband the Women Reserves Battalion on the base were formulated. The ranks of the Women Reserves on the base were dramatically reduced from their wartime peak of 661 enlisted women and 19 officers to 177 enlisted and 10 officers by April 1946. Maj. Dorothy Miller, commanding officer of the battalion, left the Marine Corps, turning over command to 1st Lt. Mary Jane Hale. The door of the women's barracks finally closed in mid-May when Cpl. Laura Picketts was the last to be discharged.

That same month, 411 base Marines prepared for armed intervention in the nation's railroad strike. President Harry S. Truman had issued an ultimatum to thousands of railroad workers who walked off their jobs May 23, 1946.

The air was tense at the base as men of a provisional battalion lined the parade grounds in full combat gear for final inspection by Col. Harry B. Liversedge, the base commander. The confrontation between Marines and civilian workers was averted at the last minute when railroad personnel returned to their jobs.

Col. Liversedge was assigned as base commander in April 1946. He was the second of three colonels to command the base during a seven-month period. Col. Miles R. Thacker had replaced Maj. Gen. Earl C. Long in January of that year, and Col. Gilder D. Jackson was base commander from June through July 1946, when Brig. Gen. Leo Hermle took command.

Before the war, Col. Liversedge was the rifle range commander at Camp Matthews, and he lived at the range again while commanding the Marine base. He organized the 3rd Raider Battalion in 1942 and was later the commander of the famed 28th Marines, the captors of Mt. Suribachi. Col. Liversedge earned the Navy Cross twice.

And Col. Jackson led the 6th Marines ashore at the taking of Guadalcanal. He held the Navy Cross, five Silver Stars and the Purple Heart.

Before World War II, the base was primarily a staging ground for Marine expeditions and headquarters for the Fleet Marine Force. But throughout World War II, the principal activity at Marine Corps Base, San Diego was recruit training. Official recognition of this new mission came Jan. 1, 1948, when the base was renamed Marine Corps Recruit Depot, San Diego. The redesignation also meant the base was removed from the immediate jurisdiction of the 11th

Naval District, and now came directly under the Commandant of the Marine Corps.

The names of other base units also changed: Camp Matthews Rifle Range became Weapons Training Battalion, Base Troops became Headquarters and Service Battalion, and Recruit Training Detachment was redesignated 1st Recruit Training Battalion.

In June 1948, seventeen World War II Mark 4s arrived at the Depot. The tanks, better known as General Shermans, were destined for the 11th Tank Battalion.

The San Diego reserve tankers unit was first organized at the Depot on Dec. 12, 1946.

"We started (the tank battalion) with a nucleus of four or five officers and maybe a dozen men," said retired Col. Phil Morell in an interview in the September 1994 edition of *Traditions: San Diego's Military History* magazine. A World War II tank commander, the colonel recalled those first months trying to organize the battalion on the base. "We had no tanks or equipment; we didn't get paid. There were only two of us with any tank experience, and the lectures we gave could have been on most anything. I used to give lectures on my World War II experiences on Guam and Okinawa. That was how the battalion got started."

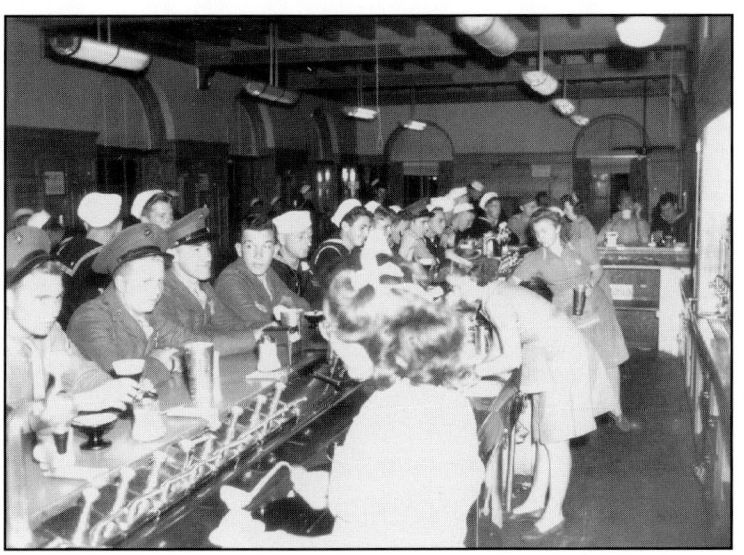

Marines and sailors crowd around the soda fountain at the Armed Services YMCA in 1953. During the Korean War years, the Y was packed with military men who found recreation and a place to sleep for short liberties.

By the time the tanks arrived during July 1948, the battalion's "A Company" had reached its authorized strength of 281 enlisted men and 20 officers. After outgrowing its single barracks building on the Depot, the battalion was assigned to the old Sea School compound. The tanks were housed in metal sheds near the bay.

Special tank-driving classes were held every Saturday afternoon. "We trained at MCRD, right at the end of the runway at Lindbergh Field," said Col. Morell. There wasn't much room for tank training at the Depot. "We had less than 20 acres to move around on." During the next two years, the battalion trained for two weeks each summer up the coast at the newly designated Marine Corps Base, Camp Pendleton. But in 1950 the training abruptly stopped.

The outbreak of hostilities in Korea in June 1950 prompted the mobilization of the reserves and a dramatic increase in the number of new recruits. Both the Depot and Camp Pendleton became staging areas for thousands of Marine Reservists and regulars, who were quickly prepared for deployment to Korea.

"That call-up was the most screwed-up call-up," confided Col. Morell, recalling his first few days back on active duty. "We went to MCRD and received all our shots; all our service and health records were updated; insurance — everything — was brought up to order, and we were ready." The next day, the battalion boarded "cattle cars" for the trip to Camp Pendleton. "We waited three days, and nothing happened," said Col. Morell. "When this guy finally did come, he took us to get socks, even though we had already been issued them. Then he took us to get physicals, then to fill out insurance papers. We complained that we already did all these things at the Recruit Depot. It was a waste of time."

Retired Lt. Gen. Victor H. Krulak also vividly remembered problems with the call-up for Korea. In his book *First To Fight: The Inside View Of The U.S. Marine Corps*, Gen. Krulak wrote, "Everything that happened, it seemed, was an enemy of the clock. The City would not permit ammunition to be loaded at its municipal piers, so every

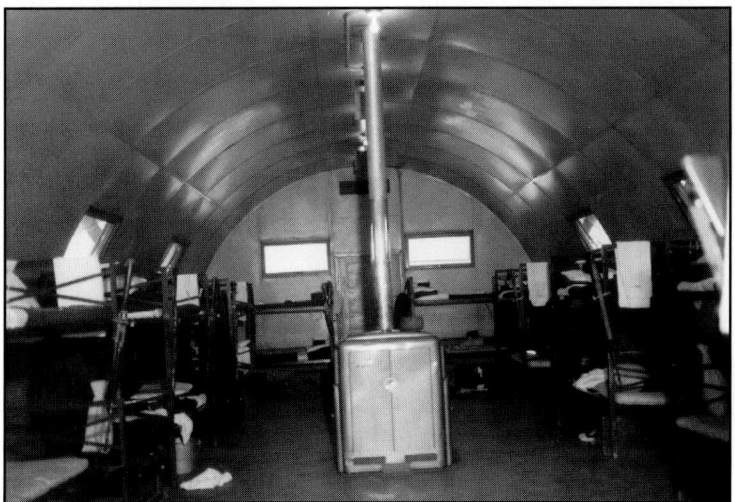

Quonset huts, like this 1970 model, were built during the Korean War as temporary housing to replace the tent city of World War II.

Top, on June 29, 1951, the MCRD base newspaper, the *Chevron*, announced the return of Marines from Korea. The photo shows their arrival at the pier in downtown San Diego, with the band playing and civilians on hand to welcome them. Above, a graduation ceremony is held at the base theater in 1956, the year the facility was named in honor of Maj. Gen. Douglas C. McDougal, Commanding General in the mid-1930s. The theater was built during World War II.

During the late 1950s, recruits in San Diego use a huge "push-ball" to aid physical conditioning and build team spirit. A recruit digs into chow balanced to increase or decrease weight as needed. Bottom, an aerial view of the base in the 1950s, looking east from the administration building in the foreground.

ship had to be moved to North Island Naval Air Station to take on ammunition."

The loading was further complicated because most of the ships were civilian-owned and had to be loaded by civilian stevedores. There weren't nearly enough stevedores to load all the ships. The Marines offered help, but the union threatened to strike. In addition, three of the civilian ships arrived late, and the Navy cargo ship, USS *Titania*, developed a bad boiler and had to be unloaded. Its cargo was transferred to other ships.

"Despite all these impediments it all came together — not smoothly, not neatly, but it all came together — Marines from everywhere moved into combat units, the hardware of war moved into ships," wrote Gen. Krulak. "The embarkation was a product of experience, improvisation, corner cutting, risk taking, and refusal to accept no for an answer."

Even though the initial buildup provided the manpower for a full-strength Marine division, the Recruit Depot was also obliged to make ready for training thousands of Marines needed for replacement drafts. The job called for the eventual expansion of the Depot from one to eight recruit training battalions.

Each battalion consisted of 25 platoons of 75 recruits each. The housing requirements prompted the Corps to seek congressional approval for major construction projects on the base totaling $2,891,268. Nearly half the money was spent on the construction of 351 Quonset huts to be used as temporary barracks. Other projects included new storehouses, messhalls, and a new cold storage building.

The 2nd Recruit Training Battalion moved into operation on Aug. 14, 1950. The new training battalion, under the command of Lt. Col. R.T. Stivers Jr., set up its headquarters in the south wing of Building 28, adjacent to the 1st Recruit Training Battalion.

Less than a month later on Sept. 11, a third battalion was organized under the command of Lt. Col. W.G. Robb. An 800 unit "tent city" was hastily erected to house the new battalion.

The 4th Recruit Training Battalion was activated under the command of Maj. V.T. Willis in late January 1951, and the base announced plans to replace the tent city with prefabricated 24-man Quonset huts, "as soon as the negotiations with civilian contractors were completed."

By mid-Spring 1951, the base personnel faced new challenges processing the thousands of Marines who began coming home from Korea.

Approximately 1,300 veterans of the Chosin Reservoir returned to San Diego aboard the transport ship USS *Sgt. Sylvester Antolak* on April 29, 1951. They were the first to come back under the Marine Corps' new rotation plan.

More than 30,000 San Diegans lined Navy Pier as the MCRD band serenaded the Leathernecks. The men boarded buses for the short ride to the Depot, where they were billeted with the 4th Recruit Training Battalion and processed for duty at posts around the country.

A Separation Center was authorized June 15. During the next two years, the center would handle thousands of Korean War veterans. As in World War II, troop strength following the Korean War dropped.

W hen compared to the drama of World War II and Korea, the mid-1950s and early 1960s were relatively peaceful times at MCRD, San Diego. But they were not without incident. During that period, *The San Diego Union* newspaper reported:

• The incinerator on the base, dubbed "old smokey," was dismantled in September 1955, and Marines began hauling their trash to city dumps.

• Two Star pines were planted in June 1956 at the entrance to the Administration building in memory of Lt. Gen. William T. Clement, base commander from 1949 to

Maj. Gen. Victor H. Krulak, the Commanding General, poses in the center of all the sergeants major of MCRD on opening night of a new staff NCO club in 1961.

President John F. Kennedy inspects the honor guard at MCRD on June 6, 1963. To the president's left is Commanding General Maj. Gen. Sidney S. Wade and Capt. Russell M. Lloyd, Jr., officer in charge of Sea School.

1951. The general, who died Oct. 17, 1955, had earned the Navy Cross during World War II.
- Sixteen Marines at the Depot were selected by movie actor Jack Webb in February 1957 to appear in "The D.I."
- Sgt. Jesse Teverbaugh, a black Marine stationed at the Depot, won a lawsuit in February 1958 against five San Diego trailer park owners for discrimination.
- Brig. Gen. Chester R. Allen held a news conference at the Depot in May 1959, proclaiming that Russian victories on international rifle ranges have "jolted" the Marines into reassessing their own marksmanship.
- A Marine corporal and two civilians robbed the post

exchange safe of $22,000 in June 1960.
• A contract between the city of San Diego and the Marines was approved in May 1961 to allow the San Diego Chargers to use the Depot's football field.
• In July 1962, Pfc. Joseph P. DiMaggio Jr., son of baseball legend Joe DiMaggio, was awarded the American Spirit Honor Medal at the Depot.
• President John F. Kennedy inspected MCRD in May 1963. A part of the Commanding General's quarters was remodeled for the visit.
• Maj. Gen. Bruno A. Hochmuth, MCRD Commanding General, announced in July 1964 that youths arriving at the Depot from civilian life left much to be desired.

Perhaps Gen. Hochmuth envisioned tough times ahead for Marines in Southeast Asia. On March 8, 1965, the Marines landed to defend the American air base at Da Nang. From that point on, there was no question that Vietnam was an American war.

The Chief of Staff of the Marine Corps, Lt. Gen. Leonard F. Chapman Jr., visited MCRD, San Diego in

Top left, a Marine private 1st class photographer demonstrates skills she learned during on-the-job training at the Depot in 1966. Left, a Marine checks produce in the cold storage room of the mess commissary storage section at MCRD in 1966. The room was part of a $2.8 million expansion program at the base at the onset of the Korean War. And above, LCpl. Nancee Vilbrandt works a "flexograph" in the disbursing office in 1965.

early April to assess recruit training. Gen. Chapman told *The San Diego Union*, "The involvement of the Marines in Vietnam up to now has not required any changes in the speed and scope of the training." But the general cautioned, "plans have been made to accelerate Marine Corps training in San Diego if the fighting in Vietnam demands a greater commitment from Marines."

On Sept. 1, 1965, the Marine Corps announced a speed-up in recruit training that, once again, put the base on a wartime footing. Recruit training was immediately reduced from 12 to eight weeks. The first draftees began arriving in November from induction centers in Detroit, Chicago, and Los Angeles.

A tent camp once again mushroomed to accommodate recruits overflowing the permanent barracks. Even the Quonset huts built during the Korean War couldn't handle the recruit population that by early 1966 had reached 13,600.

The hardback tents each housed 20 recruits and were built on the Depot's golf driving range. The tents were heated with oil stoves and there was one electric light bulb in the center. By March, there were more than 15,000 recruits at MCRD.

Gen. Krulak called the war in Vietnam the Corps' "sternest fighting test of all, where the need for adaptability was the greatest." This was also true on the home front as the Depot struggled during the late 1960s and early 1970s to adjust to the ever increasing political and cultural upheaval outside its gates.

The San Diego Union published many reports on these conflicts:

• "Opposing groups of students demonstrated at San Diego State (College) yesterday after two Marine Corps recruiters set up an information table." — May 4, 1967.

• "Go-Go girls have been banished from clubs on all Navy and Marine Corps bases in San Diego." — June 16, 1967.

• "A 17-year-old Marine AWOL from San Diego has sought and received sanctuary in the Unitarian Church."— April 6, 1969.

• "A general court-martial has been recommended for a Marine Vietnam veteran who allegedly beat six recruits on the head and face with a wire coat hanger for taking too long with meals." — Dec. 4, 1969.

• "The Marine Corps Recruit Depot reported yesterday that some 'minor incidents with racial overtones' occurred on the base over the weekend. A few Marines received minor injuries." — June 6, 1970.

• "A 23-year-old Marine went on a five-hour shooting spree early yesterday in the post exchange at the Marine

> "Plans have been made to accelerate Marine Corps training in San Diego if the fighting in Vietnam demands a greater commitment from Marines."
>
> Lt. Gen. Leonard F. Chapman Jr., Chief of Staff of the Marine Corps, April, 1965

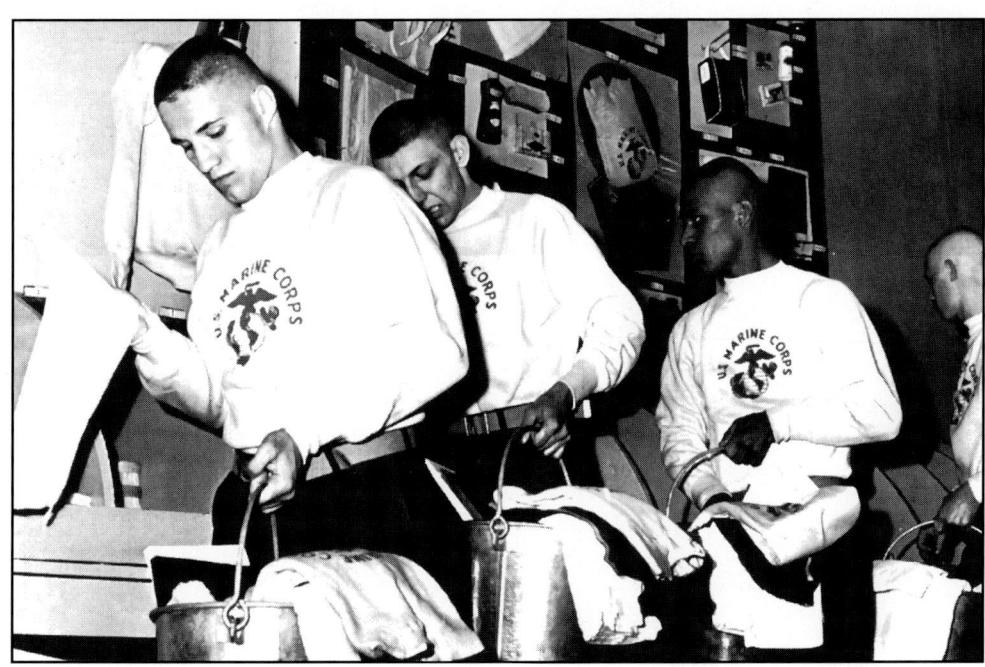

Recruits get their gear at the receiving barracks in 1968.

A rock band plays at the Depot in the 1970s, a time of turmoil both on and off the base.

Corps Recruit Depot before his buddy persuaded him to surrender. 'I'm sick of society, and I'm sick of the world,' the sobbing Vietnam veteran told Depot officials." — Nov. 22, 1970.

Col. Ernest R. Savoy, commanding officer of the Recruit Training Regiment at MCRD in 1976, was one of many Vietnam veterans assuming posts on the base in the late 1960s.

• "The Marine Corps yesterday announced a new drug amnesty policy for drug-using Marines. Commanders of the Marine Corps Recruit Depot and Camp Pendleton plan to meet next week to discuss how to implement the plan." — July 7, 1971.

The communication gap between commanders and subordinates at the Depot paralleled the rift between many fathers and sons. The Union reported, "The Commandant of the Marine Corps has called for an increase in understanding and the closing of a 'serious' communication gap now existing among Marines." The Commandant's remarks were acknowledged in a personal letter to Maj. Gen. John N. McLaughlin, Depot commander.

These incidents were a reflection of turmoil in the civilian world. But Marines also continued to prove themselves on the battlefield and were honored at MCRD for their courage. At nearly every weekly graduation ceremony, Vietnam veterans received medals for their heroism. For example, *The San Diego Union* reported on Nov. 11, 1966 that "Sgt. Francisco Trujillo, a platoon sergeant in Vietnam, received the Bronze Star Medal during the weekly parade and review at the Marine Corps Recruit Depot. Trujillo was credited with saving the lives of wounded Marines under fire." Such announcements were commonplace in the newspaper throughout the entire war.

And civilians did appreciate the job Marines were doing. Louis Kaye rounded up 123 entertainers in less than a week to welcome home the 27th Marines with a variety show. The Depot theater was used to entertain Marines fresh from the jungles of Vietnam, *The San Diego Union* reported Sept. 17, 1968. The theater was "almost rocked into rubble" as 20 Marines got up on stage and danced a "wild boog-a-loo with six USO girls in tight blue outfits."

By the late 1960s, Vietnam veterans were taking over posts on the base. For example, Lt. Col. Ernest R. Savoy, who was wounded in combat and decorated for heroism, assumed command of the 2nd Recruit Training Battalion from Lt. Col. Emerson A. Walker, who was preparing to retire after a 26-year career.

The first combat company to be stationed at the base since World War II arrived in May 1971. Approximately 200 Marines of the 1st Air Naval Gunfire Liaison Company (ANGLICO) arrived from Hawaii aboard the amphibious transport USS *Cleveland*. The Marines were trained to support ground troops by directing air and naval gunfire to enemy targets on shore.

Since the beginning of the war, American society had changed. The Corps reflected those changes in some ways. In other ways it didn't.

Reporting on life inside Marine Corps bases around the country in November 1971, *Newsweek* magazine wrote, "There are some cosmetic changes in garrison life. Quonset huts have been razed to make way for barracks resembling college dorms, and dishes are replacing the old tin mess trays. At many messhalls, Marines who miss chow can pick up a sandwich later."

Newsweek also reported, "But the boots still glisten, the green utility uniforms still crackle with starch, and scalps show through the sidewall haircuts — although off duty wigs sell briskly for $5 at Camp Pendleton's base exchange."

A tour of other Marine bases revealed that at New River Marine Air Station in North Carolina there was a formal ban on "ornaments, trinkets, symbols and other devices that are commonly worn by hippies." But at nearby Camp

Believe it ... or not! from the pages of *The San Diego Union*

24 Nov. 1965 ... Two teenagers visiting San Diego's Marine Corps Recruit Depot got into the wrong line and received recruit haircuts by mistake; D'Wayne Avila, 13, and John Mitchell Warren, 19, thought something was wrong, but what do you do when a Marine sergeant tells you to sit still and keep your lip buttoned? ... **6 Feb. 1966** ... Amateur radio operators at the MCRD are having trouble keeping in touch with one of their fellow "hams," Staff Sgt. Richard Kiter. Viet Cong guerrillas keep knocking down his antenna with mortar shells. Kiter used to be in charge of the ham station at MCRD, but since Feb. 1 he has been on the air from the Marine Base at Chu Lai in South Vietnam. ... **3 Mar. 1966** ... A drill instructor at MCRD was honored yesterday for his "courage and initiative" in rescuing a passenger from a plane that crashed at Lindbergh Field Jan. 25. Cpl. Claude E. Foster was commended in a Meritorious Mast by Maj. Gen. Bruno A Hochmuth. ... **3 Apr. 1966** ... Pvt. James L. Zimmerman, a 22 year-old recruit from Burbank, Calif., has become the first trainee at MCRD to pass his physical training test with a maximum score of 500 points. ... **22 Aug. 1966** ... A group of 72 young men inducted in the Marine Corps in Chicago and going through boot camp at MCRD are rubbing Victor Perez's shaved head for luck. They represent the largest group sworn into the Corps since the Korean War. ... **22 Sep. 1966** ... More than 1,300 Marines, many of them veterans of combat in Vietnam, arrived in San Diego from the Far East yesterday aboard the Navy transport USS *Gen. William*  *Weigel*. ... **1 Dec. 1967** ... A 17-year-old youth from Gary, Ind. insisted that it was no fault of his that he was flown to San Diego to begin Marine training when he never enlisted. "They wouldn't listen to me," said Scharod Boyd, who has been at the Depot for nearly two weeks. ... **16 Nov. 1968** ... Approximately 10 wives and children of civilian barbers at MCRD picketed the base yesterday to protest a proposed new employment policy affecting the barbers. ... **18 Sep. 1969** ... Recalcitrant recruits at MCRD have been handcuffed to a mirror and forced to look at themselves for self-examination and motivation, a spokesman for the Depot said yesterday, but the Depot categorically denies that any of the recruits were forced to stand naked while doing so. ... **16 Nov. 1970** ... What brought the fancy-dressed cowboy to the gate of MCRD Saturday at midnight? Nobody can explain it, but he was there — a cowboy in dandy dude dress shooting a six-gun into the air. ... **10 Aug. 1971** ... There's a new look at MCRD. The new look includes gourmet meals in carpeted dining halls and authorization for women Marines to wear hot pants off duty if they like. ... **8 Dec. 1971** ... A tall 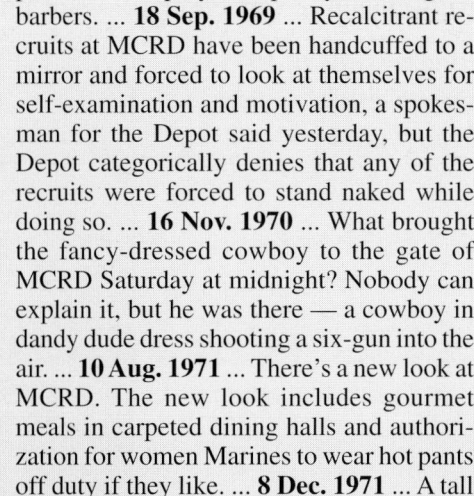 blonde girl last night outfought two AWOL Marines who tried to kidnap her at knifepoint in the employee parking lot at Lindbergh Field. ... **9 Apr. 1972** ... Women in combat? Among the gentlemanly but astonished spectators to such a development would be the United States Marines. Three battle-experienced Marines at MCRD hasten to point out that they're not against women, but American women are used to the soft life.

GySgt. R.F. Jones explains Marine Corps water survival training to the Commandant of the Indonesian Marine Corps during the Commandant's official visit to the Depot on Aug. 26, 1974.

Lejeune, Marines were allowed to put peace symbols on their automobile windows — "unless superimposed over an American flag."

At San Diego, calisthenics on the grinder were changed to take place during the cooler morning hours, and recruits no longer ran two miles around the parade field before and after every meal. "It didn't make much sense to have a lot of kids puking all the time," said Col. Edmund G. Derning, in charge of recruit training at the Depot.

The discontent and frustrations of military life in the early 1970s was unabashedly aired to the public by officers — MCRD being no exception.

As far as Lt. Ernie Marsh was concerned, the military wasn't changing fast enough to suit him. A Navy chaplain stationed at MCRD, San Diego, Lt. Marsh characterized the Marine Corps for *Newsweek* as the "last bastion of controlled thought in the United States."

Col. Derning told *Newsweek*, "Our kids come from a society that is increasingly anti-military. We get a lot of losers who come here as a last ditch. Some of them are hopeless dropouts."

The Marine Corps took action to address both the concern inherent in the colonel's remark and the problem itself — which was real.

A program initiated at MCRD, San Diego — The Marine Corps Human Relations Institute — was a direct response to such attitudes on Marine Corps bases. It was designed to improve attitudes among Marines and con-

Marine recruits in 1975 get a history lesson on the Korean War.

Commandant of the Marine Corps, Gen. Louis H. Wilson, left, inspects a member of the MCRD Honor Guard on Oct. 5, 1976, as Maj. Gen. Kenneth Houghton, right, looks on. It was the first day of the Commandant's two-day visit to the base. During a talk at the base theater, Gen. Wilson referred to Gen. Houghton as "the most combat experienced Marine in the Corps." Below, an aerial view of the base in 1970, looking southwest toward San Diego and the Coronado Bridge. In the foreground are Quonset huts and the dormitory-style barracks that were beginning to replace them as quarters for recruits.

vened its first three-month class of 90 Marines in September 1971. The idea was to provide a pipeline for highly trained human relations specialists for the Corps. "San Diego was selected over a number of other Marine Corps bases that were considered because it was located in a community with Mexican minorities as well as Negroes," said Col. John W. Haggert, the Depot's assistant chief of staff.

Eight instructors and five support personnel graduated 70 officers each year from a course that was initially 11 weeks and shortened to six weeks after Congress discontinued funds for separate service schools in human relations. The institute was disbanded July 19, 1974, and reestablished at Quantico, Va., as part of the Marine Corps Education Center.

The Corps also tackled the problem of volunteer recruits who were not ready for boot camp. According to *The San Diego Union*, in April 1973, newly enlisted Leathernecks who had trouble reading got intensive remedial instruction before they began recruit training. The catch-up course at MCRD was part of the base's learning laboratory and remedial reading center.

The latter part of the 1970s brought more criticism of MCRD. The National Athletic Health Institute described physical fitness training at the Depot in 1978 as "woefully inadequate" with outdated exercise methods. Although the Corps defended its physical training for recruits — then part of a nine-week boot camp — the criti-

Workers lay in some of the 24 lanes for a bowling alley on the base in December 1971.

cism was instigated by one of its own: Maj. Gen. Kenneth Houghton.

The general, who was base commander from 1975 to 1977, invited the nonprofit institute to evaluate physical training at the Depot and recommend changes. Gen. Houghton, a self-described "physical fitness addict," had retired by the time the institute presented its report to MCRD and to Marine Corps Headquarters, Washington, D.C. He told *The San Diego Union*, "I was concerned about our lack of (physical fitness) standards." The report criticized MCRD's program because, among other things, each physical fitness instructor had different expectations for recruits.

But Headquarters turned down the recommendation for development of a training program, saying the cost was prohibitive. The attitude at the base was two-fold. Marines believed in their training program, which had been renovated after physiological studies were conducted in 1971 by the Corps. And, in the end, it came down to the basic issue, as MSgt. Charles McCormick at the Depot told *The San Diego Union:* "Hell, we win wars don't we?"

There was more to the 1970s than internal and external strife. Living conditions improved on the base with new barracks and recreation facilities.

Officials held a groundbreaking ceremony at MCRD to mark construction of two 900-man recruit barracks costing $3.5 million in January 1971. The site was adjacent to the drill field and replaced Quonset huts and a messhall built during the 1950s.

And in March, ceremonies were held for the groundbreaking of a $750,000 bowling alley, which included 24 lanes and a Hof Brau. The center replaced the bowling alley at Midway Drive on the base.

In addition, the Depot closed a 68-acre trash dump on the base near Harbor Drive. Officials said it was a breeding place for flies and attracted sea gulls. Also a clean-burning, steam-generating plant replaced an outmoded oil-burning plant.

The 1980s brought an even more "constructive" focus to the Depot: From 1980 to 1988, one or more buildings went up almost every year, 17 in all including: Gate House 5 in 1980 at a cost of $5,000; a provost

The smoke stack behind the boiler house in Building 9, above in April 1970, comes down in 1975, at right and below, after outliving its usefulness. It was built in 1920 as part of the base's steam heating system. In 1971, the Depot began purchasing steam heat from a private company. According to the June 6, 1975, edition of the *Chevron*, the smoke stack was torn down because of deterioration and its potential as a safety hazard to air traffic from next-door Lindbergh Field.

1. Tennis Court
2. Bayview Lounge and Restaurant
3. Bachelor Officers Quarters
4. Tennis Court
5. Boathouse
6. Commanding General's Quarters
7. Family Housing, Married Officers
8. Administration Bldg. & Chapel
9. MCRD Band
10. 12th Marine Corps District
11. Library, Human Resources
12. H&S Btn. Headquarters Company
13. H&S Btn. Service Company
14. RTR: Drill Instructor School
15. Indoor Playing Courts
16. Electronic/Communications
17. Recruiters School
18. Bowling Alley/Enlisted Club
19. Legal Services/Naval Criminal Investigative Service
20. MWR Administration
21. Post Office/Exchange/Credit Union
22. Bachelor Enlisted Quarters
23. Enlisted Dining
24. Gate/Sentry House
25. Command Museum
26. Battalion HQ
27. Battalion HQ
28. Retail Exchange
29. Retail Exchange
30. Theater
31. Combat Training Pool
32. Regimental HQ
33. Academic/General Instruction
34. Dental Clinic

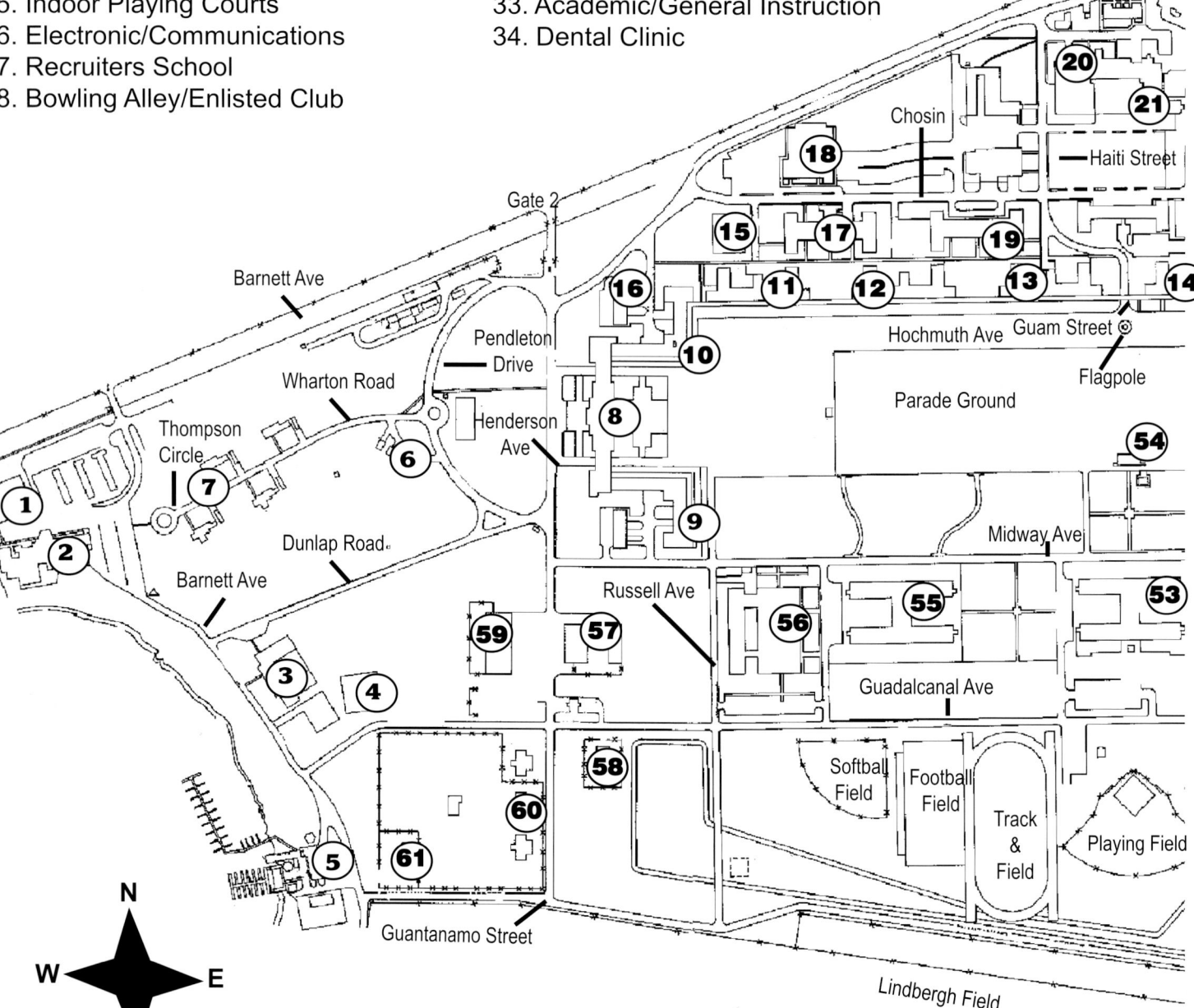

1997 Map of MCRD, San Diego

35. Visitor Reception/Storage
36. Child Care Center
37. Cold Storage Warehouse
38. Exchange, Administration
39. Warehouses
40. Child Care Administration
41. Public Works
42. Storage
43. RTR/Recruiting
44. RTR/Recruit In-Processing
45. Armory
46. Small Arms Building
47. Post Office/Recruit Exchange
48. Storage
49. Recruit Barracks
50. Recruit Barracks
51. Recruit Barracks
52. Recruit Dining Facility
53. Recruit Barracks
54. Reviewing Stand
55. Recruit Barracks
56. Medical Clinic
57. Auto Hobby Shop
58. Administration, U.S. Coast Guard
59. MWR Camping Center
60. MWR Storage
61. Administration, U.S. Coast Guard

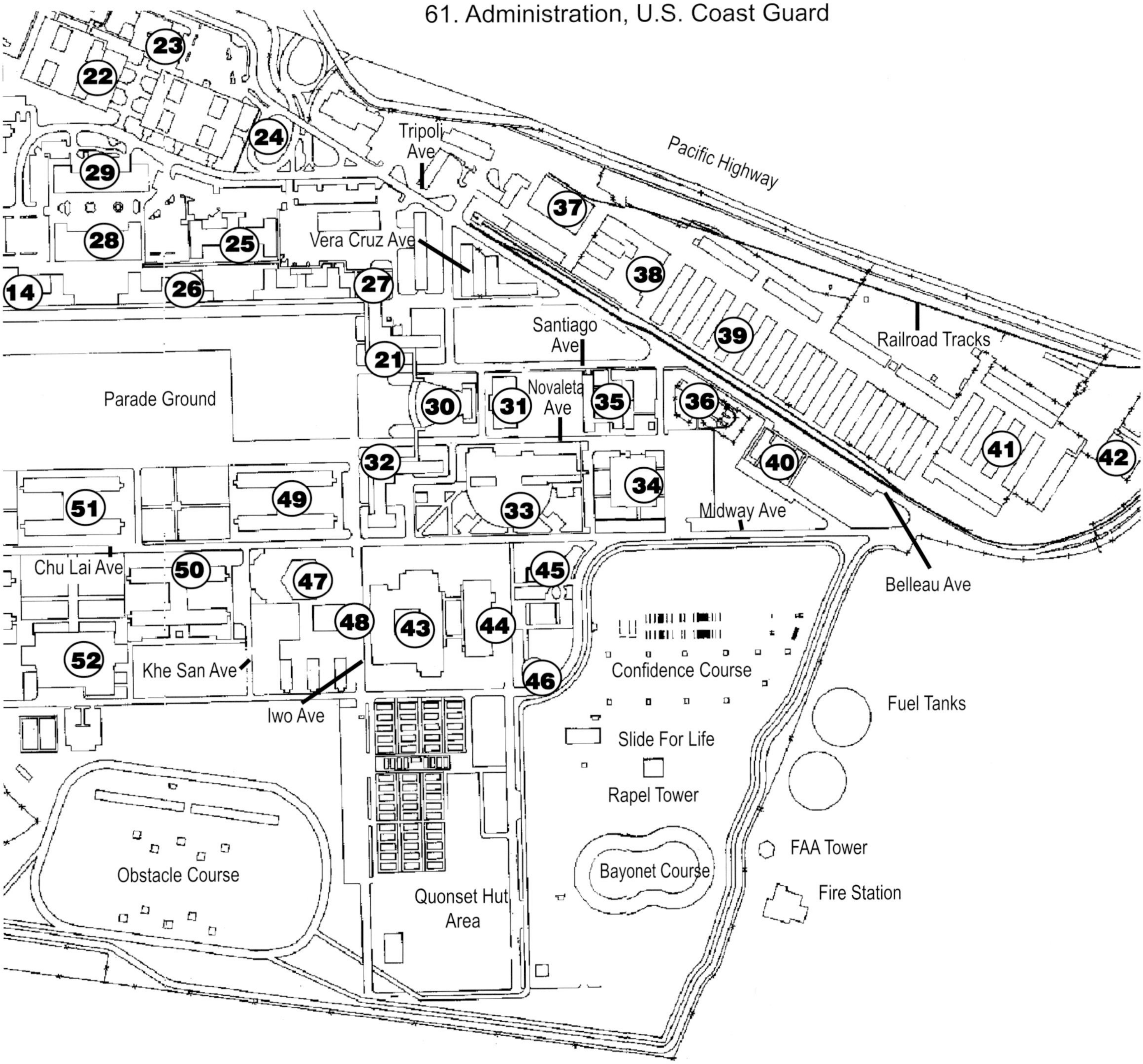

marshal's office and fire station in 1983 at a cost of just more than $1 million; an armory in 1985 valued at almost $2.7 million; six buildings in 1986, costing a total $26.1 million, including a bachelor enlisted quarters, mess hall, and recruit processing center and barracks; another bachelor enlisted quarters in 1987 cost $11.4 million; and a recruit training facility was built in 1988 at a cost of $9.6 million.

Building continued during the 1990s, although at a much slower pace. A reviewing stand was built in 1991 at a cost of $185,000, and a child care center went up in 1992 valued at $645,000. In addition, funding was authorized in 1997 to build a water survival training tank in 1998. The 44,000-square-foot facility was expected to cost $8.1 million. Depot officials put in a wish list for funding for other facilities heading into the next century, including $9.2 million for rebuilding a club; $5 million for a recruit clothing facility; $1.5 million for a fitness center; $5 million for a logistics facility; and $14.5 million for a staff NCO bachelor enlisted quarters.

Spending by taxpayers on the base was rewarded by spending off the base. When the idea of a Marine base in San Diego was first conceived in 1916, city officials knew the facility would have an enormous impact on the local economy. In 1996, the base bought $26 million worth of goods and services from local businesses and suppliers. In 1997, the base employs than 850 civilians and is home to approximately 1,900 Marines and sailors, along with 3,000 to 6,000 recruits at any one time. Most of the base's annual payroll of more than $87 million is spent in the local economy.

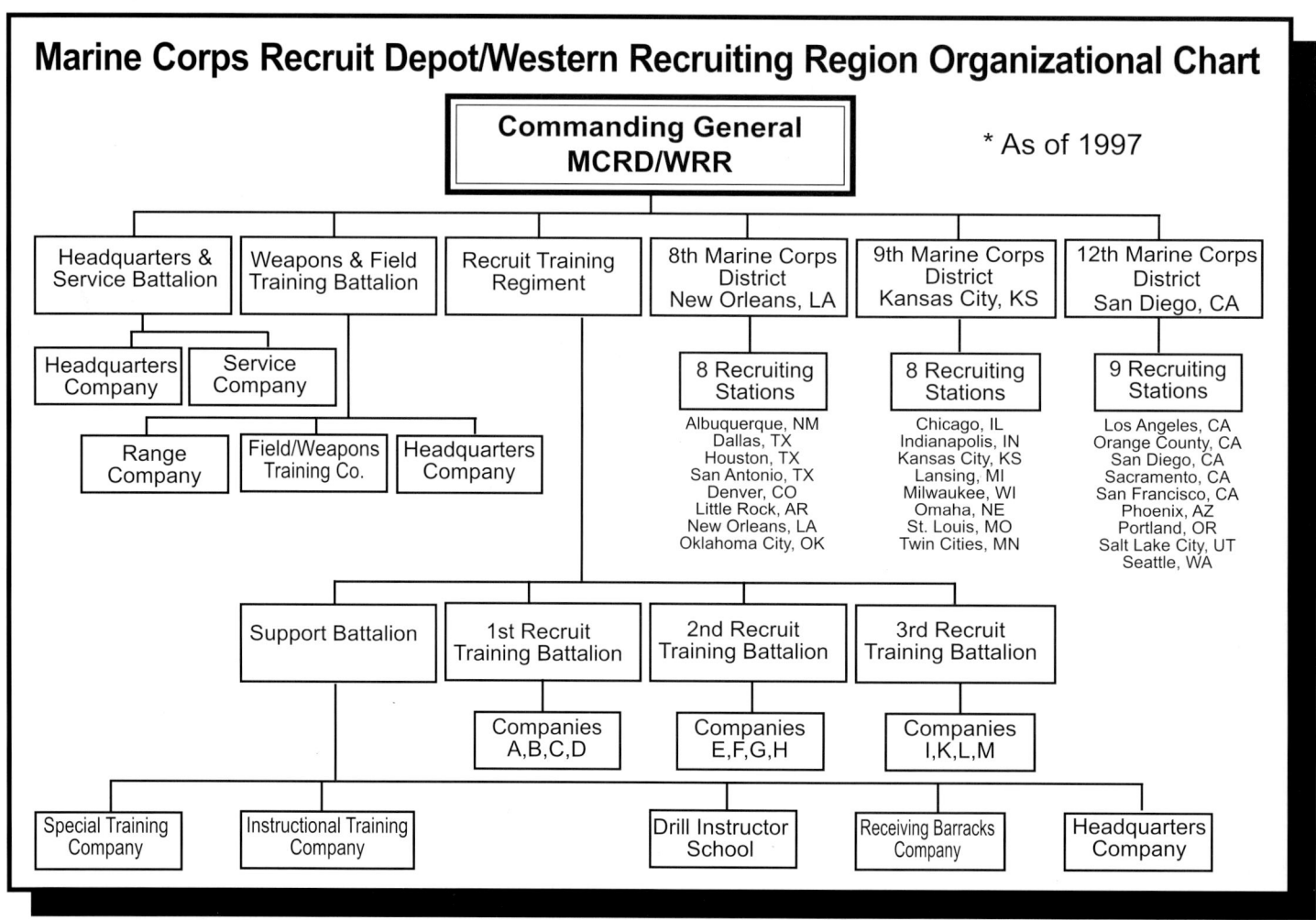

Making Marines

Recruits learn to rappel down a wooden tower that was replaced in 1994 by a cement tower.

In the tapestry of Marine Corps history, the boot arriving in San Diego during the 1990s shares a common thread with the recruit who passed through the same gates

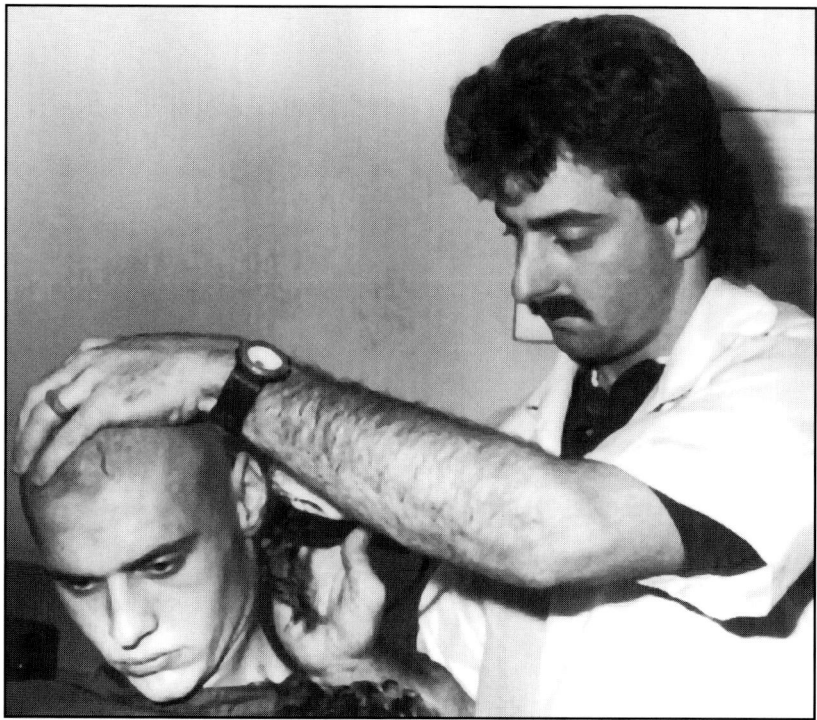

Left, a Marine shows his brother around the base in June 1973 after his graduation ceremony. This photo won second place in the feature category of the Military Photographer of the Year Contest for GySgt. Chuck McMormick. Below, a recruit's head is shaved, an initiation rite that hasn't changed from the 1920s to the 1990s.

seven decades before. Like his predecessors, he is sure to enter camp with preconceived notions about the weeks ahead. He will have heard countless stories from friends and relatives who served in the Marine Corps. He will think he is prepared for the challenges to come. But he will soon learn that the life of a recruit is not what he expected. It never was, and it never will be!

More than one million recruits have passed through MCRD, San Diego since the Depot officially opened on Aug. 11, 1923.

In those early years, the Recruit Depot was confined to a small geographic area of Marine Corps Base, San Diego and it played a subordinate role in the early history of the base. Throughout the 1920s and until the late 1940s, recruit training was overshadowed by other missions. The base was a staging area for expeditionary forces destined for Central America and the Far East. And in the mid-1930s, it became headquarters for the Fleet Marine Force.

The base did not begin to focus primarily on the task that is so familiar today until the dramatic build-up began for World War II in 1939. After the United States entered the war, with thousands of volunteers pouring into the Depot, recruit training took on new urgency. The barracks were soon at capacity. A huge tent city housed recruits as contractors raced to build hundreds of Quonset huts.

By 1941, the staging areas and advanced training facilities were moved 12 miles away to Camp Elliott, and then after September 1943 to Camp Pendleton on the north coast of San Diego County. Consequently, the Recruit Depot completely dominated the base by the end of the war. The name was officially changed to Marine Corps Recruit Depot, San Diego, in 1948.

The Korean war brought thousands of battle-hardened reservists and recruits to the West Coast. And once again, a tent camp at MCRD mushroomed near the parade ground to accommodate the new recruits. In the beginning, there was a single recruit battalion turning out one or two platoons a week. By the end of hostilities, the norm was several battalions turning out 14 platoons a week.

The pattern was repeated for the Vietnam War. And this time, recruits had to prepare to fight on two fronts — one in Southeast Asia and the other raging in the streets of America.

Recruit training over the years has changed in numerous ways. The recruit of the 1990s is better educated than his predecessor. Training methods have improved. Standard operating procedure prohibits much of the physical and mental abuse recruits once experienced. But even with

Left, recruits clean rifles in the 1940s. Below, a recruit from Platoon 272, 2nd Battalion in the mid-1950s stands at attention while his rifle is inspected. Bottom, a recruit undergoes a rifle inspection during the 1970s.

A recruit will think he is prepared for the challenges to come. But he will soon learn that the life of a recruit is not what he expected. It never was, and it never will be!

all the changes, the Marine recruit in San Diego still shares one paramount bond with his counterpart through the ages. He still has no idea what he is getting into.

Throughout the 1920s and 1930s the prescribed program for new recruits lasted eight weeks. Training used a timetable devised in 1905 by Marine Commandant, Maj. Gen. William P. Biddle. His formula was based on the idea that from the moment training began until graduation day, recruits performed under the direct supervision of a noncommissioned officer — the drill instructor. The program included drills, physical exercises, individual combat training, and qualification with the M-1903 Springfield Rifle.

The Depot's complement during the 1920s and most of the 1930s remained relatively small. For example, in 1931 there were 13 sergeants and 20 corporals. The authorized number of recruits under instruction at any given time was limited to 270.

Generally, recruits for the San Diego base have come from states west of the Mississippi River and parts of Wisconsin and Illinois. During those early years, they represented a cross section of America: farm boys from the Midwest, sons of Texas cattle ranchers, young men whose families migrated to the West Coast in search of prosperity.

Some joined the Marine Corps in search of adventure. During the 1920s and 1930s, Marines often went to exotic places such as Nicaragua, Haiti and China. But beginning in 1930, many young men joined the Corps to escape the ravages of the Great Depression. For them, life in the Marine Corps represented three meals a day and a regular job.

The Marine Corps paid for their passage West. It was the job of the hometown recruiter to put his recruits on a steamship or passenger train. And each recruit was given 10 cents for San Diego streetcar fare that would take him from the train station or dock to the base. Arriving recruits reached San Diego with little fanfare. There was no one waiting to welcome them.

For many recruits, San Diego seemed like a foreign country — the first time away from home, the first time a palm tree was more than a postcard, the cool ocean breeze, the seemingly laid-back attitude of local residents.

"It is believed that in no place will recruits gain such a pleasant impression regarding military life as here," wrote Col. Alexander S. Williams in 1926.

Col. Williams was a veteran of 25 years when he was stationed in San Diego and knew very well the realities of military life. He was with Col. Littleton W.T. Waller in 1901 on his tragic and deadly march through the jungles of Samar during the Philippine Insurrection. Col. Williams probably expressed accurately the first sentiments of most every Marine who came to San Diego: "Based on my own experiences ... nowhere else is life so pleasant as it is here in Southern California."

Recruits were told, "Streetcars numbered 13, 14 or 16 will deliver you to the main gate." For the recruit, walking through that gate meant the end of life as he knew it. For the next eight weeks, the Marine Corps would make all his decisions.

His initiation began with the first Marine he met. The sentry at the gate directed him to the Officer of the Day, who detailed a member of the guard to escort the boot to the receiving barracks. There, he was given soap and a towel, and assigned to a bunk.

The next morning he was examined by a Navy doctor. If he passed, he spent the rest of the day listening to lectures on what constitutes fraudulent enlistment. Was he concealing a criminal record, or was he married? This was his last chance to come clean.

Recruits drill on the parade deck, or "the grinder," in 1923.

He was sworn in the following day, then sent to the barber shop for a regulation haircut and ordered to see the chaplain for spiritual counseling. It wasn't until the third day that he received his uniform and equipment. The clothing was passed out under the watchful eye of an officer. If the uniform didn't fit just right, the recruit was sent to the base tailor. Finally, he was issued credits for the post exchange for "toilet articles and smoking materials."

He spent the first 21 days of boot camp in quarantine as a precaution against contagious diseases. During World War I, thousands of soldiers succumbed to influenza epidemics that spread through military bases across the country. To combat the spread, new recruits were isolated from the rest of the population.

During that time, he was assigned to a platoon and received instruction on the evolution of the infantryman. He learned facing, movements, manual of arms, close and extended order drills. Afternoons were devoted to athletics. Competition was encouraged and recruits formed baseball, basketball, and football teams.

"Only the weakling fails to derive benefits and to attain the physical perfection this training is intended to develop," according to an official publication circulated on the base in 1931.

The recruit spent the next three weeks at Marine Corps

Drilling and physical training have always been a central focus of boot camp. Below, exercising on the base in 1931; center, exercising in the 1940s; and bottom, practicing close order drill in the 1990s.

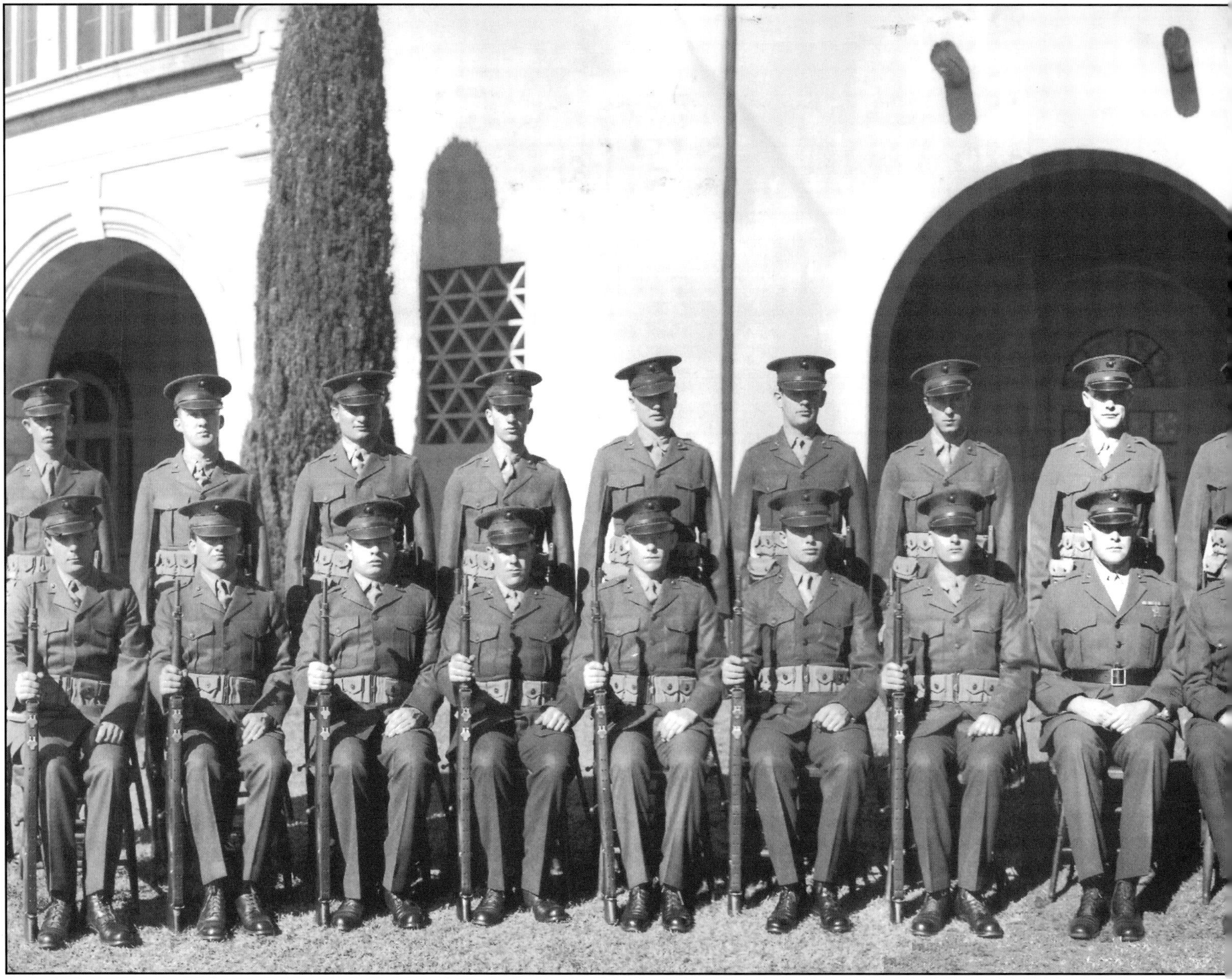

101st PLATOON U.S.M.C. SAN DIEGO
1942
U.S. MARINES — FIRST TO FIGHT

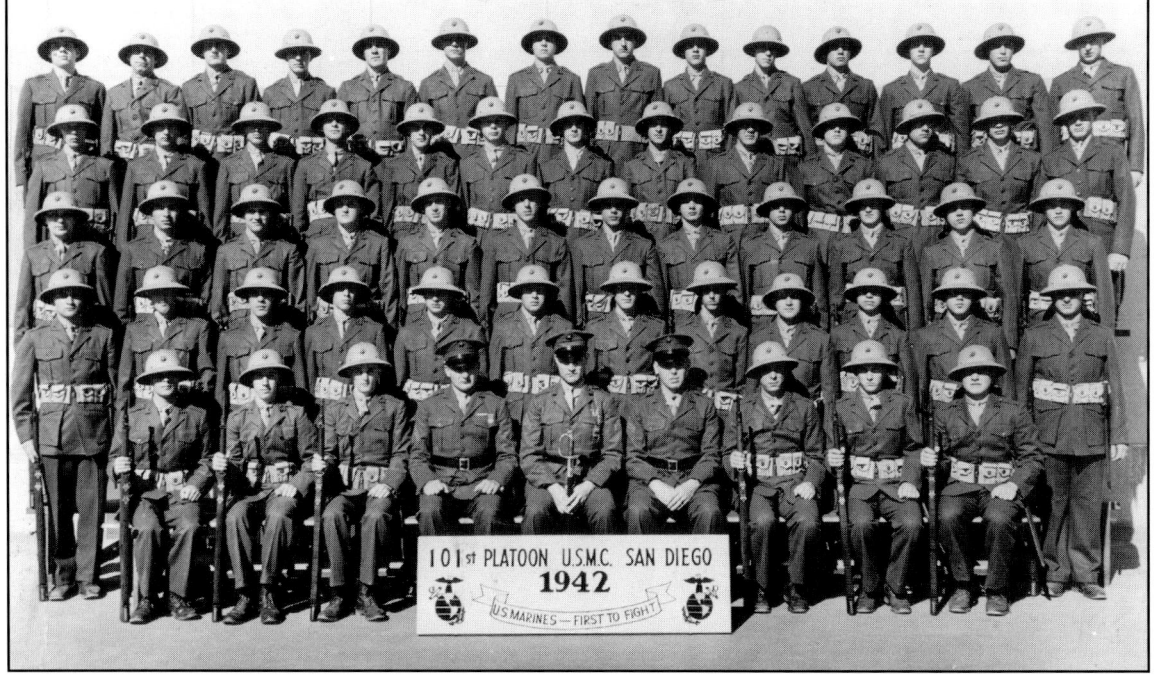

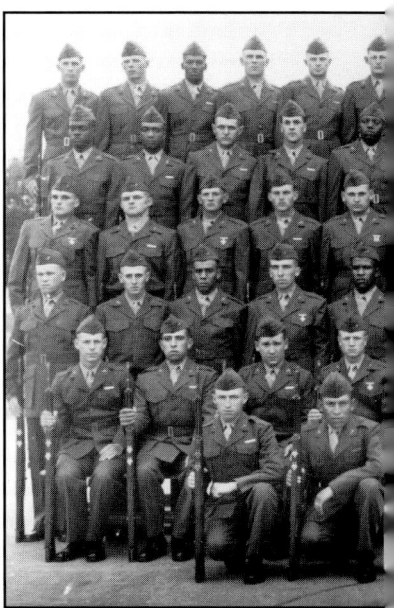

Top, the 1st Platoon in 1936 poses for a graduation photo. Below, graduation photos from 1942, 1952 and 1969.

Rifle Range, La Jolla. There he learned to fire, first on a .22 caliber rifle and then on a .30 caliber service rifle. He aimed to score enough points to make the grade of expert rifleman. The highest achievement added $5 a month to his pay. If he qualified as a sharpshooter, he was rewarded with a $3 bonus. But he had to score enough hits to make the grade as a marksman, or he would be transferred to a "special" platoon, which meant that he might not graduate with the rest of his class.

The last two weeks of boot camp were devoted to what was called "final instruction period." The recruit was expected to "qualify on the bayonet course and polish up on his infantry training." He was also required to participate in weekly parades put on by the base headquarters troops. The parades were open to the general public.

The Friday late afternoon parades became a tradition on the base. They were initiated by Gen. Pendleton during the early 1920s as a public relations gimmick. But during the early 1930s, most of the troops assigned to the base were on expeditionary duty in China and Nicaragua. So recruits were employed to bolster the ranks of the regulars.

"No onlooker would suppose that our recruit, who is about to complete his training, differs from those seasoned Marines with whom he marches on parade," stated a base publication.

Recruits of Platoon 272, 2nd Battalion await final inspection in the mid-1950s.

The graduation ceremony consisted of a full pack inspection of the class by the Commanding General, after which the platoon was broken up and each new Marine received his orders for general or special duty.

"The average age of the recruit is 20 years old, and he has completed one or more years of high school," wrote Lt. Col. Emil P. Moses in 1931. Lt. Col. Moses was the Depot's commanding officer.

He noted that under the standard procedure, "Those destined for sea duty are attached to Sea School for four weeks of additional training." But the early 1930s were particularly challenging times for the Marine Corps. The 4th Marine Regiment was still in China, and the Japanese invasion of Manchuria in September 1931 put pressure on the Depot's personnel to speed up recruit training. "The need for Marines is so urgent that seldom does a recruit remain more than one week at Sea School, and some replacements are sent to Battle Fleet with no Sea School training," lamented Lt. Col. Moses. "In some cases, recruits do not even finish their eight weeks of training at the Depot proper."

As events in the 1930s moved the United States closer to world war, emergency expansion of the San Diego base was authorized in September 1939. The frantic construction of additional storehouses, barracks, and mess facilities significantly expanded the base. But by the summer of 1941, the thousands of volunteers pouring into the base outpaced construction of new facilities. To accommodate the recruits, the Fleet Marine Force, headquartered at the base since 1935, was relocated at the newly opened Camp Elliott.

Leatherneck magazine writer James N. Wright described the Recruit Depot in September 1941: "Consisting of approximately 15 barracks, two mess halls, 1,100 tents, an amphitheater, and several storerooms, the layout is in reality a city within itself." Referring to the staff, Wright wrote, "The responsibility of completely training and transferring several hundred men per month rests with a staff of 12 officers and 150 especially qualified enlisted men. An additional hundred enlisted men are necessary to handle all other functions associated with the Depot." In conclusion, Wright wrote, "It is now possible to handle the 3,500 men (recruits) at the Depot without confusion or unnecessary interruptions."

Lt. Col. John Groff was in charge of the Depot during the build-up for the war. He is credited with modernizing the Depot, introducing a public address system that no Marine could escape. All the buildings were wired, as were the parade grounds, and athletic and drill fields. The entire Depot was connected to the Duty NCO office.

Dec. 7, 1941, ignited the entire nation, and new recruits were caught up in the excitement.

"A be-medalled officer swore us in," a recruit told

Platoon 105, 1st Battalion in 1960 learns to swim, left, and breaks for chow.

Leatherneck in May 1942. "Individually, we said 'I do' and a few hours later we were on a fast train bound for the coast. On that cross-country trip we saw the exciting picture of a nation arousing itself for war. At night the trains were blacked out. Soldiers guarded bridges. The trains were full of soldiers. Everywhere we looked we saw soldiers. Khaki britches. In refreshing contrast was the uniform of the grey-haired, salty old (Marine) sergeant who met us at the station and escorted us to the base."

At the beginning of the war, basic training was reduced from eight to four weeks. The rapid growth in the Marine Corps from 27,000 to 450,000 men forced the decision-makers to cut the training cycle.

According to Lt. Gen. Victor H. Krulak, the Depot's Commanding General from 1959 to 1962, shortening the training cycle in the early days of World War II "was a mistake that generated many problems and was quickly reversed."

In his book *First To Fight: An Inside View Of The U.S. Marine Corps* Lt. Gen. Krulak wrote, "It took every bit of eight weeks to screen out the misfits who came into the Marine Corps through the Selective Service System, and the pressure on the drill instructor to cope with the functionally illiterate, the physically marginal, and the emotionally unmotivated was immense." Gen. Krulak emphasized that paternalism and "rigorous physical punishment" increasingly became part of the recruit training formula.

Recalling his boot camp experience in 1943, Lenly Marvin Cotten said, "I never knew such frustration or anger. I had never been called such names without a fight. But they (DIs) know how to take the fight out of you and keep you so dog-tired and scared that you couldn't keep up."

In his book, *The Brig Rat*, Cotten confesses that many recruits were consumed by thoughts that they might not survive the rigors of boot camp. "That's the biggest fear — failure!"

Said Cotten, "One part of our training that was hard to understand was the shaking us out of our sacks at three a.m., to run to the sea for a pail of water. If your pail was not full enough or you had not run fast enough, you were ordered to dump your pail and run back for more."

At the time, Cotten said, recruits thought the water drill was cruel punishment meted out simply because the DI had had a bad day. But years later reflecting on the incident in his book, Cotten wrote, "Now we know, it was to make us follow orders, no matter what."

Gen. Krulak believes that, although recruit training had its faults, it was successful in accomplishing its mission. "The young man who completed the training had clearly acquired some of the precious virtues of commitment and obedience, and he met the extreme challenge of combat from Guadalcanal to Okinawa with poise and steadiness."

The training schedule expanded to 10 and then 12 weeks following World War II. And, although the same training formula was followed, new methods were introduced.

Recruits no longer received all their training directly from their drill instructor. MCRD established a special instructor staff of highly qualified teachers. These instructors took over most of the classroom and field classes.

When the Korean War exploded in 1950, a new tent camp mushroomed near the parade deck to handle the expanding number of recruits. Some of the men were raw boots, but many were combat veterans of World War II.

Recruits practice with pugil sticks on the Bridge Over Troubled Waters. The water was replaced with sawdust in 1993.

Thousands of former servicemen had become slightly stale in civilian life, and needed to be retrained.

Training was cut back to eight weeks. Subjects such as field tactics, advanced phases of combat conditioning and combat principles were dropped because similar courses were being taught at Marine Corps Base, Camp Pendleton.

With the end of the Korean War, the training cycle went back to 10 weeks. During the ensuing years, the makeup of recruits was changing, and so, too, was the training they received. "The recruit that now comes to us is better fed, better housed, and better educated," Col. George R. Newton, commanding officer of the Recruit Training Regiment, told *Leatherneck* magazine in 1961. "As always, he'll need to use his muscles; but he'll need to use his mind too in today's Marine Corps."

The buildup for the Vietnam War started slowly. But on Sept. 1, 1965, the Marine Corps announced a speed-up in recruit training that put MCRD on a wartime schedule. The new schedule reduced training from 12 to eight weeks and went into effect immediately.

Two months later, the first draftees since the Korean War came to MCRD from induction stations in Detroit, Chicago, and Los Angeles. Reportedly, the recruits had expected to go into the Army and were less than thrilled about being in the Marine Corps.

The Depot's barracks were filled to capacity by February 1966, and base officials announced that a tent camp would be erected to accommodate the recruits. The hardback tents were built on the base's golf driving range, and 700 recruits occupied the tents. "Wartime urgency has invaded the Depot," proclaimed *The San Diego Union* correspondent Robert Zimmerman. "Supplies have been moved out of the Quonset (World War II) huts so they can be used for barracks. Vehicle traffic is being detoured from Depot streets passing through recruit training areas. Training battalions have been enlarged."

Zimmerman called the new recruits products of a "younger generation that probably has been analyzed, worried about and criticized more than any other."

Opposition to the war had grown by 1967, particularly on college campuses. On May 5, 1967, *The San Diego Union* reported that Marine Corps recruiters at San Diego State University were harassed by students opposing the war.

"Being a recruiter back in the 1960s was like living on another planet," recalls retired MSgt. Raymond Cieslinski, historian for the West Coast Chapter of the Drill Instructors Association. "At the time, we saw it as us against them (civilians). We didn't hold civilians in very high esteem. We knew we had a job to do. We had to take that kid that got off that bus and give him the tools he needed to survive in Vietnam. We had only eight short weeks to do it in."

During the Vietnam War, Marine Corps strength peaked at 310,000 men and women. Recruit strength at the Depot topped 20,000 in 1968.

The recruit population at MCRD, San Diego fluctuated between 4,000 and 6,000 men through the mid-1990s. Approximately 51 percent of the men who enlist in the Marine Corps take their 12-week training course in San Diego. More than 97 percent of today's recruits are high school graduates and approximately 7 percent are married.

Since the first recruits came to San Diego in 1923, the Marine Corps has kept pace in a dramatically changing world. But the basic recruit training formula remains virtually intact.

Why? Because it is a system that works — a dependable formula that has served Marines, the United States, and the free world through four major conflicts. By fine-tuning through the years, the legendary Marine Corps training has never failed to mold recruits into the best-trained fighting men in the world.

Right, recruits from Platoon 105, 1st Battalion in 1960 tackle the Confidence Course. Below, a recruit shows his spirit with a war cry in the 1960s. Bottom, company, series, and platoon honormen present guidons during their graduation parade in the 1990s.

In 1940, recruits at Marine Corps Rifle Range, La Jolla (later known as Camp Matthews) demonstrate the four positions used in firing a .30-caliber rifle. From left: prone, sitting, kneeling and offhand, or standing.

Riflemen All

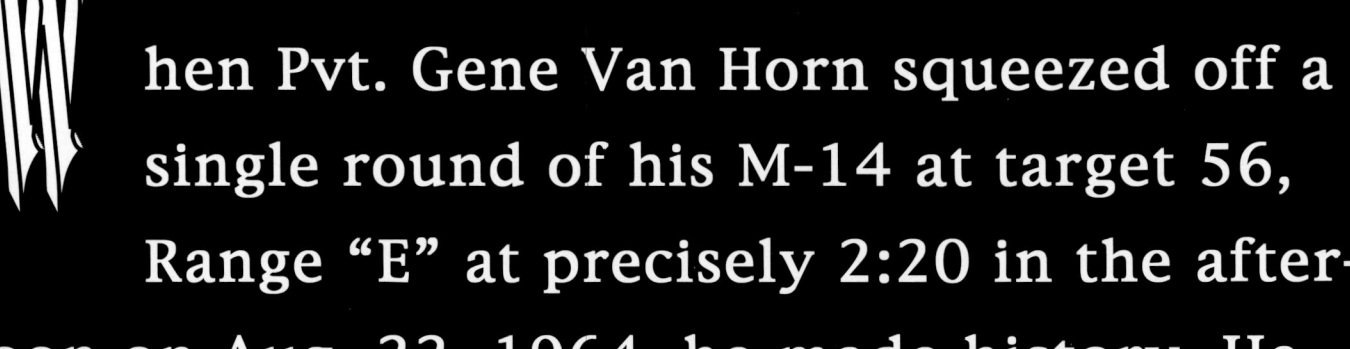

When Pvt. Gene Van Horn squeezed off a single round of his M-14 at target 56, Range "E" at precisely 2:20 in the afternoon on Aug. 22, 1964, he made history. He

At right, Cpl. Shannon takes aim with his Springfield .03 rifle at Marine Corps Rifle Range, La Jolla in 1926. The camp was built in 1918 and renamed Camp Matthews in 1942. Below, officers check Marines' scores during target practice during the 1930s at Marine Corps Rifle Range.

was the last man to fire his rifle at Camp Matthews. Van Horn joined the ranks of more than one million Marines who fired an estimated 300 million rounds as part of their recruit training at Camp Matthews in La Jolla.

Five days earlier, Pvt J.R. Ibarra of Platoon 161 also made history when he fired his M-14 at 2:17 p.m. at Edson Range. This marked the beginning of an era of qualification at the new Stuart Mesa facility at Camp Pendleton.

During that week, 96 instructors worked double-duty to ensure a smooth transition between the two rifle ranges. After spending their mornings coaching the last groups of recruits to train at Matthews, the instructors boarded buses for the 30-minute ride to Camp Pendleton, where they made sure the targets at the new facility operated flawlessly.

The closing of Camp Matthews was not without sentimental reminiscences. Maj. Gen. Bruno Hochmuth, the Recruit Depot's Commanding General, spoke for many of its alumni:

"To me, this is a sad event. None of us has witnessed the final hour of a training facility that has played such a vital part of the training of so many Marines for such a long period of time."

Because every Marine is a rifleman, it's typical of the Corps that San Diego Marines had a rifle range before they had a permanent home. Groundbreaking ceremonies for what is now the Marine Corps Recruit Depot were held March 15, 1919, but the Marines had been firing at Camp Matthews since 1918.

The creation of Camp Matthews logically followed the Marine Corps loss of its North Island rifle range in 1916 when the Army Air Corps took over the property. After inspecting several potential sites, the Marines settled on 544 acres of land they leased from the city in 1917. Capt. (later Maj. Gen.) E. C. Long was charged with building the first range in late 1918. It was known initially as Marine Rifle Range, La Jolla. Twenty-four years later in wartime April 1942, the range was renamed Camp Calvin B. Matthews in honor of Brig. Gen. Calvin B. Matthews, a well-known coach of Marine rifle and pistol teams and

A Marine receives a Springfield rifle at the armory for the Marine Corps Rifle Range, La Jolla during the 1930s.

Recruits learn the basics of handling the .30-caliber water cooled machine gun at Marine Corps Rifle Range, La Jolla during the 1930s.

a strong advocate of Marine marksmanship.

At first there was only one range — "A" Range. It was built using an old mule scraper combination and a "modern" one-lung "breakdown" concrete mixer. The sand and gravel for the butts were secured from a nearby dry stream bed, and the range detachment supplied the construction labor. The construction men cooked their meals under the protection of a fly tent and used the ground for a table. But because recruit training didn't begin in San Diego until 1923, shooting details at first consisted of Marines requalifying with their .30 caliber Springfield rifles.

Inasmuch as there was no permanent detail at the range until 1923, Marines using it had to march the 12 miles up Rose Canyon from San Diego, pitch tents, spend the night, shoot the course as long as they needed, and then march back to Marine Corps Base. In November 1920, a Capt. Martin was put in charge of a permanent range detail consisting of one NCO in charge, one cook and 10 privates. The NCO was MGySgt. Thomas J. Jones, who later became one of the Marine Corps' all-time great shooters and marksmanship instructors.

"Those days all we had was 10 targets, with a small mess hall, a head and a few tents," MGySgt. Jones said in a 1964 interview with the *Chevron*, the Recruit Depot's newspaper. Records show that a detachment of the 1st Separate Battalion, 5th Brigade, and Brigade Headquarters moved from Balboa Park to become the first troops

> "Those days all we had was 10 targets, with a small mess hall, a head and a few tents."
> MGySgt. Thomas Jones
> on the rifle range during the early 1920s

85

Photos on Pages 86 and 87, counterclockwise from left: Marines trudge up "Agony Hill" at Camp Matthews during World War II. Below: Headquarters area at Camp Matthews in 1943. Bottom right, Marines at the rifle range are filled with the fervor of World War II sentiment against Japan after that country's attack on Pearl Harbor in 1941. And right, during World War II Camp Matthews chief range officer Maj. J.E. Snow poses with a Japanese trophy headed for the U.S. government's program of melting down scrap metal for bullets. Maj. Snow won the cup at a Japanese shooting match in Tientsin, China, during 1926. Before the 12-guage shotgun competition began, the Japanese boasted the Americans didn't have a chance of winning. But then-Capt. Snow won the competition with 96 of a possible 100 points, seven points higher than his nearest Japanese competitor. This caused the Japanese a great deal of embarrassment, and they refused to allow Capt. Snow to take the Emperor's Cup — a 3-foot silver loving cup — with him. Instead, they gave him a small trophy and a Browning automatic shotgun. But for years, the incident bothered Maj. Snow. And in 1943 he got his chance to consign his "phony" trophy to its proper fate.

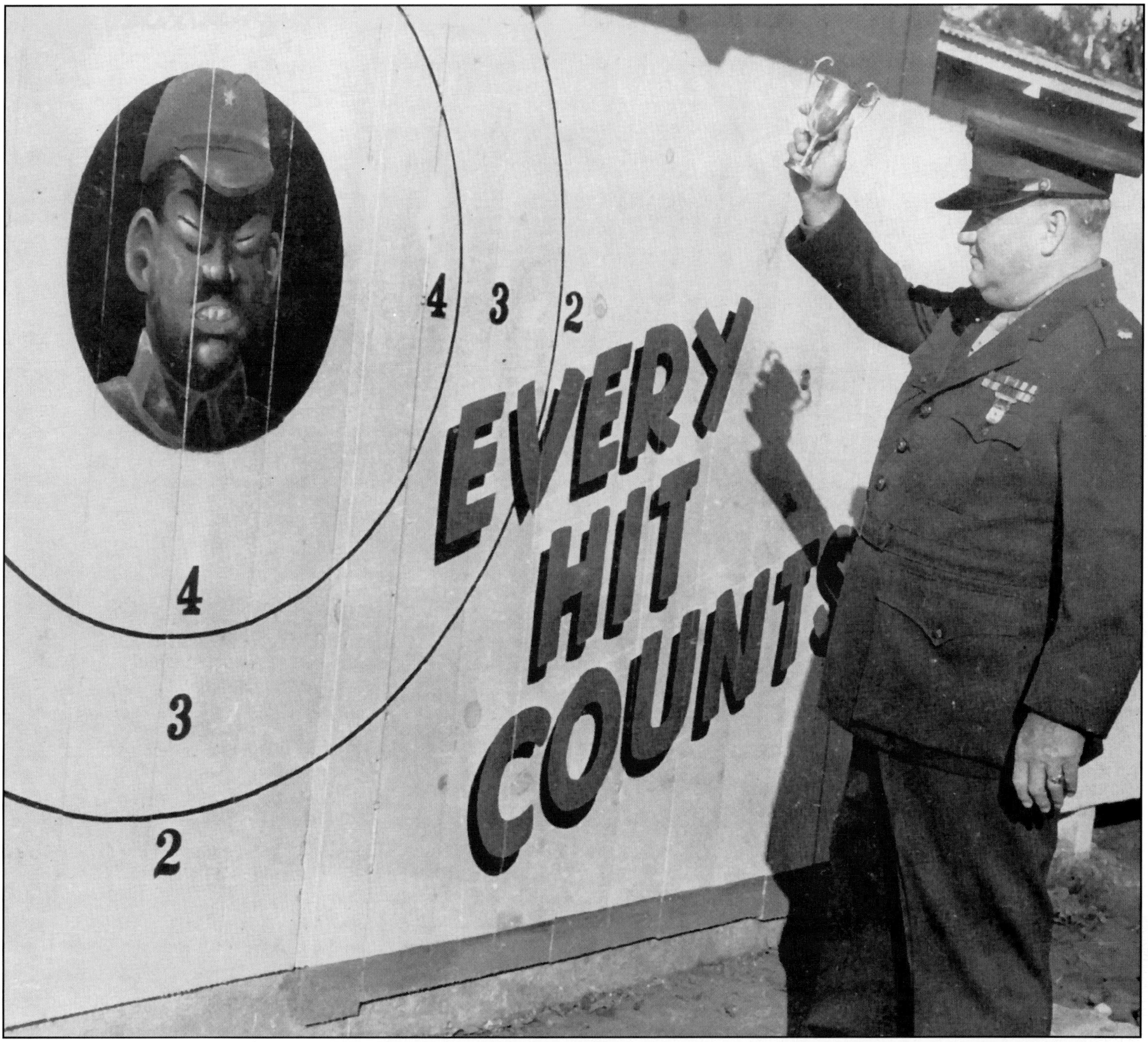
4 3 2
EVERY
HIT
COUNTS
4
3
2

EVERY
HIT
COUNTS
What YOU learn HERE pays off
in DEAD JAPS over there!

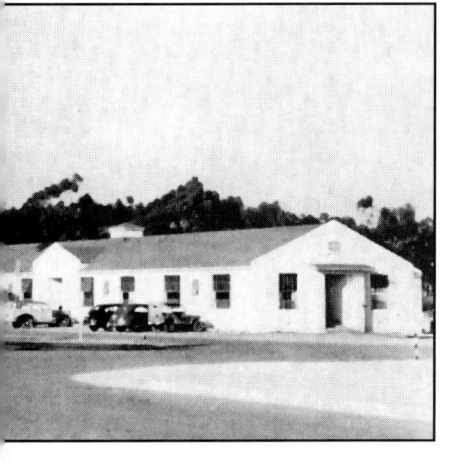

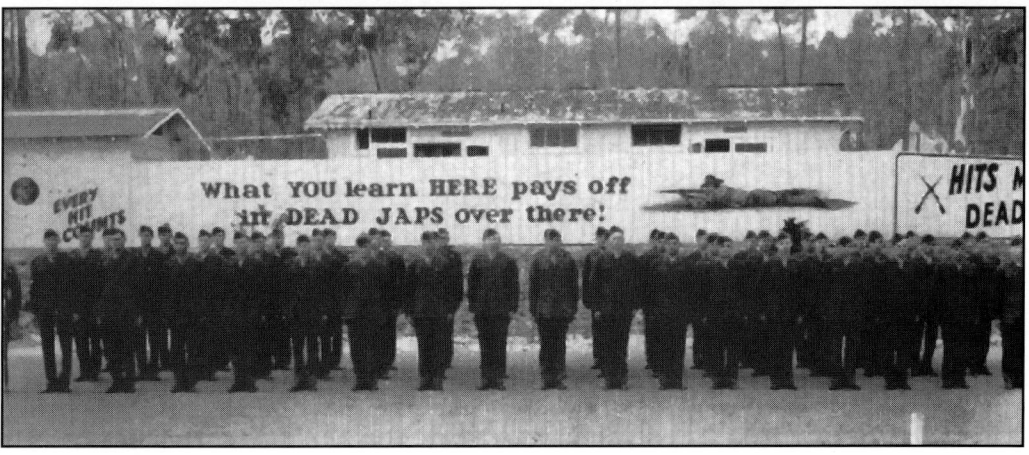

An aerial view of Camp Matthews in the 1950s. In August 1956, the La Jolla Town Council asked the San Diego City Council to "remove Camp Matthews from the vicinity of the San Diego metropolitan area."

to occupy the newly-built rifle range permanently in December 1921.

Recruits spent three weeks on the rifle range, according to Jones. There was no established weapons school or snapping-in (dry firing exercises). "Mostly they were shown very briefly the rifle firing positions," MGySgt. Jones recalled, "given a little snapping-in and then they started shooting the course."

One platoon of about 30 men would go to the range at a time. MGySgt. Jones said, "We trained in small platoons because only four or five recruits arrived a day for boot camp." Not until the late 1920s and then again during the late '30s was there more than one boot platoon there at a time. Requalifiers had no set snapping-in periods in the beginning either, said MGySgt. Jones. And, instead of securing for the day after firing, as Marines do today, the requalifiers picked up shovels and picks and went to work building and rebuilding. This practice remained for many years. But by 1924, a set training program was established for the recruits and requals.

They snapped-in the first week and started shooting the second week. Recruits were also taught windage, elevation and everything else they needed to improve their marksmanship.

Facilities in the 1930s at the rifle range hadn't expanded much since 1920. There were only six buildings: a 40-man barracks, a headquarters building, office building, a quartermaster storage building, weapons training building, and a mess hall. Recruits lived in two-man tents.

There was a small seven-hole golf course where the Camp Matthews' "B" Range was later located. That range was built in 1936. By then, requalifiers were snapping-in with their units before going to the range for one week of firing before record day. With war clouds gathering in Europe and the Japanese on the march in Asia, the Marine Corps started expanding and developing Camp Matthews in the late 1930s, preparing to meet the needs of a growing Corps.

"B" Range was built in addition to pistol and Browning Automatic Rifle (BAR) ranges. A 1,000-yard line was added earlier to "A" Range to provide the proper facilities for competition shooting. On March 25, 1941, Maj. Gen. Thomas Holcomb, Commandant of the Marine Corps, fired the first shots on what was then the largest single rifle range in the Western United States. It was "E" Range, and its hundred targets brought the total number of .30 caliber targets to 185 at the rifle range.

The size of the range detachment increased rapidly. In 1941, there were generally three to four platoons in training at a time with two arriving and leaving weekly. Buildings, barracks, huts, tents, and mess halls were constructed. By June 1941 there were 54,539 officers and men in the Corps.

The outbreak of World War II necessitated a rapid expansion of the range. Thousands of men poured through its gates, overtaxing the facilities so much so that 5,000 West Coast Marines who had enlisted just prior to December 1941 were sent north to San Luis Obispo for rifle training. Camp Linda Vista was established in 1943 approximately 10 miles east of Matthews. It was never more than a tent camp. The Marines there took their rifle training at nearby Camp Elliott (along present-day Interstate-15).

During the peak of the war in 1944, as many as 9,000 men qualified at Camp Matthews every three weeks. Camp personnel mushroomed to more than 700. The size of the facility also increased dramatically.

A large school range was built near the main camp area under the direction of MGySgt. Jones. "F" Range was established with 75 targets. A camp area arose to house recruits between "E" and "F" Ranges.

During the initial weeks of World War II, rifle training lasted only two weeks as recruits were hurried through before transfer to Camp Elliott for combat training and then rushed to the front lines. Later, training at Camp Matthews expanded to the standard three weeks. Platoons arrived on Sunday, drew equipment, received a lecture on range routine, rules and regulations and moved into their quarters. At 6:30 the next morning, the platoons assembled and marched to their respective school ranges or other activities.

Besides snapping-in, recruits learned sights, sight settings, blacking of sights, trigger squeeze, what to do in case of stoppages, safety precautions, use of combination tools and ruptured cartridge extraction, score books, windage rules, estimations of wind, zeroing of rifles, and rapid fire operation, functioning, and safety of the .22 rifle and BAR. They had to master all of this before ever firing a

Firing on the pistol range at Camp Matthews during the 1950s.

Above, a Marine practices with an M-1 Garand rifle during the 1950s. The Garand was introduced during World War II. Below, a drill instructor checks a recruit's position at Camp Matthews during the 1950s.

Marines pull targets Aug. 2, 1952, at Camp Matthews.

Recruits clean their rifles at their tents at Camp Matthews in the 1950s.

round.

The famous Garand M-1 rifle was introduced in 1943. Qualification average with the M-1 that year was 78.7 percent. But by 1944 — despite the great turnover of coaches and DIs who were shipped overseas — the qualification average rose to 88.1 percent. In 1944 more than 100,000 individuals fired at Camp Matthews, including 12,172 experts, 33,049 sharpshooters and 49,175 marksmen.

Firing went all day from dawn to dusk. One day on "E" Range more than 1,600 persons fired. That impressive achievement translates into 100 targets and at least 16 relays on the line awaiting their turn to shoot. Training was also given in the BAR, hand grenades, carbine and .45 caliber pistol.

The first WRs (Women Reserves) arrived at Camp Matthews in 1943. "The barracks were brand new, just waiting for us," said Lucy Shank, who worked in the records office. "It was my job to record the M-1 rifle, Browning automatic rifle and pistol scores." Most of the WRs were assigned to the Quartermaster Corps and motor transport, said Shank. "We never got to fire the M-1s, but we did many poses for publicity photos for our hometown newspaper."

By the end of the war, coaches and other range personnel could point with pride to how well they had done their jobs. The Marine and his rifle had advanced right up to Japan's doorstep. Demobilization after the war drastically reduced the Corps, but it never again was as small as "the Old Corps." Permanent personnel assigned to Camp Matthews were reduced to about 120 by 1947. An increase in activity at Camp Matthews coincided with the expansion of the Corps during the Korean War.

The rifle range detachment was redesignated as Weapons Training Battalion (today known as Weapons Field Training Battalion) on Jan. 1, 1948.

By the end of 1943, the M-1 rifle had completely replaced the renowned .03 Springfield. But in the minds of many Marines the M-1 was an inferior weapon. During World War II, "old-timers" in particular had little faith in the accuracy of the M-1. But it was the rifle instructors' job to change prevailing attitudes.

"You can't build up a man's confidence in a new weapon by knocking it," said MSgt. Victor L. Woods in a 1949 interview with *Leatherneck* magazine. "Then, too, it's here to stay and there's no use beating our teeth about it."

Even though the Marines were holding their ground in Korea, they were slowly losing the war back home over Camp Matthews. The post World War II boom in San Diego resulted in a surge of new home construction. The suburbs were expanding and local officials and politicians saw the sprawling rifle range as a rich resource for commercial and residential development.

In August 1956, the La Jolla Town Council asked the San Diego City Council to "remove Camp Matthews from the vicinity of the San Diego metropolitan area." The Marines said they had no intention of closing the camp.

But public pressure continued to mount. U.S. Congressman Bob Wilson (R-San Diego) asked the Corps in June 1957 to relocate the facility. Wilson introduced a bill on July 31, 1959, authorizing the Secretary of the Navy to convey title of Camp Matthews to the University of California. The Navy opposed the bill. Following a three-year legal battle, the Navy dropped its opposition, and on Oct. 7, 1964, Camp Matthews was turned over to the University of California, San Diego.

The expansion of the college campus erased nearly all traces of Camp Matthews during the next three decades. A handful of the old, wooden, World War II buildings

An aerial photograph shows a view of Camp Matthews looking east during 1962. The camp was turned over to the University of California, San Diego during 1964. Among the meager reminders of the range still intact on the UCSD campus are a guard post, the administration building and a memorial plaque.

still stand along with the guard house at the rear gate of the camp. The fitting, enduring memorial to the rifle range is a bronze plaque embedded in a boulder on the university lawn. It is dedicated to the more than one million Marines who qualified at Camp Matthews.

The new Marine rifle range carried with it the seeds of the old — literally. Landscape architects arranged to have about 60 valuable trees from Camp Matthews transplanted to the new site, called Camp Stuart Mesa, at Camp Pendleton on San Diego County's north coast.

The transplanted trees included 31 Phoenix Date, 16 Washingtonia, six Gaudalupe, five Cocos Australis and two Draco, according to the Sept. 9, 1964, edition of the *Chevron*. The trees were expected to complement large spreading Palms — adding to the natural beauty of the site and guarding against erosion, the newspaper reported.

Along with four 50-target ranges, A, B, C and D, there were 11 buildings for: administration; staff NCO club and quarters; a general-purpose building that included a barber shop, dispensary, PX, laundry and enlisted men's club; a mess hall; recruit barracks; camp maintenance, motor transport and supply; armory; target factory; school and classrooms; RTR Range Liaison Office; and range personnel quarters.

When the range opened officially on Aug. 22, 1964, it was named for Maj. Gen. Merritt A. (Red Mike) Edson, the commander of the 1st Marine Raider Battalion, also known as Edson's Raiders, during World War II. Like his predecessor, Gen. Matthews, Gen. Edson was also known for his accomplishments as a rifleman.

It didn't take long for Marine platoons to start posting 100 percent qualifications.

Sgt. A.J. Teson, senior drill instructor of Platoon 380, was so certain that L Company, 3rd Recruit Training Battalion, would make a clean sweep that on Oct. 6, 1964, he pulled out his calendar and wrote "ice broken at Stuart Mesa Range by 380" on the page for Oct. 23. When his prediction came true, he told the *Chevron*, "The platoon is well-disciplined, and I just had a feeling they would do it. The drill instructors felt the same way. There just wasn't

An aerial view of the Edson Range during the 1970s, looking west. The range was established in 1964.

any doubt."

The platoon followed in the footsteps of the last one to qualify 100 percent at Camp Matthews: Platoon 354, which fired Aug. 14, 1964.

It didn't take long for the range to be overtaxed. The Vietnam War increased pressure on training facilities, so a portion of Camp Margarita at Pendleton was turned over to Weapons Training Battalion, along with one 150-target range at Chappo Flats, less than half a mile away. During the first quarter of 1966, approximately 25,000 recruits took rifle training at the three ranges, compared with 27,957 for all of 1965.

For most Marines, their weeks as recruits spent on the rifle range represented a welcome respite from the daily travails of boot camp. Years later they still remember it all — the constant snapping-in on the school range, that first signal that a "bull" had been scored, that choking tensed-up feeling the night before record day, the elation that finally came from qualifying, and the pride in wearing that silver medal. Many Marines credit the lessons learned at the rifle range with saving their lives. At the very least, the range molded them into Marine Corps riflemen.

Rewards for riflemen

The David S. McDougal Memorial Trophy was presented during a ceremony at Camp Matthews to Maj. Gen. Leo D. Hermle, Commanding General of MCRD, on April 12, 1947, by retired Maj. Gen. Douglas C. McDougal, who was Commanding General from 1935 to 1937. The trophy was named in memory of Gen. McDougal's son, Lt. Col. David S. McDougal, who was killed in action on Okinawa in 1945. He was a member of the winning National Rifle Team in 1940. The trophy was awarded to winners of the Marine Corps Rifle Match.

The San Diego Perpetual Trophy, a bronze bear on a redwood base with the seal of the city of San Diego, was presented in 1921 to Brig. Gen. Joseph Pendleton by various local civic organizations. It was designed by Dr. Alonzo D. Jessop, a member of the board of J. Jessop and Sons Jewelers, who said Gen. Pendleton was so impressed with the gift that he "paraded it up and down D Street on a gun carriage."

Brig. Gen. Calvin Matthews' career highlights

The Marine Corps Rifle Range, La Jolla, was named for Marine Brig. Gen. Calvin Bruce Matthews during World War II.

Gen. Matthews was an enthusiastic proponent of marksmanship throughout his long career, and he served as captain of several Marine national match teams. Every year at Camp Matthews, the Marine recruit with the highest rifle score was awarded a trophy bearing the general's name.

Gen. Calvin B. Matthews

Born in Loudon County, Tenn., on Sept. 10, 1882, Brig. Gen. Matthews was commissioned a second lieutenant on Dec. 6, 1904.

He served two tours from 1906 to 1910 as a battalion adjutant with the 2nd Marine Regiment at Camp Elliott in the Canal Zone in Panama. Upon his detachment, he became commanding officer of the Marine Guard, USS *Rhode Island*. This was followed by duty in connection with Marine Corps rifle teams.

From 1915 throuch 1918 he was detailed to the Marine Legation in Beijing, China. In February 1920, he was ordered to Haiti with the Haitian Gendarmerie as chief of staff. He was awarded the Distinguished Service Medal by the president of Haiti.

In 1930 he was named "el jefe" (the director) of the National Guard in Nicaragua. He was awarded the Medal of Distinction by a grateful Nicaraguan government for his relief work during the Managua earthquake in March 1931. Matthews also received the Distinguished Service Medal from the U.S. government for his service in Nicaragua.

In part the citation reads: "From 6 February, 1931 to 2 January 1933 a period of continuous state of warfare existed on the far-flung borders of the country against well-organized, heavily armed groups of bandits under capable guerilla leaders who were attempting to overthrow the Government, pillage the country and rob the peaceful and law-biding citizens. ... The Guardia National carried on continuous operations against these organized bandits, defeating them in many combats."

Six years following his service in Central America, Brig. Gen. Matthews died on Aug. 20, 1939, from injuries he received in a car accident while serving as president of the Marine Corps Examining Board in Washington., D.C.

Maj. Gen. Merritt Edson's career highlights

The rifle range at Marine Corps Base, Camp Pendleton was named in honor of Maj. Gen. Merritt A. "Red Mike" Edson on Jan. 25, 1965.

Gen. Edson received the Medal of Honor for service during World War II. But there was another good reason for naming the rifle range for him: his long association with small arms marksmanship.

His accomplishments included:
- Firing member of the winning Marine Corps National Match Rifle Team in 1921 at Camp Perry, Ohio.
- Assistant team coach for the 1927, 1930 and 1931 Marine Corps National Rifle and Pistol Teams.
- Team captain and coach of the 1932 and 1933 Marine Corps rifle teams.
- Captain of the winning Marine Corps National Match Rifle Teams in 1935 and 1936.

In addition, after his retirement on Aug. 1, 1947, Gen. Edson was elected president of the National Rifle Association.

Following are highlights of Gen. Edson's 30-year career in the Marine Corps.

He was commissioned a second lieutenant Oct. 9, 1917, and he sailed for France during World War I in 1918 with the 11th Marines.

He was the commanding officer of the Marine detachment aboard the USS *Denver* beginning in late 1927. Edson earned his first Navy Cross with this unit during February to May 1929 in Nicaragua battling the Sandino-led rebels.

During his service in Nicaragua, Edson was nicknamed "Red Mike" for his red hair and beard. The nickname became a code name several years later during the battle to defend Henderson Field on Guadalcanal.

Lt. Col. Edson took command of the 1st Battalion, 5th Marines at Quantico in June 1941. The battalion became the 1st Raider Battalion in early 1942. It was also known as Edson's Raiders.

In September 1942, the 1st Raider Battalion along with other Marine units successfully defended Henderson Field, which was crucial to the survival of five Marine battalions on Guadalcanal. Col. Edson received the Medal of Honor.

Edson was named chief of staff in August 1943 of the 2nd Marine Division, which was then preparing for the invasion of Tarawa in November. His estimate of the situation proved accurate and became a classic in Marine Corps military literature. He was promoted to brigadier general.

In February 1947 to Marine Corps Headquarters, where he participated in planning that established the Corps as a permanent arm of the military.

A leading candidate for commandant, he retired in 1947 to lobby publicly against unification of the Corps with the Army or Navy. Because he was such an ardent opponent of unification, he is credited by some with saving the Corps' independence. Gen. Edson was promoted on retirement to major general.

Maj. Gen. Edson died Aug. 14, 1955, at the age of 58. He died of carbon monoxide poisoning in the garage of his home in Vermont.

Gen. Merritt A. Edson

> "It is incredible to me that it took the Corps a century and a half to awaken to the extraordinary importance of the drill instructor's task."
>
> retired Lt. Gen. Victor H. Krulak

The Drill Instructor

A drill instructor, wearing his field hat and carrying his ceremonial sword, barks out an order at MCRD, San Diego in 1975.

Training in the Marine Corps has always been the strictest and most demanding of all the services. Historically, the Corps has set uniformly high standards of performance to sustain its image as

A drill instructor in 1968 listens to a recruit in Platoon 1106, 1st Battalion. On the wall is the DI's creed.

an elite fighting unit — a force in readiness to fight at a moment's notice.

At the center of this rigorous training program is the drill instructor.

It is his responsibility to instill in the recruit the skills, knowledge, discipline, pride, and self confidence that makes a Marine. No easy task.

The DI of the mid-1990s is prescreened for job suitability. Would-be DIs must be at least a corporal and at most a gunnery sergeant. Candidates for DI school must be between 21 and 37 years old, high school graduates and have received not more than one non-judicial punishment within the last 12 months. They must meet medical, physical and emotional standards, and comply with appearance and weight standards. And being a DI must not cause undue hardship for the candidate's family.

Candidates attend a rigorous 56-day training program over a period of 11 weeks. During a period of mobilization for war, the DI's training is shortened to 34 days. Approximately 80 would-be DIs make up each class, which is held four times a year. The course emphasizes cultivation of leadership abilities, Standard Operating Procedures, close order drill, and physical conditioning. While in school, candidates spend more than 80 hours on the parade deck, where they are evaluated on their execution of close order drill. Their leadership abilities are tailored toward working with young, immature recruits.

Because of high selection criteria, an average of less than 10 percent of DI candidates dropped out of the program between 1990 and 1995.

This process is a reflection of the difficult task of molding young recruits. But the arduous training DIs go through is also the fine tuning of a system that historically fostered the notion that the DI was in a world of his own.

The DI's image over the years — cultivated by the Corps and reinforced by Hollywood — had become somewhat larger than life. Viewed as a

Top, drill instructors in 1943 gather in the tent city erected during World War II. Above, DIs do some administrative work inside a tent in 1943. Below, DI Hugh O'Brien in 1943. After leaving the Marines, O'Brien went on to fame as an actor in movies and television.

into combat.

quintessentially rugged, disciplined and sometimes brutal Marine, this stereotype influenced many drill instructors to assume the role.

Under intense pressures to turn boys into men in a few short weeks, some DIs employed tactics that led to abuses and embarrassment to the Corps.

The great majority of these abuses were petty; nevertheless, a few isolated incidents led to the deaths of recruits. Such tragic episodes became the catalysts to significant changes in recruit-training methods.

But over the years one basic tenet has remained intact: The DI plays the paramount role as the central figure for instructing and supervising new recruits.

During 135 years of Marine Corps history, no formal training program existed for recruits. Noncommissioned officers at Navy yards throughout the country were expected to teach new recruits basic drills and how to use a rifle.

Marine Corps Commandant, Maj. Gen. William Biddle determined this training was inadequate, and in 1911 authorized recruit depots at Norfolk, Va; Mare Island, Calif.; and Puget Sound, Wash. Gen. Biddle also is credited with instituting the concept that drill instructors would stay with recruits from the time they entered boot camp to the moment they graduated.

During World War I, drill instructors had complete authority over recruits in their charge. The eight- to 10-week program was physically demanding, and DIs felt no remorse about using physical punishment as a means to discipline recruits, according to retired Lt. Gen. Victor Krulak in his book *First to Fight: An Inside View Of The U.S. Marine Corps.*

The enormous buildup for World War II from 27,000 to 450,000 Marines put an additional burden on DIs. Initially, the training period was cut from eight to four weeks to get as many Marines as possible

The Marine Corps began receiving the bulk of its per-

> "There had been a widespread perception, among recruits and drill instructors alike, that a recruit platoon was a little world in itself with the drill instructor as supreme and answerable only to God."
>
> — retired Lt. Gen. Victor Krulak

sonnel from the Selective Service System in December 1942 with the termination of voluntary enlistments for men of draft age. As a result, DIs were forced to deal with more than the usual number of recruits who were physically and mentally unsuited to becoming Marines. In addition, the influx of so many recruits created a shortage of qualified DIs, forcing the Corps to mobilize inexperienced corporals and privates as drill instructors.

For the most part, DIs were left to run their platoons as they saw fit.

"We had very little supervision," Henry Meyer, a DI in San Diego during World War II, said in a documentary video on MCRD, San Diego. "We were lord amongst ourselves. We knew what we were supposed to do. Our first contact was the First Sergeants Office. He was the key man; he was God as far as we were concerned."

A formal school for drill instructors was established in 1942.

On Sept. 1, 1943, Col. George T. Hall, commanding officer of the Recruit Depot, issued the following guidelines for DIs: "Drill instructors shall not lay hands on recruits except for the purpose of making corrections. They shall not strike, kick, curse or in any way mistreat a recruit. The practice of using swagger sticks or a cane in making corrections is prohibited." Even so, many DIs continued to rely on physical intimidation.

Emotional intimidation was also part and parcel of recruit training. E.B. Sledge recalled in detail his World War II drill instructor nearly 40 years after his boot camp experience in San Diego.

A corporal met Sledge and his fellow recruits when they got off the bus in 1943, Sledge wrote in his book *With the Old Breed at Peleliu and Okinawa*. The DI ran the men up and down the streets, then "put his hands on his hips and looked us over contemptuously. 'You people are stupid,' he bellowed. From then on he tried to prove it every moment of every day."

But the recruit training formula worked well despite its shortcomings, according to Gen. Krulak, the Depot's Commanding General from 1959 to 1962. "The young man who completed the training had clearly acquired some of the precious virtues of commitment and obedience, and he met the extreme challenge of combat from Guadalcanal to Okinawa with poise and steadiness," Gen. Krulak wrote.

Sledge agreed, writing, "This seemingly cruel and senseless harassment stood me in good stead later ... ."

In 1944, a new policy was announced that clearly acknowledged the stress of the DIs' wartime work: DIs who had been at the Depot more than a year were relieved by returning combat veterans.

The DI school at San Diego closed at the end of World War II, but was re-established at the outbreak of the Korean War. Once again, the recruit training cycle was reduced to eight weeks, and DIs were given the enormous responsibility of molding young draftees into Marines within a compressed time frame.

Former California Congressman Pete McCloskey Jr. credits rigorous boot camp training with saving his life

Swagger stick had more than one use

Following is an article originally published in the Chevron *on Feb. 21, 1942, by Cpl. Charles O. Wood. The headline was "Daring Reporter Tells Why D.I.s Carry Sticks."*

It's really not important at all, but have you ever wondered just what the stick carried by the drill instructors means to them? Well if you made a point of asking some old-time DI, he'd probably lead you to believe that it means more than a first casual glance would indicate.

For a subject, we chose Sergeant Robert A. Morehead. Bob has served with us for over eight years and intends to serve for at least eight more, barring an act of Japs. During those eight years, he's seen service in China waters, aboard the "Augie," most of Europe aboard the *Indianapolis* and several U.S. posts which normal transfers dictate.

The Sergeant is a typical Marine and when we asked him about that 40-inch stick he carries at all times he explained that he "just couldn't get along without it." When we approached him he was eating chow with, believe it or not, the stick across his knees!

Morehead explained that the stick is used primarily to measure the proper distance between ranks. It also helps entice the men who habitually fail to heed verbal instructions. "It really doesn't hurt," says Bob, "but I guess it does smart a little."

Marine recruits have been the same for years according to Morehead. "They're a lot of 'Play prettys' who drink their coffee with crooked little fingers when they first enlist, but in a few weeks they step right in with the very best Leathernecks.

Just a minute, Sarg — "Hey you! Square yer hat!"

If you would like to meet Morehead, don't go to the first guy you see carrying a 40-inch stick — it might be someone else, 'cause all the DIs carry them.

Brig. Gen. A.L. Bowser, Commanding General of Recruit Training Command, with Capt. (later Maj.) John Buck in 1956 in front of Building 28. The howitzer has since been moved to stand in front of the Command Museum.

and the lives of Marines under his command in Korea. "We were literally saved on one occasion because another regiment, the 1st Regiment of Marines, was able to climb a 2,700-foot hill in about five minutes less time than it took the (Chinese) 3rd Field Army to climb that hill," McCloskey told the Congressional Committee on Armed Services in 1976. "That particular battle may have saved the 1st Marine Division in Korea, and it was entirely the result of physical training, arduous physical training."

The success Marines achieved on the battlefield underscored the attitude in the Corps regarding boot training — "if it ain't broke, don't fix it."

But the Corps was forced to re-evaluate its training program when six recruits at Parris Island drowned during a disciplinary session on April 8, 1956. Known as the Ribbon Creek Affair, the incident compelled the Corps to question the latitude DIs were given during boot training.

Gen. Krulak wrote: "Certainly, one of the most beneficial results of the Ribbon Creek Affair, was the reaffirmation of a truth well known in the Corps — that a solid chain of command, with appropriate responsibility at every level, is essential.

"There had been a widespread perception, among recruits and drill instructors alike, that a recruit platoon was

Drill instructors at MCRD, San Diego during the 1960s pose for a photo. During the Vietnam War, South Vietnamese military personnel were brought on base to learn the fine points of being a drill instructor.

a little world in itself with the drill instructor as supreme and answerable only to God."

As a result of Ribbon Creek, the Recruit Training Command at MCRD, San Diego was established May 11, 1956, under the direct command of the Marine Corps Commandant, rather than the Depot's Commanding General. Brig. Gen. (later Lt. Gen.) Alan Shapley was the first commander and established the headquarters in Building 28. The establishment of the command set up a chain of commissioned officers to work closely with drill instructors. Four or five platoons were formed into a "series" with a series commander who was charged with the evaluation of daily training exercises.

The Recruit Training Command (redesignated Recruit Training Regiment in 1960) also began supplying most of the instructors for the DI School, which averaged approximately 60 students in 1963. These instructors were expected to serve for at least one year and were required to be "thoroughly proficient" in at least one subject on the syllabus, but be ready to conduct any class.

At the beginning of U.S. involvement in the Vietnam War, the recruit training program was fixed at eight weeks and DI School was expanded to eight weeks. The barracks were overflowing by early 1966, and the Depot was required to house 700 recruits in hard-backed tents.

During the Vietnam War, 12,000 to 15,000 recruits were trained monthly from 1965 to 1973 in San Diego, and for the third time the Selective Service System provided a portion of recruits. By the late 1960s, the controversy surrounding the Vietnam War had taken its toll on recruits and DIs.

"To tell you about being a drill instructor during the Vietnam period is like talking about being on another planet in another time," said retired MSgt. Raymond Cieslinski in the MCRD video. "We didn't hold civilians in high esteem, and it made training these kids difficult."

To complicate matters, Project 100,000 required that each service accept a certain number of recruits who could not meet induction mental standards. Many of these recruits were poorly educated and required remedial training. By the height of the Vietnam War, these substandard recruits made up approximately one quarter of the total population of Marine recruits.

According to the Standard Operating Procedures of the early 1970s, DIs could not maltreat recruits in any manner. "We could not touch a recruit; we could not swear at a recruit. But that was overlooked," MSgt. Cieslinski said.

The result was summed up succinctly by a former DI. "Well, it went too far, and we caused our own heartburn," Sgt. Roger Roll told *The New York Times* in 1977. "A kid got killed out in San Diego."

In 1975, Pvt. Lynn E. McClure was forced to fight several successive pugil-stick bouts at MCRD, San Diego. The injuries he received during the exercise proved fatal. He died a few months later in 1976 of a brain hemorrhage. The incident led to new restrictions being placed on drill instructors.

In 1977, Marine Corps Commandant, Gen. Louis H. Wilson told *The New York Times*, "It's absolutely forbidden for a drill instructor to put his hands on a recruit in any way. We've cut the daily training schedule ... we've reduced the hours that the DIs work with recruits ... ." The Marine Corps also increased supervision of DIs, with two officers assigned to each series, or group of 1,300 enlisted men, the newspaper reported. "Before these changes, officers were like a handle on a pot, but not in it," said Col. Gary Wilder, the head of a task force on recruit training at Parris Island, S.C.

The Corps wanted to put a stop to abuse of recruits, but it also wanted to stop abuses of the system, such as "heavy barreling" and "flight pay." According to a history lesson DI candidates receive today, "DIs are famous for heavy barreling. Examples of this are giving a recruit all the answers to the academic test, switching recruits on qualification day ... and using illegal substances to clean weapons." Flight pay, the lesson explains, "is an expression for payment of gifts wrongfully solicited by a drill instructor ... in order (for a recruit) to graduate."

One result of the changes: Some DIs left the Corps. Sgt. Lee Dickinson, a DI, told *The New York Times*, "Some DIs couldn't adapt to the new rules. They were good Marines and they went down the tubes. There was a lot of overreaction, Marines saying that they were now teaching Sunday School, that they didn't want to work with officers. These Marines have gone, the old-timers."

The curriculum for a drill instructor in 1997 might well leave some of those old-timers speechless. It includes,

In March 1960, a recruit from Platoon 105, 1st Battalion gets a lesson in how to address a drill instructor.

Drill instructors provide instruction on everything, down to the smallest details of Marine Corps living, whether it's shining shoes or making bunks, as seen in these photos taken during the mid-1970s.

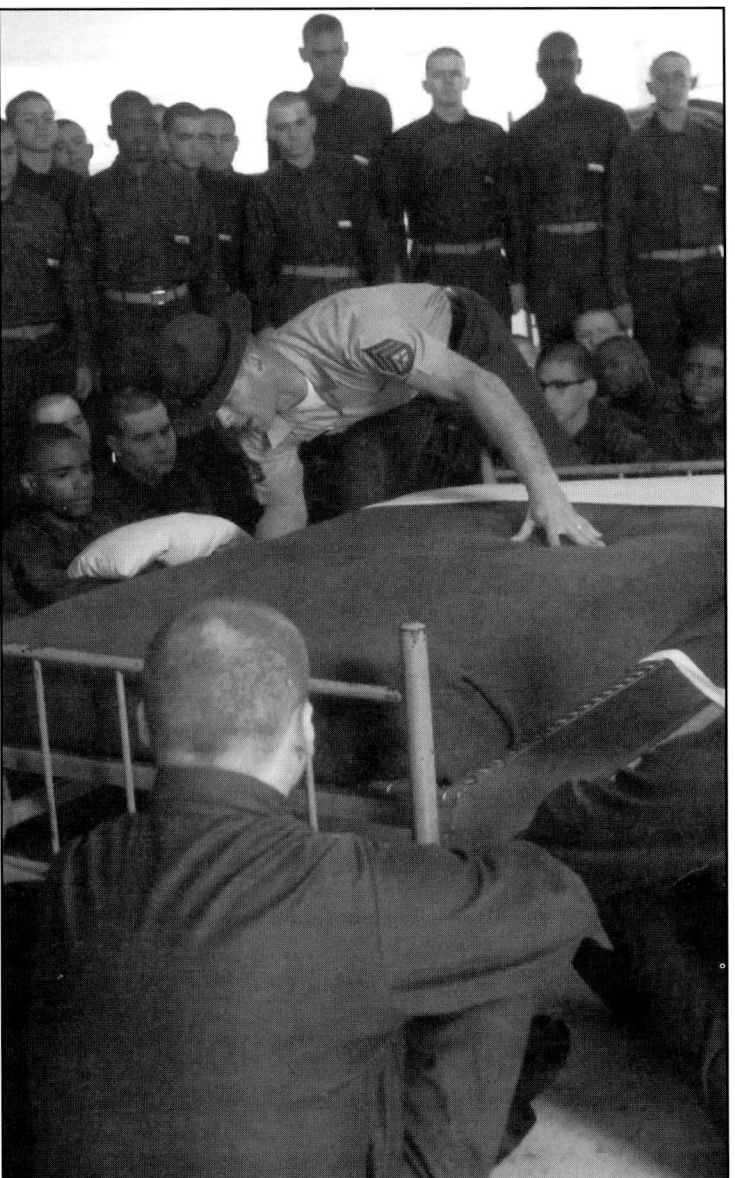

for example, a statement of recruit training principles: "When a recruit signs a contract with the Marine Corps, there is an expectation that each recruit expects the Marine Corps to fulfill. That expectation is to make him a Marine by providing organized, challenging training, professional supervision and fair treatment."

Drill instructors now follow a program of instruction with standardized, written guidelines and objectives. The meaning of fair treatment is spelled out as well. Today, the would-be drill instructor learns that a recruit has seven rights, including the right to eight hours of sleep, the right to eat and the right to medical attention. The curriculum explains, "These are common rights we would give to a prisoner during wartime, but because a few recruit trainers in the past have attempted to take these basic rights away, we have had to formalize them within the regulations for recruit training. Remember, absolute power corrupts absolutely."

After learning these kinds of lessons, "Today's DIs produce a basically trained Marine who is better trained and more physically fit than at any time in our history," said Maj. S.A. Packard, director of the MCRD, San Diego Drill Instructor School in 1997. The training, he said, is accomplished, "without resorting to the negative techniques that have been used at times in the past. Today, we train smarter, better, fairer."

The DI of the 1990s no longer relies on the tough-guy image fostered in the heat of war and polished by Hollywood.

MCRD's Commanding General, Brig. Gen. Garry Parks, said in a 1996 documentary video: "Our approach is to use firmness, fairness and dignity as we train Marines. Our DIs use leadership by example in their approach."

Left, DIs oversee pugil stick practice in the mid-1970s. Below left, a drill instructor gives a lesson in close combat methods in 1968. Below right, recruits follow a DI's movements during rifle training in 1975.

Left, a Sea School student at San Diego trains on gunnery equipment in 1944. Above, students of a 1967 teletype operators course in the Communication and Electronics School pose for a class photo.

The Schools

Training Marines has been an integral part of the San Diego base ever since Sea School moved from Northern California two years after the post opened. Over the years, the base has been home to both large and small schools, in which

Marines take a class on Navy insignia at the San Diego Sea School on March 10, 1944.

thousands of Marines have received valuable instruction.

Among the major schools on the base, Sea School was the most long-lived, taking its place alongside recruit training in 1923. For more than half a century, the school prepared Marines for service aboard ship.

Numerous schools emerged on the base during World War II. Hundreds of Marines received training in such diverse specialties as truck mechanics, signalmen, radio operators, and record clerks.

In terms of sheer numbers, Communication and Electronics was, by far, the largest school. The school was officially established on the base in 1950 and grew to approximately 4,000 instructors and students by the height of the Vietnam War.

In their barracks, Sea School students learn knot-tying, a skill they will share with their sailor shipmates on sea duty.

Recruiters School is the most recent addition to the list of those that have operated on the base. Operating as a tenant command, it is responsible for training all personnel who operate the hundreds of recruiting stations throughout the United States.

"A ship without Marines is like a coat without buttons."
                                    Adm. David G. Farragut

Sea School

On Nov. 10, 1775, the Second Continental Congress, meeting in Philadelphia, authorized the formation of two battalions of Marines to serve aboard American ships. The resolution stressed that Marines should be former seamen or have knowledge of maritime affairs.

Nearly four years later, after his victory over the H.M.S. *Serapis* in the Battle off Flamborough Head on Sept. 23, 1779, John Paul Jones credited Marine marksmen aboard USS *Bonhomme Richard* with "clearing the British deck with its gun crews."

The traditions of the sea-going Marine were firmly entrenched in the annals of military history by the time Sea School was established in San Diego in 1923. Originally located at Mare Island, Calif., Sea School was moved to San Diego along with the Recruit Depot.

Most candidates enrolled in Sea School directly upon completion of their recruit training. "His first day is a memorable one," Col. E.P. Moses, the Recruit Depot's commanding officer, told *Leatherneck* magazine in the June 1932 issue. "He learns for the first time that the barracks has no floor or ceiling, and other items quite foreign to the land soldier ... . He is taught the proper way hammocks are triced up to permit comfort for sleeping ... . He is given instructions in the loading, pointing and training drills of 5-inch .51 caliber rifles (sic) ... . He is made to realize the importance of cleanliness in the compartment at sea."

A department under the jurisdiction of Sea School was the Field Music School, where Marines were taught the drum and trumpet. The school had 40 students in 1932.

San Diego's Sea School in 1940 was under the command of Capt. William R. Hughes. Each three-week class instructed approximately 90 students. Sea School candidates usually were in the top one third of their recruit training platoon and were nominated by their drill instructors.

Sea School students in San Diego practice on gunnery trainers in 1944.

Using a scale model of a cruiser in 1942, Marines train on shipboard procedures at San Diego.

The curriculum in 1940 included 60 hours of lectures, covering topics such as "Relations with the Navy" and "Sea Terms and Expressions." In addition to drills on the 5-inch Navy guns, sea-going Marines were expected to be proficient with .50-caliber anti-aircraft machine guns and .45 caliber pistols.

Attesting to the high standards of Sea School, 1st Sgt. Robert W. Thompson Jr., who was a Sea School instructor in San Diego, told *Leatherneck* magazine in June 1940, "Of the 781 men who entered the school (in 1940) two deserted, 100 were transferred as unfit for duty afloat, and 679 were transferred to Marine Detachments in the fleet."

Marine Headquarters, Washington, D.C., decided to deactivate Sea School in San Diego in 1941 to consolidate training on the East Coast. The school was closed shortly after World War II began, but the need for increased numbers of sea-going Marines soon became evident. Col. William H. Rupertus, the base commanding officer, ordered the school reopened in January 1942. The first class had 100 Marines, and was under the command of Lt. R.L. Powell.

In August 1942, the Commandant of the Marines Corps, Maj. Gen. Thomas Holcomb, issued an order forbidding Marines from wearing their blue uniforms aboard ship. The move may, in part, have been an austerity measure, but it also had to do with the fact that during the war the primary job of Marines aboard ships was as gunners. The same proclamation was issued at the beginning of World War I. During peacetime when the Marines performed more ceremonial duties, they were allowed to revert to their colorful blue uniforms.

During World War II, Sea School Marines participated in the production of several Hollywood films. Paramount Studios came to the base in June 1942 and employed the services of two Sea School gun crews, who re-enacted the defense of "Wake Island," on the shores of nearby Imperial Beach. Sea School Marines were enlisted nine months later by Metro-Goldwyn-Mayer to lend a hand in "Salute To The Marines."

All the publicity may have prompted a story in the December 1943 issue of *Leatherneck*, describing San

Diego's sea-going Marines as "show-outfits" who in the prewar Sea School days "were seen marching about doing trick drills in Technicolor blues with the sun glittering on highly polished buttons."

The *Chevron*, the base newspaper, called Sea School Marines "one of the most colorful units on the Marine Base." On July 4, 1942, the newspaper also noted: "Their life is a series of drills, inspections and classes, with polishing and shining thrown in to make it interesting."

Sea School lasted four weeks at the beginning of World War II. Graduates were usually assured of the sea duty they requested, although most sea-going Marines were required to perform a month of guard duty at the San Diego base while awaiting transfer.

By August 1942, Sea School was extended to five weeks, so that Marines could spend a week training on 20 mm and 44 mm guns at the Navy's newly opened anti-aircraft school in nearby Pacific Beach.

The Marine Corps' only other Sea School, located in Norfolk, Va., closed in 1945. On March 21, 1946, the *Chevron* reported that Maj. Derek W. Price was in command of the San Diego school. The paper also announced that a new "3A-2 trainer" was on the base. "Two gun mounts are equipped with sights into which the gunners look and pick up their targets. Enemy planes appear coming in at various bombing angles ... . Sound effects of the planes also incorporated into the trainer accustom him to actual battle noise."

The attraction of travel and adventure on the high seas lured Marines into Sea School during peacetime. With the war over, the emphasis at Sea School was no longer on gun proficiency, but rather on guard and orderly duty, ceremonies and naval customs. "One eight ball can foul-up the small 40 or 50 man detachments," reported *Leatherneck* magazine in August 1949. "High ranking naval officers may judge the whole Corps by the caliber of their Marine orderlies."

The outbreak of the Korean War placed gunnery skills at the top of list once more. The curriculum during the war also included classes in shipboard fire and damage control. The faculty in 1952 consisted of 12 NCOs and three sailors under the command of Maj. Richard L. Moore. During the Korean War, entire ship detachments went through Sea School as a unit and were often assigned to Navy vessels that were taken out of mothballs.

Sea School was reduced again to four weeks by 1962. Located near the present-day administration building, the school resembled the other old Spanish-style barrack buildings in the area, with the exception of a ship's bell and a large sea horse conspicuously placed at the entrance.

GySgt. Mel Jones described Sea School's interior in the March 1962 issue of *Leatherneck:* "Practically every inch of the walls (bulkheads, sir) are covered with artwork. Most of the creative decor is composed of ceiling to deck murals tracing naval history almost from the days of the canoe. There are replicas of medals, photos of ships, letters of appreciation, portraits of former Commandants

> By 1987, only five ships manned by Marine detachments required gun crews. The few Marine gun crews needed were trained aboard ship or sent to Navy gun-loaders schools.

Marines practice on a 5-inch gun at Sea School, San Diego in October 1936.

Sea School at San Diego in the mid-1960s: above left, a Marine rings the Sea School bell; above right, students leave their living area "topside" for morning inspection; and left, a student salutes an officer at the school's entrance — a mock-up of a ship's quarterdeck.

and, looking like a mad cartoon in the Louvre, the four letters EXIT."

Jones noted there was brass work everywhere. "Even light fixtures on the ceiling (overhead — darn it) twinkle like a South African diamond mine." Some of the rooms at Sea School were designed to simulate life aboard ship. Thirty Marines were assigned to a compartment, each with his own sea locker.

Particular attention was paid to uniforms. Aboard ship, Marines were expected to stand countless formations as honor guards for visiting dignitaries. To assure compliance with strict uniform standards, four pages dealing with the wear and care of clothing were issued to each Marine. One suggestion: "At small expense to you but at great saving to the life of your trousers, you should have a small piece of cloth sewn to the inside of the cuff where it wears against the heal of your shoe." Other suggestions included: "Have a tie for each shirt and send them to the cleaners together" and "Your coat should be tailored while you're standing at attention."

In 1968 with the Vietnam War in full swing, nearly all students for Sea School in San Diego were coming directly from the Second Infantry Training Regiment at Camp Pendleton. Following boot camp in San Diego, most Marines received advanced training at Camp Pendleton before shipping out to Vietnam.

Sea School's commanding officer was Capt. Robert A. Vostry, and 1st Sgt. Charles E. Johnson was the school's senior noncommissioned officer. Many of the school's instructors were previously DIs, who gave away their former careers by the way they barked orders.

Sea School acquired its own mascot in May 1971 —

San Diego Sea School students demonstrate the loading and firing of a 20 mm twin gun mount Feb. 25, 1953. The guns had been recently installed.

Left, Staff Sgt. Hector M. Flores, 1st Detachment commander, and Sgt. William D. Harris stand at parade rest during the last Sea School graduation and the deactivation ceremony Dec. 8, 1987.

Ike Puller, a 4-year-old English bulldog. Reportedly, Ike took great pleasure in four things: "eating, sleeping, trotting alongside the double-timing troops, and chasing MP trucks." The latter was officially frowned upon by Capt. Larry Snead, the school's commanding officer.

Class size in 1971 was about 70 men. The usual courses were taught with the addition of a new class in drug awareness. That year, there were more than 800 Marines serving two-year assignments aboard ships. Aircraft carriers normally had a detachment of 55 Marines. Cruisers had 39 and sub tenders had 23 Marines.

First Lt. R.A. Palena was the school's commanding officer in 1982. By then, all Sea School instructors were required to take a formal instructors course at the Landing Force Training Command, Pacific, across the bay at Coronado, Calif.

The advent of the nuclear Navy drastically reduced the need for Marine gunners. By 1987, only five ships manned by Marine detachments required gun crews. The few Marine gun crews needed were trained aboard ship or sent to Navy gun-loaders schools.

The Marines' new mission was guarding nuclear weapons aboard ships against terrorist attack.

During the late 1980s, the average class size was 120 and lasted four weeks. The school's commanding officer was Capt. Thomas Reimann, who previously served as the CO of the Marine detachment aboard USS *Blue Ridge*. With the advent of more sophisticated weapons systems, the emphasis at Sea School shifted to academics. "When they get here from Infantry Training School (at Camp Pendleton)," Reimann told *Leatherneck* magazine in April 1987, "they're suffering from the 'DI Syndrome.' They've been yelled at in boot camp; they've been yelled at at ITS. They're used to being yelled at. We try to get across early that this is an academic environment."

Sea School in San Diego was deactivated on Dec. 8, 1987. Capt. Michael F. Reineberg was the school's last commanding officer. Sea School closed because many of the shipboard duties once performed by Marines were taken over by sailors. Marines would remain responsible, however, for ship's security and supervise Navy guards, who would perform most duties. As a result, the training of sea-going Marines would be the responsibility of Marine Security Force Battalions located at Norfolk, Va., and Vallejo, Calif.

During World War II, Marine Corps Base, San Diego trained Marines to work with telephone lines and transmit messages via semaphore. The base also provided training on radios and walkie-talkies.

"The students seem to toss around expressions like 'AMSG-1,' 'Rectifier,' 'Cathode,' and 'AN/CPS-5' with careless familiarity."

Chevron, Oct. 6, 1950

Communication and Electronics School

On Jan. 7, 1950, the Signal and Track Vehicle School Battalion, then the largest of the Marine Corps' formal schools, began moving from Marine Corps Base, Camp Pendleton, Calif., to MCRD, San Diego. In a sense, the school was coming home. During the 1930s, Signal

Battalion at San Diego taught Marines about different aspects of various communications systems and how to keep them functioning. Classes in semaphore, telephone lines, radio, and walkie-talkies were given. In 1941, Signal Battalion transfered to Camp Elliott, a few miles northeast, and then moved to Camp Pendleton during World War II.

The formal signal school was activated during World War II at Quantico, Va., as the primary location for training radio and track vehicle operators and repairmen.

Quantico's Signal and Track Vehicle School Battalion was relocated to Pendleton's Camp Del Mar in 1947.

Three years later, the school moved to MCRD, San Diego. The *Chevron* proclaimed in bold headlines: "First Contingent Arrives From Del Mar." During the next 24 days, approximately 1,100 Marines moved from their makeshift accommodations at Camp Del Mar and occupied more than a dozen buildings at MCRD. The move was intended to give the school a more permanent home.

Col. George R. Ruffin Jr. was the battalion's commanding officer. Several schools operated within the battalion's structure.

Capt. D.F. McGeehan commanded the Amphibian Tractors Mechanics School. Marines who took the six-month course worked on LVT-3s (Landing Vehicle, Tracked) and LVT-A5s. This component of the battalion, however, moved back to Camp Pendleton during September 1950. According to the *Chevron*, the move was made because of the Korean War and a shortage of space at MCRD. The scope of the training at Del Mar was broadened to include tank mechanics.

In July 1950, the battalion schools remaining at MCRD began operating their own radio station — W6YDK. The amateur radio station was maintained primarily for train-

The *Chevron* announces the arrival of Communication and Electronics School at MCRD in the Jan. 13, 1950, edition.

ing. The station was powerful enough to reach the East Coast, and anyone who was attached to the base was encouraged to send private messages. An ad running in the *Chevron* said, "Anyone wishing to send a message of a personal nature through this station call 2nd Lt. Breeze at extension 239, and leave a message including the phone number and address."

Other courses included the high- and low-speed operators classes. High-speed or Morse code operators often worked aboard ships. They were in great demand because of their ability to work extremely fast under a lot of pressure. Their specialties were either in receiving or transmitting Morse code — never both. At the other extreme was the low-speed or field operator. Known as the "Comm. Man," these operators carried a 25-35 pound radio and followed their units into combat.

During the 1950s, most Marines considered the Radar Technicians Course the "roughest" to pass. The 18-week course included classes in analytical geometry and differential calculus. Students for the course were handpicked by Headquarters, Marine Corps, and sent to Great Lakes Naval Training Station, Ill., for basic courses in radio and electronics before being transferred to MCRD.

As the Corps' needs expanded and new classes were added, the signal component of the school was redesignated Communication-Electronics Schools Battalion on Oct. 1, 1953.

The three main schools within the battalion were: Operational Communications, Electronics, and Communications Material schools. There were 18 courses in all centered around radar and radio technologies.

Technological advances made during the early 1960s in communications and electronics forced an expansion of the school. By the mid-1960s, the number of departments in the school had increased dramatically, and the student population was approaching 4,000 — nearly double what it had been before the Vietnam War. The school's growth demanded more classroom and storage space than MCRD could realistically provide.

Night classes were introduced to alleviate the overcrowding. Nevertheless, construction began in January 1966 on a new Communications-Electronics School at Marine Corps Air-Ground Combat Center at 29 Palms, Calif.

Headquarters, Marine Corps, decided to move the school from MCRD in phases over several years. The move began in 1966 with the transfer of schools for Tactical Air Control and Defense System, Electronics and Marine Tactical Data Systems Maintenance.

San Diego's growth as a major metropolitan area presented other problems. For example, communications between civilian planes and air traffic controllers at nearby Lindbergh Field were interfering with the school's radio frequencies. Conversely, the equipment used by Marines at the school was interfering with commercial broadcasting stations.

"We (Marines) were told that we could not operate our radios a great deal because of interference of commercial radio and TV stations in the City of San Diego area," said Sgt. Maj. Stephen D. Allermann, who was a PFC taking the Field Radio Operators Course in November 1970. "Of course, it did not take a great deal of time for a bunch of privates and

A classroom in Building 317, the Electronics School, at MCRD, San Diego in April 1970.

Marines at MCRD, San Diego take a break from classes at the Communication School, Building 239, in April 1970.

PFCs to figure out what this meant. This was an opportunity to explore!" Allermann said that during breaks between classes, he and other Marines "surfed the 920 channels" on their AN/PRC-25 and AN/PRC-77 radios.

"In no time, we found two TV stations, several taxicab base stations, and a few local San Diego business bands. This was an opportunity to test the MIJI (Meaconing, Intrusion, Jamming and Interference) training. In no time classmates were ordering up cabs and sending pizzas."

Apparently, word got out about these opportunities to explore the radio bands, and shortly thereafter, according to Sgt. Maj. Allermann, field training was moved to Naval Air Station, Miramar — a few miles north of MCRD but relatively undeveloped.

"Each morning we would load up 'cattle cars' with all our equipment," Sgt. Maj. Allermann said. "We then traversed the highways to the 'Back Forty' at NAS, Miramar. Here, we conducted training in the high frequency radios. Radio frequencies were assigned, and we communicated with ourselves. Surfing these frequencies was a bit tougher. There were over 10,000."

The radio operators also had a chance to practice their skills in the field at other locations.

"Volunteers were sought to act as communicators at the San Diego golf course for a big PGA tournament," Sgt. Maj. Allermann said. "The radio operators that were assigned, myself included, were shuttled to the golf course to act as radio operators to rebroadcast scores during each hole so that the scoreboard was kept accurate and up to date. This was an opportunity to practice operating the radios as well as view the scenery — girls."

Shortly after Sgt. Maj. Allermann was reassigned to Camp Lejeune, phase two of the move began in January 1971 when newly constructed facilities at 29 Palms were ready. More than 2,000 personnel and dozens of truckloads of classroom and electronics equipment were moved.

Headquarters, Communication-Electronics School Battalion left San Diego on Feb. 1, 1971, and, on the same day, reactivated the school at 29 Palms.

But according to Sgt. Maj. Allermann, the Field Radio Operators Course was still at MCRD when he returned from Vietnam in 1973. "While there, volunteers were sought to instruct the Field Radio Operators Course. ... I volunteered and assisted during some classroom and field training."

> "It is no simple mission, for he must be constantly thinking, scheming and conceiving ideas which will outwit the competition and at the same time keep the Marine Corps fresh in the minds of the public."
>
> Guide to Administration
> U.S. Marine Corps
> 1st Lt. Walter R. Hooper, 1943

Recruiters School

"The Marines are looking for a few good men" — 21,207 to be exact. That's how many new Leathernecks were recruited by the Western Recruiting Region in 1996. The figure represents the number of recruits who came to MCRD, San Diego from states west of the Mississippi River — approximately 52 percent of the total manpower needs of the Marine Corps.

The recruiters, who are assigned to fill that quota, work

Former Marine J.T. Malcom, left, helps recruiter MSgt. J.L. Barnes persuade Malcom's son, Eddie, to join the Corps in the early 1930s by showing off his old uniform. Malcom was on active duty from 1905 to 1914.

at the recruiting substations across the West. They are the Corps' top sales staff. To sell their product, these Marines in blue uniforms must truly believe they work for one of the best "companies" in the nation. They must understand how to sell the entire Marine Corps — all the fields and every program. That's where the Recruiters School at MCRD, San Diego plays an essential role.

The school was activated in San Diego in early October 1971 in buildings 317 and 394. This replaced the Recruiters School at Parris Island, S.C., which had been operating since August 1947. From November 1971 through August 1972, schools operated at both depots.

The first six-week course at San Diego began Nov. 2, 1971, with nine instructors and 120 students. Marines were expected to become proficient in such subjects as community relations, career benefits, officer selection, and substation management. But the core classes were recruit screening and public speaking. Approximately 40 hours of public speaking classes required recruiters to develop presentations suited for students as young as eighth-graders.

For Marines accustomed to the decorum of military life, it can be an enormous challenge to operate in a world of civilians where the stripes on your shirt sleeve mean little.

"It's tough and sometimes discouraging work," wrote Tom Clancy in *Marine: A Guided Tour Of A Marine Expeditionary Unit*. "Just five years after the victory in the Persian Gulf, all the services are scrambling to keep up the recruit pool required to sustain our forces."

The Marine Corps of the 1990s has the smallest per capita advertising budget for recruiting of any of the services. In recent years, television and print advertising has played an important role in targeting high-school and college age men and women. The recruiters of the late 20th century employ many of the same techniques their counterparts did in the 1970s — visiting schools on career day, working out of a booth at military air shows and exhibitions, and cold calling on potential recruits recommended by friends and family. But the differences between the 1990s and 1970s could be summed up in a simple phrase — the legacy of the Vietnam War.

Perhaps the most difficult period of recruiting in Marine Corps history was the 1970s. The advent of an all-

This 1970s Marine Corps poster uses a photo of then-Commandant Gen. Louis H. Wilson. In the wake of the death of a recruit in 1976, recruiters were being blamed for bringing unqualified young men into the Corps.

Sgt. Linda N. Clark of the MCRD Recruiters School welcomes Commandant, Gen. Louis H. Wilson on Oct. 5, 1976. Speaking to a congressional committee that was investigating recruitment practices earlier that year, Gen. Wilson called recruiters "the lifeline of the Corps."

volunteer military in 1973 coupled with the lingering sentiments of the anti-war movement severely reduced the recruiting pool. The Marine Corps dramatically increased the number of substations in a move to extend the potential pool of recruits. But the expansion was not enough, and some recruiters resorted to enlisting men who were unqualified to be Marines in order to reach individual goals.

The death of a San Diego recruit in 1976 sparked a congressional investigation into recruiting and recruit training practices. One former Marine Corps recruiter told the committee recruiters were under "terrible" pressures and that in his opinion, "It was standard practice to rig physical, mental and other tests to clear unqualified recruits for entry into the Corps." He told the committee he and other recruiters believed that failure to meet quotas meant fines and even court-martial.

Although the Marine Corps never endorsed any such policy, this perception among the ranks caused Commandant, Gen. Louis H. Wilson to tell the press, "There'll be a concerted effort to counter the serious misconceptions that keep Marines from volunteering to become Marines or recruiters."

Gen. Wilson also addressed the congressional committee, candidly admitting that there were incidents of abuses among recruiters and drill instructors. "I accept the full responsibility for the unacceptable actions of a few Marines," he said. The general said that the Marine Corps was aggressively working to "remove" and "punish" recruiters who violate regulations. "In fiscal year 1975, 252 recruiters were relieved for reasons which range from indebtedness to incompetence to malpractice." The Commandant pointed out that at the recruiter's school in San Diego the rules and regulations that govern recruiting are clearly defined.

In defending his Marines, Gen. Wilson called recruiters "the lifeline of the Corps."

"The Marines who perform these duties work long and difficult hours, and in general, I am extremely pleased with their performance." The Commandant pointed out that even Congress recognized this fact by authorizing special duty assignment pay.

On June 1, 1976, the Marine Corps responded to the criticism by placing the nearly 2,000 recruiters around the country under the direct supervision of the two recruit depot commanders: Maj. Gen. Kenneth J. Houghton at MCRD, San Diego and Maj. Gen. Arthur J. Poillon at Parris Island, S.C. The reorganization officially began April 1 when Gen. Houghton assumed control of the 8th Marine Corps District and was completed in June when he took over control of the 9th and 12th Districts. The recruiters previously had been under the jurisdiction of area commanders, whose main job was coordinating reservist activities. Recruiters were also made responsible for the qualifications of their recruits.

Gen. Houghton spent several months touring the districts and talking to recruiters. "I tried to impress on them the need for quality, to focus on the 75 percent high school graduate for next year," the general told the *Chevron*, MCRD's newspaper.

Several more changes occurred in 1977. The Corps required recruiters to put their promises to new recruits in writing. Also, recruiting methods were standardized throughout the country to lessen the work load, and to help recruiters track and analyze their work. Previously, each recruiting district developed its own system. Some recruiters even developed unorthodox styles of their own.

For example, MSgt. Jean "Cheesey" Neil combined his extraordinary talents in athletics with recruiting. The legendary sports figure at the San Diego base in the 1930s worked as a recruiter in the early 1950s. MSgt. Neil enlisted star athletes from his recruiting station inside the main Post Office in downtown San Diego. Sometimes he even snatched them from the jaws of the Army.

Bob Skinner, who later played for the Pittsburgh Pirates, recalled his unconventional entrance into the Marines. "The Korean War was on, and I just got my draft notice from the Army. But Cheesey made another arrangement," said Skinner in the September/October 1996 edition of *Traditions: San Diego's Military Heritage* magazine. "He fixed it so I could enter the Marine for two years of active duty (en-

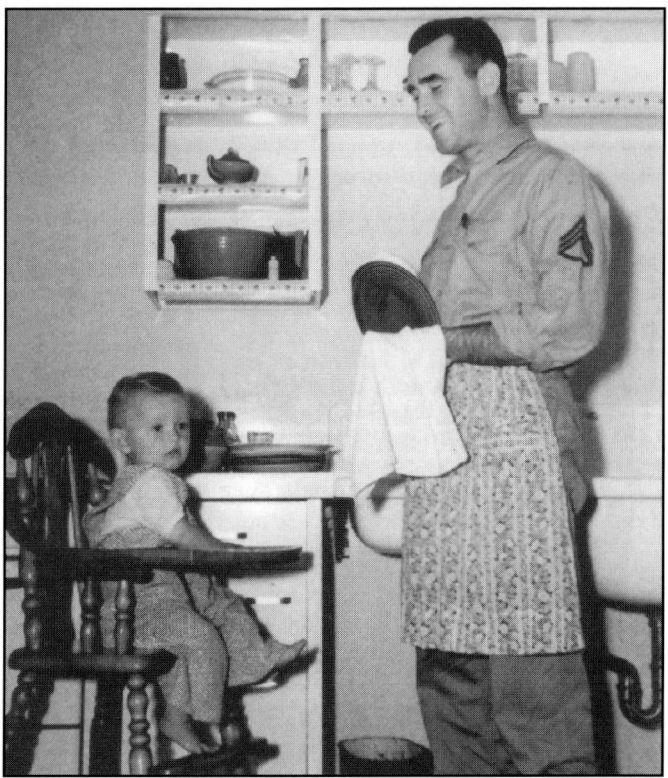

Sgt. Jean "Cheesey" Neil, shown at home with son Mike, was an unorthodox recruiter in the 1950s. His presentation of Marine Corps life was so persuasive, however, that even his son joined. Mike Neil advanced to brigadier general in the Marine Corps Reserve.

listments were for three years at the time) followed by a stretch in the active reserves.

Recruiters school at MCRD, San Diego moved in the spring of 1977 to Building 27. The school initially occupied only the second floor, which had been used as a medical facility. The first floor continued to function as a mess

Instructors at the Recruiters School at MCRD, San Diego pose for a 1997 group photo.

hall.

"There was no money allotted for the move," said MSgt. D.D. Gronke, a school instructor in 1997. "Recruiters School students moved everything in the school over the weekend, using Marine Corps MC35A2C trucks." The school expanded to the first floor in 1985.

Beginning in 1979, the Corps introduced a FEX or field exercise training program as a way of getting recruiter students to interact with civilians. Col. James Guerin initiatied this new approach, sending students to local recruiting stations for two days to apply their classroom skills. During his tours at MCRD, Col. Guerin was director of the Recruiters School, commanding officer of the Recruit Training Regiment and Chief of Staff to the Commanding General.

"I once thought that if a recruiter just sat in the office, people would walk in," said Capt. Ronald Dalton in a February 1991 interview with *The San Diego Union* newspaper. Capt. Dalton confessed that his most daunting task as executive officer of the Mission Valley station, located just a few miles from the Depot's gate, was keeping in contact with 220 high schools throughout Southern California. "Those high school lists (of students) are the only tools we have." California education laws allow school districts to supply recruiters with the names of students. However, many will not.

Still, the atmosphere has improved for recruiters of the 1990s. MGy. Sgt. Chauncey Franklin, a recruiter at the Mission Valley station, told *The San Diego Union*, "The climate today is tremendously more pro-military than it was in the Vietnam era. Then, the draft was still in effect."

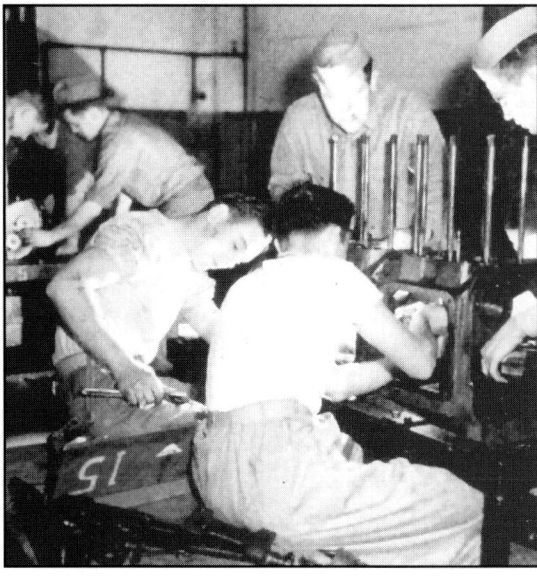
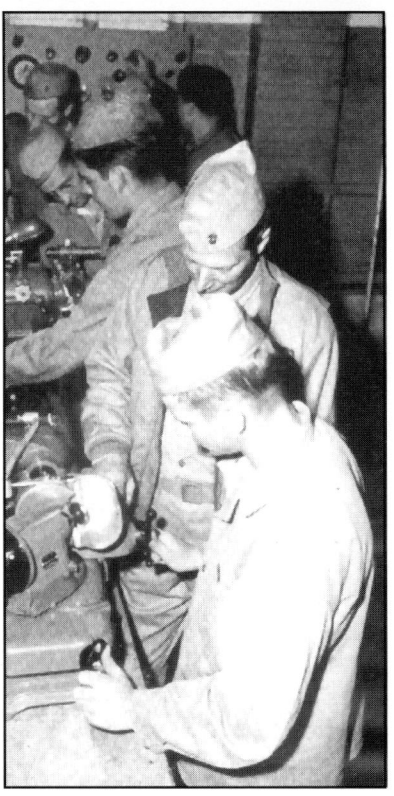

Below, Marines learn to overhaul engines and, bottom, take a machine shop class at Marine Corps Base, San Diego in 1943. These courses were among several that were taught on base during World War II.

World War II Schools

MCRD, San Diego was also home to numerous smaller schools at various times, such as the First Sergeants, Clerical, Motor Transport, and Military Police schools. Most were organized during World War II and closed at the end of hostilities.

The First Sergeants School was established in San Diego in March 1942 by Warrant Officer Ford E. Wilkins. The average class size was about 40 students. The school trained first sergeants to keep service record books, muster rolls, reports, and to understand court-martial procedures. Candidates for the eight-week course were selected by their company commanders. The school closed in June 1944. During its 27 months of operation, the school graduated 559 NCOs for the Fleet Marine Force, and other Marine units. Warrant Officer Robert W. Teorey was the officer in charge when the school closed.

The 12-week Clerical School was open to all enlisted Marines. The school offered courses in typing, shorthand, and operating equipment such as the teletype machine. The average class size was approximately 80 Marines.

The Motor Transport School was operating on the base by May 1943. The 12-week course trained Marines to drive Jeeps, and light and heavy trucks. The school also taught Leathernecks who had worked as auto and truck mechanics in civilian life how to repair military vehicles.

The Military Police School was conceived by Gen. Edward A. Craig in 1941, while he was a colonel assigned as Base Provost Marshal.

Gen. Craig wrote in his memoirs, "On 17 October 1941, a Guard Battalion was organized. This was probably the first unit trained essentially as Military Police in the Marine Corps. A Military Police School was organized and I trained my men in their duties getting assistance from the San Diego Police traffic officers and the Federal Bureau of Investigation. With the arrival of the Jeeps for issue, I arranged for motorized patrols of the base which was filling up with troops and equipment as the war became a reality."

Marine Base football players (from left) Don Beeson, team captain Cothrane, and Cooper talk with coach Johnny Blewett (second from right) circa 1930.

Sports Legends

Alan Shapley, later a Marine general, gets a hit in the 1930s.

The football team from San Diego State Teachers College routed the San Diego Marines 18-0 in 1922. This marked the beginning of a rivalry that spanned more than four decades. During those years, the Marines in San Diego would field some of the most talented service teams in the country.

It didn't take long for sports to take hold at the new Marine Base in San Diego. Athletics have flourished there — with only short breaks — for more than 75 years. Competitive and recreational pastimes have included most sports during this period.

But football was the glamour sport, drawing thousands of civilian supporters to the games. During the 1930s, San Diego Marines played and defeated some of the best college teams in the nation. Although the team was discontinued during World War II, the 1950s and early 1960s were the defining years for Marine Corps football in San Diego. Under the guidance of their coach, CWO Robert "Bull" Trometter, the Marines compiled one of the best won-lost records in service sports.

Even though baseball never attracted the huge crowds that followed football, the San Diego Marines excelled at the nation's pastime, routinely winning the 11th Naval District Championship. Beginning in the 1950s, many of the Depot's star players went on to achieve success as major-league baseball players.

The first team of any consequence to play football at Marine Corps Base, San Diego was organized in 1924 and coached by Capt. (later Gen.) Elmer Hall.

Capt. Hall was a former University of Oregon football star who enlisted in the Marine Corps at the beginning of World War I. He played football at the Marine Barracks on Mare Island, Calif., in 1917 on a team that was considered the best in the country. The team was invited to the Rose Bowl classic in Pasadena, Calif., following an undefeated season against the highest ranked college and services teams on the West Coast. That year the Marines trounced the University of Southern California, 34-0, and the University of Oregon, 28-0. In the Rose Bowl, they beat the 91st Division Army Team from Camp Lewis, Wash., 19-7.

Capt. Hall was ordered in 1924 to report to San Diego to start a football program. Although no statistics for the year are available, the Marines played in the 11th Naval District Service League. The district encompassed a geographic area that included Southern California and parts of Arizona. (By the mid-1990s the district had been redesignated Naval Base, San Diego.)

In 1924, the Marines also registered their fourth straight loss against San Diego State College, a rivalry that would last until 1963. During those years, the Leathernecks beat San Diego State 17 times, lost 9 games and tied once.

In 1925, Capt. Hall became assistant coach to make room for his old friend Capt. Johnny Beckett, who had been player-coach of the 1917 Mare Island team. Capt. Beckett earned the job of organizing the All-Marine Team at Quantico in 1921. The All-Marine Team was a powerhouse, combining the best football players and coaches from all the bases, a practice that drained San Diego of its finest prospects. The custom of sending the best players on the West Coast to the East Coast continued until 1931.

The San Diego Marines finished with a 7-3-1 record in 1925, lining up against teams such as: Naval Training Station, Naval Air Station, Destroyers Squadron, and the West Coast Army. GySgt. Willis Ryckman, known as the grand old man of service football, was the leading ball carrier for the Marines. The highlight of the season was a 25-12 victory over a powerful West Coast Army team. That year, the Army defeated the West Coast Navy Team for the Coast Service championship.

Running back Albert "Red" Woods gained recognition as one of the first players to have taken his recruit training in San Diego. He played for San Diego during the

Above, Lt. Col. Elmer Hall in the 1930s with mascot James Jolly Plum Duff. Right, the spirits of veterans are watching over a game in the cover illustration for the Nov. 11, 1932, program for an Armistice Day game between San Diego State College and the Marine Corps Base.

The offensive line and backfield of a San Diego Marines football team pose for the camera in the 1930s at Hall Field.

1925 and 1926 seasons. After a short tour in Nicaragua in 1927, he was transferred to Quantico for the All-Marine Team.

The 1926 season was the first year the San Diego Marines won the West Coast Service Championship, finishing with a 5-1-2 record. The year also marked the beginning reign of the Poppleman brothers — Raymond J., Lyle H., and Clyde M. The brothers were high school football stars in San Fernando, Calif. Raymond joined the Marine team right out of boot camp in 1926. An outstanding full-

A late 1920s Marine Corps Base, San Diego football team makes a stop on the way to Los Angeles. The next day, the Marines beat Army 10-7. Standing at far left, coach Johnny Blewett, and far right, Don Beeson.

> MCRD football coach Maj. Allan "Scotty" Harris
> said his job at the base was made simple by the fact
> that most of the commanding generals "were jocks."

Robert "Bull" Trometter during the 1938-39 football season at Marine Corps Base, San Diego. Trometter went on to become one of the best coaches in the Corps.

back, he was transferred to Quantico, where he played on the All-Marine Team in 1927-1928. Lyle and Clyde joined the San Diego team in 1928 and played until the early 1930s.

There was no football on the base in 1927 with many of the players on expeditionary duty in Nicaragua and China.

The next year was a time for rebuilding. The Marines hired Johnny Blewett, a civilian, to lead their young and inexperienced squad. Blewett had played football for the University of California, Berkeley. With Blewett at the helm from 1928 to 1930, the San Diego Marines posted a 12-12-2 record. In 1929, the Leathernecks posted another upset over a powerful West Coast Army Team. The game was played at the Coliseum in Los Angeles. With the score tied at 7, the Marines won the game in the final two minutes with a 35-yard field goal.

Blewett resigned in 1931 when the Corps instituted a policy that all coaches must be active-duty Marines. At the same time, the All-Marine teams that had been assembled at Quantico since 1921 were abolished. This action allowed San Diego to develop and keep its best players.

The new coaching staff of Capt. Johnny Beckett, Capt. Harry Liversedge (later a base commanding officer) and Lt. W.O. Thompson led the Marines to a 7-4 season that was climaxed by a 7-0 win over Loyola University.

Jean "Cheesy" Neil was a star player on the 1931 squad. His career in San Diego spanned 30 years, beginning as a player in

San Diego Marines play Loyola at Balboa Stadium in 1933. Service teams often played until in stadium until it was taken over by the San Diego Chargers in 1961.

1929 and ending when he retired as a coach at MCRD, San Diego in 1959. Although best known for football, Sgt. Neil also excelled in basketball, baseball, tennis, and track and field.

Football in San Diego reached a higher plateau during the 1930s when the Marines adopted a more rigorous schedule, thanks to the efforts of Maj. Charles McL. Lott. College teams such as UCLA, Brigham Young, Arizona State, and USC became formidable opponents.

Maj. Lott, credited with bringing a new era of "big time" football to the base during the early 1930s, also brought American football to North China. He also coached the 1922-1923 American Legation, Peking, China, Marine teams.

As athletic director at the San Diego base, Maj. Lott promoted Marine Corps football around the West Coast. He also coached the San Diego Marines from 1935 to 1938. During that period, the Marines won 26, lost 14 and tied 4 games. Under his direction in 1936, the Marines whipped USC, 20-0; San Diego State, 14-0; and the University of California, 19-0.

Marine football in San Diego reached another milestone in 1939 with the first undefeated team. The

Football wasn't the only award-winning sport on the base. Left, the 1929 swim team shows off a trophy. The team won the 11th Naval District title and the service class title at San Diego's Silver Gate Swim. Right, the 11th Naval District champs in volleyball in 1930 stand proud. With coach Johnny Blewett (standing left), and athletic officer Maj. Charles McL. Lott (standing right) are Jean "Cheesy" Neil (next to Lott) and Don Beeson (kneeling right).

Marine Corps CheVron—Page Five

Battle of the boot camps

Of all the gridiron legends forged by MCRD Marines, few could match the hoopla of the short-lived annual face-off with their counterparts from Parris Island. For three seasons, the teams from the two recruit depots met to "settle the age-old boot camp controversy," reported the *Chevron*. The two teams fought it out in 1949, 1950 and 1951 at the Boot Bowl on the Marine Corps birthday for the honor of taking home the Boondocker trophy. In 1949, San Diego lost 19-13, despite a 70-yard touchdown run by "Skeet" Quinlan. The next year, however, San Diego got its revenge, drubbing Parris Island 57-18. It was San Diego's ninth successive win of that season and was played before a capacity crowd at Balboa Stadium. In 1951, although the *Chevron* reported that "both teams just about fumbled themselves off the field," San Diego lost 16-9.

BOONDOCKER TROPHY. The "Boondocker Trophy," awarded to the winner of the annual "Boot Bowl" fray between MCRDep and Parris Island, was presented three years ago by the Staff NCO club of the local Recruit Depot. As can be seen by the inscription, PI took possession of the trophy last year.

1952 Boondocker Fray On National Television

(Continued from Page 1) Toro and Camp Pendleton, and Parris Island is expected to cop the East Coast championship. The lone hurdle remaining is Camp Lejeune and the date of the game is set for Thanksgiving Day, November 27. PI tripped Quantico early in the year, 22-7, while Camp Lejeune bounced Quantico last week, 25-2. Quantico was rated in pre-season polls as one of the powerhouses in the east.

The visitors have a strong offense centered around quarterback Sam Vacanti, former University of Iowa and Purdue University great. The little passing wizard has flipped 98 aerials for 54 completions and 914 yards. He has thrown 10 touchdown passes.

His favorite target this year has been right end Bob Schnelker, formerly of Ohio State University. Schnelker has gobbled up 23 tosses for an amazing 422 yards and six touchdowns. Bill Hayes and Spec Granger are also rated top pass receivers, snaring eight and 10 respectively.

ELTER LEADING GAINER

The team's leading ground gainer is Leo Elter who has scampered 492 yards for an average of 6.6 yards per try. Bill Hayes has romped 434 yards, making an average of 5.2 yards per carry, and Bill Mixon has gained 348 yards, averaging 3.7 yards on each attempt.

PI will send an offensive line into the game averaging 210 pounds per man, one pound less than the average for the Depot's offensive forward wall. The Islanders' offensive backfield will average 193 pounds per man, as compared to the Depot's 196 pounds per man.

The Parris Island defensive forward wall, including the linebackers, will tip the scales at an average of 213 pounds per man, and the Depot's average will be 212 pounds. PI's defensive backfield also outweighs MCRDep's, 186 to 184.

PROBABLE OFFENSIVE STARTERS

MCRDep		Parris Island
Tom Evans	LE	Spec Granger
Tex Lawrence	LT	Louis Harrelson
Ed H. Brown	LG	Bull Stovall
Bob Griffin	C	George Radosevich
Chuck Cusimano	RG	Billie King
Marv Beguhl	RT	Rex Boggan
Bob Bell	RE	Bob Schnelker
Tom Kingsford	QB	Sam Vacanti
Tom Carodine	LHB	Billy Mixon
Ron Hoenisch	RHB	Leo Elter
Bob Goode	FB	Bill Hayes

Cartoon and article from the Oct. 31, 1952, edition of the *Chevron* before a match with Parris Island.

MARINE CORPS CHEVRON

Published By Marines At The Marine Corps Recruit Depot, San Diego

Vol. 10 — Friday, October 12, 1951 — No. 41

Battalion Plans Costume Dance For Halloween

H&S Battalion will stage a Halloween masquerade and hard time costume dance at the Mission Beach ballroom Oct. 31 from 9 p.m. to midnight. All personnel of the battalion and their guests are invited. Prizes will be awarded for the best costumes. Music will be furnished by the Depot dance band under direction of MSgt Pat Mulligan. Transportation will leave from the front of the administration building at 7:30.

COSTUMES REQUESTED

1stLt Harry J. Nolan, Battalion Recreation Officer, said "the only form that won't be allowed is swimming suits." Other than that personnel may wear anything, including field boots, blue jeans and logger shirts. However, 1stLt Nolan said that he would like as many personnel as possible to come in suitable Halloween costumes. He advised personnel to begin planning and preparing their costumes as soon as possible.

A baby sitter service will be provided at the Staff NCO club nursery. When a child enters the nursery his parents will receive a ticket that will allow them to leave the Depot, through either gate 2 or 4, after midnight to get the child.

DECORATIONS PLANNED

Depot Devildogs Tackle State College's Unbeaten Grid Team

Staters Slight Favorites In Traditional Clash

MCRDep's thunderous Devildogs, riding on the crest of two smashing victories over service foes, collide with the unbeaten, untied Aztecs of San Diego State College tomorrow night in a Shrine-sponsored charity contest in Balboa Stadium. Kick-off time for this intra-city feud which dates back to 1922 is scheduled for 8:15 p.m.

Coach Mark Rainer's Marine grid-craft expects to find rough sailing in its encounter with the collegians, but will be going all-out to hold the edge gained by a 28-14 victory last year.

Going into that battle, the Marine-Aztec series was knotted at six games apiece with the 1925 tilt ending in a draw.

QUINLAN STARS

The Devildogs were sparked by Volney "Skeet" Quinlan, who played the full 60 minutes and was all over the field setting up two TDs and passing for another. He also inflicted damage

---

Leathernecks were coached by now-Brig. Gen. Hall.

The 1939 season also produced one of the most memorable comebacks in Marine Corps history. The Marines trailed 14-9 and were down to their final play in a game against Redlands College, when they pulled out all the stops in an amazing 28-yard play. Back Arne Arneson lateraled the ball to back Max Tafoya, who lateraled to end Cliff Griffin, who lateraled to end Al Montrief, who immediately fumbled the ball only to have Griffin recover it in the end zone.

The 1939 squad was filled with great players such as Warren "Locker Box" Jones and Robert "Bull" Trometter, who later went on to coach MCRD football and baseball. Trometter, who received the nickname "Bull" because of his charges up the middle line, was a triple threat as a player, excelling as a passer, runner, and kicker.

While playing for the base in the 1930s, Trometter moonlighted for the professional San Diego Bombers football team. Trometter had to play under the alias Murphy because Marines were forbidden to engage in

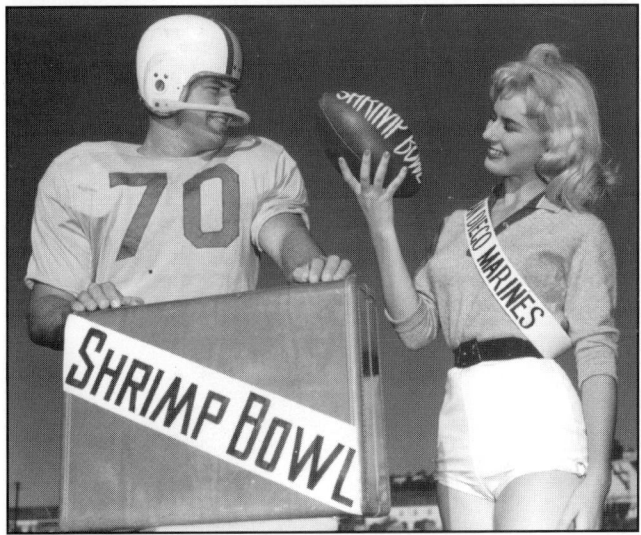

Above, the *Chevron* touts a game with rival San Diego State College in its Oct. 12, 1951, edition. Right, Gay Cowie, winner of the 1955 Fairest of the Fair pageant, gives the MCRD team a sendoff to the Texas Shrimp Bowl.

professional sports.

Football was discontinued at the beginning of World War II and resumed in 1947. The Marines played on Hall Field, named in honor of Gen. Hall. The 6,000-seat football field was located almost in the center of the of the south side of the base between Midway and Guadalcanal streets.

During the postwar era, the San Diego Marines produced some outstanding teams and one of the most successful coaches in Marine Corps history — CWO Bull Trometter. During five seasons at MCRD, San Diego, Trometter compiled a 52-7-1 record.

Trometter posted a perfect 10-0 record in 1959, his last season in service football. He believed his success was partly attributable to the fact that Marines were usually better prepared physically and mentally than most of their opponents. But the real key to his success at MCRD was talented players such as Volney "Skeet" Quinlan and Billy Martin. Both Marines were exciting breakaway running backs. Quinlan averaged 7.6 yards per carry and would eventually play for the Los Angeles Rams. Martin ended up signing a contract with the Chicago Bears.

In 1958, a packed house saw MCRD embarrass Camp Lejeune in the first Leatherneck Bowl game in San Diego's Balboa Stadium. The Marines attracted huge crowds to the 20,000-seat stadium built for the 1916 Panama-California Exposition.

The San Diego Marines continued their winning ways in the 1960s under the leadership of coach Maj. Allen "Scotty" Harris. MCRD posted 10-1 records in 1963 and 1964. Maj. Harris joined the Marines during World War II. After the war, he went to Ohio State University and subsequently returned to active duty as an officer. Wounded in Korea, he turned to coaching. Many of his players, such as Perry Rodrique, eventually formed the nucleus of Brigham Young University's powerhouse teams of the 1960s. And others, such as Herb Traveno — who would become the San Diego Chargers top place kicker — turned pro.

Maj. Harris said his job at MCRD was made simple by the fact that most of the commanding generals "were jocks."

The Vietnam war put an end to football at MCRD. Maj. Gen. Bruno Hochmuth, the Commanding General, called off the 1965 season. He was concerned about public reaction because of the needs of the Marines on the battlefront.

Organized baseball at MCRD, San Diego was also a casualty of the Vietnam War. But its roots go back to the year the base opened when the Marine team won the 1921 District Service Championship. The biggest game of the year was against the team from the USS *Charleston*, which was the holder of the Fleet championship at the time. The game was played for a purse of $3,500, and the Marines won 10-6. Professional baseball player Grover Cleveland Alexander was one of the umpires.

Marine Corps Base, San Diego baseball teams had mediocre years from 1922 to 1925, coming in second or third to the Destroyer Base (later Naval Station, San Diego) and the Naval Air Station on North Island.

The 1926 winter-season team posted a 14-2 record against service teams, winning the 11th Naval District Championship. After the season, five of the players were sent to Quantico to play for the All-Marine baseball team.

All major sports were discontinued at the Marine Corps Base in 1927 because of a lack of personnel. Baseball returned to the base in 1929 under the coaching of Johnny Blewett, who engineered a 39-9 record. The season was not completed that year because the other teams in the 11th Naval District league lost so many players to transfers.

Former Commandant, Maj. Gen. John Lejeune offi-

Above, MCRD quarterback John Proctor hands off to Mike Davis in 1963. Right, Marine Billy Martin in 1959. He was later drafted by the Chicago Bears.

Above, Chief Warrant Officer Robert Trometter, front row center, with his stand-out 1959 football team. Sitting to Trometter's right is Maj. Gen. Victor Krulak, MCRD's Commanding General, and to Trometter's left is Brig. Gen. Bruno Hochmuth, then Commanding General of the Recruit Training Command on the base. Below, Maj. Allen "Scotty" Harris, second row, fourth from left, who coached MCRD football teams in the 1960s. His teams posted 10-1 records in 1963 and 1964, the base's last gridiron seasons. The 1965 season was canceled because of the Vietnam War.

Above right, former Commandant, retired Maj. Gen. John Lejeune in 1929, the year he threw out the first ball of a game between the Marines and the Fleet Air team, officially opening the 1930 season. Above left, a 1930s baseball team. Right, baseball field at the Marine Corps Base circa late 1920s.

cially reopened the Service League season June 15, 1929, pitching the first ball between the Marines and Fleet Air. The Leathernecks won 1-0 behind the two-hit pitching of LeBoyd White.

The Service League was not organized the following year, so the Marines played in the Inter-county League, consisting of eight other teams from Southern California towns. Under coach Blewett, the Marines posted a 26-8 record. Outfielder Don Beeson led Marine sluggers with a .438 batting average.

In 1931, the 11th Naval District Service League got going again. The Marines dominated the league, posting an 11-1 record. Throughout the 1930s, the difference between average Marine baseball teams and outstanding squads was determined by international affairs. Many of the best players often found themselves on expeditions in Central America and the Far East.

MCRD's golden age of baseball began in 1952, when the San Diego Marines won the All-Marine Championship in a five games series against Parris Island. Bob Skinner was the series star for the San Diego Marines. Born and raised in nearby Pacific Beach, Calif., Skinner batted .400 in the series. He later played outfield for the Pittsburgh Pirates and St. Louis Cardinals, posting a life-time major league batting average of .277.

"There was a lot of prestige involved," said Skinner in the September/October 1996 edition of *Traditions: San Diego Military Heritage* magazine.

"Parris Island had a damn good team, and it was a dogfight all the way. We played like it was the World Series. After we won the last game 4-1, a huge celebration broke out," said Skinner, who was a major league scout in 1996. "The stands emptied and everybody, including the brass, was grabbing us and slapping us on the back. Even the Commanding General (Brig. Gen. William J. Whaling) was hugging us, a complete breakdown in the usual Marine Corps decorum."

The Marines posted a 60-18 record that year against

service and college teams. They even played in Tijuana, Mexico, against the Mexican all-stars.

"The fans were so excited, those rickety old wooden stands were quivering. We thought sure they would fall down," said Jerry Dahms, who played for MCRD in the early 1950s.

After the game, the Marines were invited to attend a celebration hosted by the Governor of Baja California, Mexico. "Tijuana's mayor and a lot of brass were there," said Dahms. "One of our pitchers, Bruce McKelvey, who had a bit to drink, decided to teach the mariachi band the Marine Corps Hymn. Pretty soon, there he was, half drunk, conducting those mariachis as they played the hymn. I'm sure it was never performed like that before or since. It caught everybody by surprise. We all snapped to attention and tried like hell not to laugh."

MCRD, San Diego baseball produced a number of major league players during the 1950s. Boston Red Sox pitcher Earl Wilson played for the base in 1957 and 1958. In 1957, he posted a 15-0 record with three no-hitters. The team also included a flashy centerfielder named Floyd Robinson, who would go on to play for the Chicago White Sox, and Ray Oyler, who later played shortstop for the Detroit Tigers.

"The big Marine Corps baseball program stopped in the 1960s because it became too expensive," said Joe King, the Depot's recreation director in 1997.

"Many bases didn't have big baseball fields, though this one did. Beeson Field used to have stands, dugouts, and locker rooms." But the stadium was torn down and the era of big-time baseball gave way to intramural sports. "They wanted more participatory not competitive playing," said King, who was a master gunnery sergeant on the base from 1973 to 1975.

Although baseball and football dominated the sports pages of the base newspaper at MCRD, other sports also have been well-represented through the years on the base, such as basketball, swimming, track and field, racquetball, wrestling, tennis, golf, and volleyball. All these sports continued in an intramural program throughout the 1970s, '80s and '90s. Soccer was part of the line-up during the mid-'90s.

In 1975, King coached the MCRD team that won the Armed Forces softball championship, winning the base's first interservice gold medal in 10 years.

Men's and women's softball is currently the most popular sport at MCRD, with an average of 13 or 14 teams culled from 1,900 base personnel, King said. And many teams have had more than the standard 15 players. MCRD's basketball team won the West Coast Regional Championship during 1994 and 1995, King said.

The base continues to field outstanding individual

Above, Women Reserves softball players in 1945 gather for a team photo. They were the 11th Naval District champs that year. Below, Col. Harry Lay congratulates Donald M. Beeson, 1929 11th Naval District tennis champ. Beeson's 20-year athletic career beginning in 1928 also included baseball, football and basketball. On April 26, 1950, the baseball field at MCRD was named in his honor. Maj. Beeson retired from the Corps in 1948.

athletes. Staff Sgt. Fred Waddell at MCRD was a member of the All-Marine Softball Team for 1994, '95 and '96. Moreover, the base produced the 1995 female athlete of the year for the Marine Corps and the Armed Forces: triathlete Capt. Karen Kraijeck.

Right, San Diego Marine first baseman Bob Skinner stretches for the ball in 1952, the year MCRD beat Parris Island. Below, Chicago White Sox centerfielder Floyd Robinson in 1962. He got his start at MCRD in 1958.

Below, MCRD, San Diego's winning 1952 baseball team members with their trophies. Kneeling from left: Ray Oyler, Pete Walski, Tom McCollum, Al Dorow, Bob Whitworth, Floyd Robinson, Bill Lachemann, Billy Capps and John Miller. Standing from left: Ted Ellis, Chuck Matthews, Ray Tabacchi, Col. Bruno Hochmuth, Maj. Gen. Thomas A. Wornham, coach Robert Trometter, Jim Knerr, Jack Osborne, Jim Pyles, and Earl Wilson.

Semper fido! Mascots win Marines' hearts

A small riot broke out at a Marine-Navy football game, and the instigator was none other than Gen. Smedley Butler coming to the defense of Jiggs — the bulldog mascot of the Quantico, Va., Marine Corps Base.

Reportedly, a Navy drum major kicked the base's mascot down the field to accentuate the sailors' 42-0 rout of the Marines. Infuriated, the general led the rush from the stands onto the gridiron intent on avenging the Corps' honor. The general received a split lip during the melee that followed between Marines and sailors.

The English bulldog has been the Corps' mascot ever since Gen. Butler introduced Jiggs in 1921 to the Marines at Quantico, Va. Over the years bulldogs have come to symbolize the grit and resolve that Marines have displayed on the battlefield and in athletic competition.

While bulldogs have reigned supreme most of the years since the base opened, other canines of questionable heritage have also earned the title of Marine mascot.

Soochow was buried with honors on the base in 1948. The mixed-breed terrier was first adopted in the late 1930s by the 1st Battalion, 4th Marines when the unit was on duty in Shanghai, China. Soochow accompanied the Marines to Corregidor and spent World War II at a POW camp. After the war, the dog was brought back to San Diego with the released prisoners. Soochow became the base mascot, replacing the bulldog Jolly Plum Duff, who had just been killed in an automobile accident.

More than 800 Marines turned out on Aug. 11, 1950, to witness the dedication of a mascot memorial. "The Marine Corps has always been a very closely knit family," said Gen. William T. Clement at the dedication. "Included in that family, our mascots and war dogs have played an important part. In dedicating this memorial to our mascots, I do so with the firm conviction that those we honor here today had a very definite influence on the Marines who have known and cared for them."

Royalty graced the Depot during the early 1950s with the reign of Rolwal Red Rival. The English bulldog was the offspring of two of the greatest show dogs in the Southwest — Seven Gable Vici and Bailey's Dream. Even so, the royal canine soon became "Smokey," thanks to the Marines' penchant for bestowing nicknames.

Smokey won the affection of the Marines and was promoted to corporal. As with most Leatherneck mascots, Smokey became a personality in his own right, so much so that on Oct. 31, 1952, he was credited in the base newspaper with writing an article about his life at MCRD. "When a *Chevron* reporter attempted to interview Smokey, he was met by silence," announced the *Chevron* on page 8. The paper went on to explain that the "pup" wouldn't release any information unless he could write it himself.

"I make my residence at the little red house next to the athletic office at Beeson Field," wrote Smokey. "My hobby is riding around the Depot in a truck or car. I usually hang my head out of the window and sneer at recruits. I can't complain much about Marine Corps chow, for I usually eat steak, eggs and cottage cheese."

Shockingly, Smokey admitted that at times he wished he had been a civilian dog. "I went over the hill a couple of times, but managed to beat the rap on each occasion," wrote Smokey, who was annoyed because he had been confined to quarters following the mishaps.

On Nov. 10, 1994, Po' Boy's Smokin' Joe became the base mascot. A present from the Big D chapter of the Oklahoma City, Okla., Marine Corps League, the dog was received by Brig. Gen. Edwin C. Kelley Jr., the base Commanding General.

Joe has a military identification card and his own uniforms. He promotes the Marine Corps at official events off the base and reviews graduations ceremonies. Joe's handler, LCpl. Fred Zimmerman, says, "He's the most photographed Marine around here."

Duffy was buried in April 1945 near the baseball field centerfield fence.

Po' Boy's Smokin' Joe is MCRD's current mascot.

Brig. Gen. Smedley Butler, CG at Marine Corps Base, San Diego during 1926-27, poses with mascot Jiggs.

Base Commanders

Marine Corps Commandant, Gen. Louis H. Wilson shares a laugh with Maj. Gen. Kenneth H. Houghton, MCRD's Commanding General, during the Commandant's visit to the base Oct. 5, 1976.

Maj. Gen. Joseph H. Pendleton

Commanding General, MCRD — March 1 - June 1, 1924.

Born June 2, 1860, at Rochester, Pa. — Died Feb. 2, 1942, in Coronado, Calif.

Commissioned a second lieutenant July 1, 1884, he was promoted to brigadier general Aug. 29, 1916, and major general Dec. 10, 1923. His career included distinguished service in Nicaragua in 1912 and in Panama in 1916 during revolutions in those countries. He was awarded the Navy Cross in 1920 for service in the Dominican Republic. He retired June 2, 1924. Camp Pendleton Marine Corps Base was named in his honor Sept. 25, 1942. (For more information on Gen. Pendleton's career, see Page 12.)

Brig. Gen. Dion Williams

Commanding general, MCRD — July 10, 1928 - April 4, 1929

Born Dec. 15, 1869, in Williamsburg, Ohio. A resident of Washington, D.C., he died Dec. 11, 1952, at Bethesda Naval Medical Center, Md.

Commissioned a second lieutenant in July 1893, he was promoted to brigadier general in June 1924.

He participated in the Battle of Manila Bay during the Spanish-American War in 1898, and was in command of the company of Marines at Cavite, Philippine Islands, that hoisted the first American flag to fly over Spanish soil during the war.

In 1902, he wrote the first report that developed advanced-base doctrine for the Corps. He advocated the use of Marines to garrison naval stations and predicted it would be necessary to establish temporary bases in a naval campaign. Much of his thinking was eventually adopted. He was Fleet Marine Officer of the U.S. Atlantic Fleet during "The Great White Fleet's" world cruise during 1907. In 1924, he was Commanding General of the Marine Corps Expeditionary Force at Quantico, Va., that marched to the Civil War battlefield at Antietam, Md. There, the force performed field exercises under simulated war conditions. From 1924 to 1933, Gen. Williams was on duty at Headquarters, Marine Corps, Washington, D.C. During that period, his assignments included three years as assistant to the Commandant. He retired Jan. 1, 1934.

Maj. Gen. Smedley D. Butler

Commanding General, MCRD — Feb. 25, 1926-March 3, 1927.

Born July 30, 1881, in West Chester, Pa. Died June 21, 1940, in Philadelphia, Pa.

Known as "Ol' Gimlet Eye," he was appointed a second lieutenant in May 1898 at the age of 17 for the war with Spain. He became a brigadier general in March 1919 and was promoted to major general in July 1929.

Gen. Butler served during the Boxer Rebellion in China in 1900, when he was wounded in battle. For this service, Gen. Butler became one of the few Marines to be decorated with the Marine Corps Brevet Medal. In 1912, he took part in action in Nicaragua. As commander of the landing and occupation force at Vera Cruz, Mexico, in 1914, he received his first Medal of Honor. He received his second Medal of Honor for bravery and forceful leadership in Haiti during 1915 as commander of a detachment of Marines and seamen from the USS *Connecticut*. For service during World War I in France, he was awarded the Army Distinguished Service Cross, Navy Distinguished Service Medal, and French Order of the Black Star. He retired Oct. 1, 1931. The USS *Butler*, a high-speed minesweeper, was named for Gen. Butler in 1942.

Brig. Gen. Robert H. Dunlap

Commanding general, MCRD — Jan. 31, 1930 - Dec. 25, 1930

Born Dec. 22, 1879, in Washington, D.C. Died May 19, 1931, at La Farinière, Cinq-Mars-la Pile, France.

Gen. Dunlap was appointed a second lieutenant in August 1898 for the Spanish-American War. He was promoted to brigadier general in November 1929.

He participated in the Battle of Tientsin in China in 1900 during the Boxer Rebellion, and in 1914 he took part in the occupation of Vera Cruz, Mexico. During World War I, he commanded the Army's 17th Regiment of Field Artillery and took part in the Meuse-Argonne Offensive and the march to the Rhine. He was cited by the commander-in-chief of the American Expeditionary Forces for exceptionally meritorious and conspicuous service. In 1928, he commanded the 11th Marines and exercised control over the northern area of Nicaragua, a disaffected section of the country. For this, he received the Distinguished Service Medal. In France in 1931, while Gen. Dunlap was preparing to take a course at the French War College, a landslide imprisoned a woman in a cave. During a rescue attempt, Gen. Dunlap saved her, but was killed by a subsequent landslide.

Maj. Gen. John H. Russell

Marine Corps Commandant — 1934-1936

Commanding General, MCRD — Dec. 26, 1930 - Nov. 22, 1931

Born Nov. 14, 1872, in Mare Island, Calif. Died March 6, 1947, in Coronado, Calif.

Appointed a second lieutenant in July 1894, he was promoted to brigadier general in January 1922, major general in September 1933 and to Commandant of the Marine Corps March 1, 1934, serving until his retirement Dec. 1, 1936.

Including his time at the Naval Academy (1888-1892), Gen. Russell's 48 years of service was more than any other officer in the Army, Navy or Marine Corps at that time.

Gen. Russell served aboard the battleship USS *Massachusetts* during the Spanish-American War in 1898. From November 1910 until April 1913, he commanded the Marine detachment, American Legation, Peking, China, during that country's transition from an empire to a republic. He was appointed American High Commissioner to Haiti with the rank of Ambassador Extraordinary, serving from 1922 until 1930. While he was assistant to the Commandant, he was instrumental in creating the Fleet Marine Force. His awards include the Distinguished Service Medal and Navy Cross.

Maj. Gen. Douglas C. McDougal

Commanding General, MCRD — May 6, 1935 - May 18, 1937

Born April 23, 1876 in San Francisco, Calif. Died Jan. 20, 1964, in La Jolla, Calif.

Gen. McDougal was appointed a second lieutenant in March 1900, and was promoted to brigadier general in March 1934, and major general in October 1939. As a young man, he served first as an ensign in the Navy and then as a cadet in the U.S. Revenue Service, the forerunner of the U.S. Coast Guard.

He particpated in Boxer Rebellion operations in 1900 in China. From 1909 to 1911, he served at Headquarters, Washington, D.C., principally as an instructor in rifle marksmanship. He was captain of the first Marine Corps Rifle Team to win the National Match, and in 1928 he was captain of the American International Rifle Team that competed in The Netherlands. He participated in the occupation of Vera Cruz, Mexico, in April 1914. During the ensuing years, he saw service in Haiti, Santo Domingo, and France. From March 1929 to January 1931, he was director-in-chief of the Guardia Nacional de Nicaragua, and for his service was awarded the Distinguished Service Cross. While at MCRD, he was also Commanding General, Fleet Marine Force. He retired Jan. 1, 1940.

Brig. Gen. Frederic L. Bradman

Commanding General, MCRD — Dec. 7, 1931 - April 30, 1935

Born Jan. 18, 1879, in Newark, N.J.

He was appointed a second lieutenant for the war with Spain in 1898 and was promoted to brigadier general in 1931.

During World War I, Gen. Bradman served as Fleet Marine Officer on the USS *Pennsylvania*, flagship of the Atlantic Fleet. During June 1930, he was sent to Managua, Nicaragua, to command the 2nd Marine Brigade, which was engaged in the task of establishing order and peace. On March 31, 1931, an earthquake destroyed Managua, and then-Col. Bradman began organizing reconstruction and relief measures for civilians. His work was recognized by his superiors as well as the National Red Cross, and he received the Medal of Merit from the Nicaraguan government. He is a graduate of the Army and Navy War Colleges. He retired Dec. 1, 1938.

Maj. Gen. Louis M. Little

Commanding General, MCRD — May 19, 1937 - Aug. 15, 1939

Born Jan. 17, 1878 in New York. Died July 16, 1960, in Newport, R.I.

Gen. Little was appointed a second lieutenant in July 1899, and was promoted to brigadier general in January 1934 and major general in July 1935.

During the summer of 1900, he was a member of the 1st Brigade, China Relief Expedition, which fought its way to beleaguered foreigners in Peking during the Boxer Rebellion. He commanded the 8th Marines and troops in the field in Haiti from 1919 to 1921. His service was recognized by the Haitian government with its Medal of Honor and Merit with a citation that read in part: "An officer of a generous and courageous character. Acquired great popularity in the regions where he had combatted to re-establish order." He was a graduate of the Naval and Army War Colleges. He was director of Marine Corps operations and training from 1927 to 1931, and then was posted to Haiti to serve as Commanding General, 1st Brigade, returning in 1934 to Headquarters. In 1937, he was named Commanding General of the Fleet Marine Force and MCRD. He retired Feb. 1, 1942.

Maj. Gen. Clayton B. Vogel

Commanding General, MCRD — Aug. 16-31, 1939

Born Sept. 18, 1882, in Philadelphia, Pa. Died Nov. 26, 1964, at the U.S. Naval Hospital, Philadelphia, Pa.

Gen. Vogel began his 42-year career in the Corps as a second lieutenant in August 1904. He was promoted to brigadier general in March 1937 and to major general in April 1941.

He saw duty abroad in China, the Panama Canal, Cuba, Nicaragua and Haiti. During the early 1930s in Haiti, he was made Commandant of the Garde d' Haiti until the Marines were withdrawn in August 1934. From 1937 to 1939, he was Adjutant and Inspector of the Marine Corps. He was then ordered to San Diego as Commanding General of the 2nd Marine Brigade, and was in command of the 2nd Marine Division from its formation on Feb. 1, 1941 through October. Following a tour in the South Pacific as Commanding General of the I Marine Amphibious Corps in 1942 and 1943, he returned to San Diego in August 1943 as commander of the Fleet Marine Force, Pacific. In May 1944, he assumed his final active duty assignment as Commanding General, Marine Barracks, Parris Island, S.C. He retired from that post in January 1946.

Brig. Gen. Richard P. Williams

Commanding General, MCRD — Sept. 1, 1939 - Sept. 19, 1939

Born June 20, 1879 at Fort McPherson, Atlanta, Ga. Died March 14, 1950 at Savannah, Ga.

Gen. Williams was appointed a second lieutenant in October 1899, and was promoted to brigadier general in September 1934.

During World War I, he was assistant chief of staff with the Army's 90th Division stationed in France, serving with that organization during the Meuse-Argonne offensive. After the war, he commanded the naval prison at Parris Island, S.C., from 1921 to 1923 and again from 1925 to 1929. During the latter period he was often in command of the entire Parris Island base. He was named commanding officer of the 2nd Regiment stationed in Haiti in May 1929, and a few months later he assumed command of the Garde de Haiti. He returned to the United States in 1933 and graduated from the Army War College. In 1934, he was appointed officer-in-charge of the Marine Corps Reserve at Headquarters. Three years later, he became Commanding General of the 1st Marine Brigade, Fleet Marine Force, at Quantico, Va. In 1939, Gen. Williams took charge of the Department of the Pacific in San Francisco, Calif., the post from which he retired April 1, 1940.

Maj. Gen. William P. Upshur

Commanding General, MCRD — Sept. 20, 1939 - Dec. 7, 1941

Born Oct. 28, 1881, in Richmond, Va. Died Aug. 18, 1943, near Sitka, Alaska.

Gen. Upshur was appointed a second lieutenant in February 1904. He was promoted to brigadier general in June 1938 and to major general in October 1939.

After expeditionary duty in Cuba, Panama, the Philippines, and China through 1914, he assumed command as a captain of the 15th Company, 2nd Marines at Port au Prince, Haiti. In that island nation's mountains, he led Marines against revolutionaries who were trying to oust the American-backed government. The Marines captured and destroyed Fort Dipitie, for which Gen. Upshur received the Medal of Honor. During World War I, he served in France with the 13th Marine Regiment, commanding the American Military Prison and American Guard Camp. After the war, he served at various foreign shore stations and aboard ships. He was a graduate of the Army and Navy War Colleges. His last station was commanding general of the Department of the Pacific in San Francisco, Calif., beginning in January 1942. He was on an inspection tour during the summer of 1943, when he was killed in a plane crash near Sitka, Alaska.

Brig. Gen. Matthew H. Kingman

Commanding General, MCRD — April 27 - Aug. 8, 1944

Born March 1, 1890, in Humeston, Iowa. Died Nov. 16, 1946, at Bethesda Naval Hospital, Md.

Gen. Kingman was commissioned a second lieutenant in November 1913 and was promoted to brigadier general in August 1942.

He was commander of a machine gun company and later a battalion in France during World War I, and participated in five major engagements. He also took part in the march to the Rhine and the occupation of Germany. He was wounded by German machine gun fire June 6, 1918, at Belleau Wood. After the war, he served in Haiti, Nicaragua, and Panama. He was executive officer of the 5th Marines, Fleet Marine Force at Quantico, Va., in 1936. He was executive officer of the 2nd Marine Brigade, Fleet Marine Force at Marine Corps Base, San Diego from 1939 to 1940. He retired April 1, 1940, as a colonel, and returned to active duty Feb. 11, 1942, when he was named commander of the training center at Camp Elliott, San Diego. In late March and early April, he was in command of MCRD. His decorations include the Croix de Guerre, two Silver Stars and Purple Heart. He retired in October 1944.

Lt. Gen. James L. Underhill

Commanding General, MCRD — April 3, 1942 - March 31, 1943

Born June 12, 1891, at San Francisco, Calif. Died Oct. 7, 1991, in Monterey, Calif.

Gen. Underhill was appointed a second lieutenant in November 1913. He was promoted to brigadier general in August 1942, major general in May 1944, and lieutenant general in November 1946.

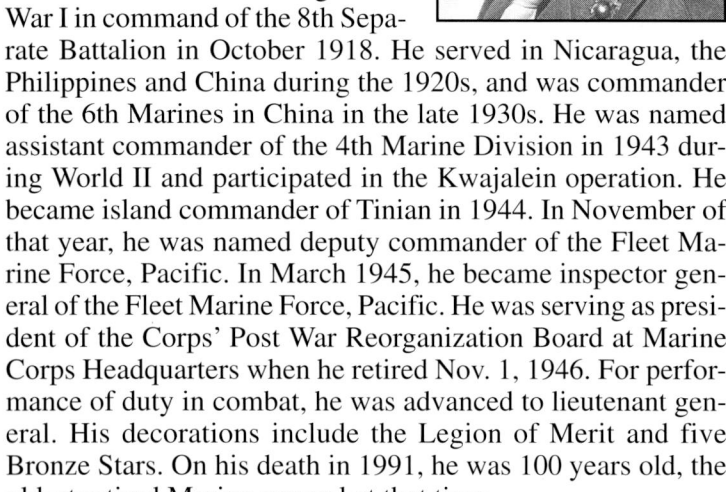

He went to France during World War I in command of the 8th Separate Battalion in October 1918. He served in Nicaragua, the Philippines and China during the 1920s, and was commander of the 6th Marines in China in the late 1930s. He was named assistant commander of the 4th Marine Division in 1943 during World II and participated in the Kwajalein operation. He became island commander of Tinian in 1944. In November of that year, he was named deputy commander of the Fleet Marine Force, Pacific. In March 1945, he became inspector general of the Fleet Marine Force, Pacific. He was serving as president of the Corps' Post War Reorganization Board at Marine Corps Headquarters when he retired Nov. 1, 1946. For performance of duty in combat, he was advanced to lieutenant general. His decorations include the Legion of Merit and five Bronze Stars. On his death in 1991, he was 100 years old, the oldest retired Marine general at that time.

Maj. Gen. Earl C. Long

Commanding General, MCRD — July 1945 - April 1946

Born Nov. 4, 1883, in Clayton, N.J.

Appointed a second lieutenant in August 1909, Gen. Long was promoted to brigadier general in August 1942 and major general in November 1944.

Prior to accepting his commission, he graduated from the University of California with a degree in engineering. He served aboard the cruiser USS *Charleston* for eight months during World War I. He saw service in the Philippines from 1920 to 1922, and went on to posts in Nicaragua, Mexico, and China. During World War II, he was commanding general of the supply service for the I and later V Marine Amphibious Corps and, subsequently, the Service Command, Fleet Marine Force. His decorations include the Legion of Merit with gold star, Nicaraguan Campaign medal, Mexican Service Medal, Victory Medal with France clasp, Yangtze Service Medal and Marine Corps Expeditionary Medal. He retired Aug. 1, 1946.

Maj. Gen. Archie F. Howard

Commanding General, MCRD — Aug. 9, 1944 - June 12, 1945

Born Jan. 29, 1892, at Clay Center, Kan. Died June 24, 1964, in Coronado, Calif.

A graduate of the U.S. Naval Academy, he was commissioned a second lieutenant in 1915 and was promoted to brigadier general in August 1942 and major general in July 1945.

During World War I, Gen. Howard served ashore in Siberia and afloat with the Asiatic Fleet. In 1918, he commanded the Marine detachment aboard the Fleet's flagship, USS *Brooklyn*. He took 30 Marines ashore in Vladivostok, Russia, to protect the American consulate and to join an international force patrolling the city at a time of great disorder in Vladivostok between the Bolsheviks and their opponents, the White Russians. He became assistant commandant of the Marine Corps Schools at Quantico, Va., in 1939. From May 1941 to July 1943, he served as chief of staff of the I Marine Amphibious Corps. He was thereafter named island commander on Guadalcanal and later New Georgia, for which service he was awarded the Army Distinguished Service Cross. He retired in November 1946.

Lt. Gen. Leo D. Hermle

Commanding General, MCRD — July 29, 1946 - Aug. 31, 1949

Born June 30, 1890 in Hastings, Neb. Died Jan. 21, 1976, in La Mesa, Calif.

Gen. Hermle was commissioned a second lieutenant in August 1917, and was promoted to brigadier general July 15, 1943, major general in December 1946 and lieutenant general in September 1949.

As a member of the 6th Marines during World War I, he participated in the defense of the Verdun Sector, where he was gassed. He also took part in the St. Mihiel and Meuse-Argonne Offensives, where he was gassed and wounded in action. He was awarded the Distinguished Service Cross and Distinguished Service Medal for extraordinary heroism. In 1941, as commanding officer of the 6th Marines at Marine Corps Base, San Diego, he deployed with the regiment to Iceland. In 1943 during World War II, as assistant commander of the 2nd Marine Division, he participated in the Tarawa invasion. As assistant commander of the 5th Marine Division, he participated in the assault and capture of Iwo Jima in 1945. His World War II medals include the Navy Cross, Legion of Merit and Bronze Star. He retired Sept. 1, 1949. For performance of duty in combat, he was advanced to the grade of lieutenant general after his retirement.

Lt. Gen. William T. Clement

Commanding General, MCRD — Sept. 1, 1949 - Nov. 30, 1951

Born Sept. 27, 1894 in Lynchburg, Va. Died Oct. 17, 1955, in Bethesda, Md.

Gen. Clement was appointed a second lieutenant in April 1917. He was promoted to brigadier general Oct. 3, 1942. By 1948, he was a major general and was promoted to lieutenant general on retirement May 1, 1952.

In 1917, he joined the 2nd Marine Regiment in Haiti, which was fighting revolutionary forces. He was executive officer of the Recruit Depot at San Diego from 1929 to 1930. At the outbreak of World War II, he participated in the defense of the Philippine Islands and received the Navy Cross. In November 1944, he was named assistant commander of the 6th Marine Division and participated in the assault on Okinawa. His second Legion of Merit with a gold star was awarded for, in part, "his daily visits to the front line elements, his aggressiveness and the coolness and courage he displayed under fire." He was commanding general of the Fleet Landing Force at Yokosuka (Tokyo Bay) Occupation Force, which landed on Japan on Aug. 30, 1945. His decorations also include the Bronze Star.

Maj. Gen. William J. Whaling

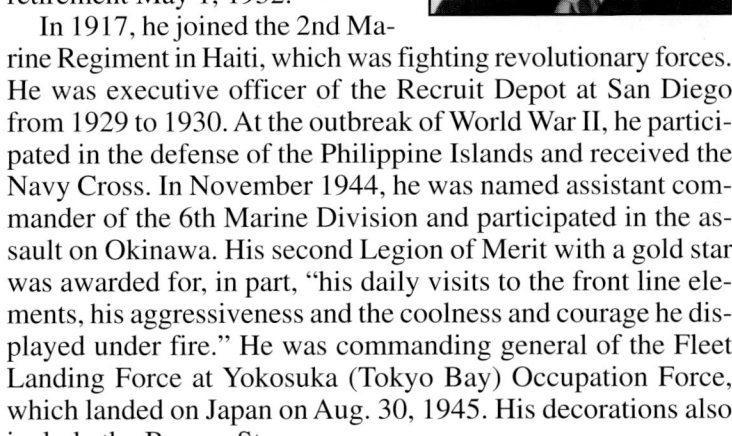

Commanding General, MCRD — April 22 to Sept. 12, 1952

Born Feb. 26, 1894, in St. Cloud, Minn. Died Nov. 19, 1989, in Lyons, N.J.

Gen. Whaling enlisted in May 1917 and was commissioned a second lieutenant in August 1918. He was promoted to brigadier general in July 1949, and major general upon retirement July 1, 1954.

He saw action during World War I with the 6th Marine Regiment in France and received the Silver Star. He was gassed in June 1918 and was awarded the Purple Heart. He was a member of 11 Marine rifle and pistol teams, including the 1924 Olympic pistol team. He also coached and commanded teams from 1935 to 1939 that were rated among the best in the world. His 1939 rifle and pistol team won numerous competitions, including the National Pistol Match and the Wimbledon Cup Match. He participated in combat during World War II at Guadalcanal, New Britain and Okinawa. He was awarded the Navy Cross for "extraordinary heroism" on Okinawa while serving as a regimental commander. He also won the Bronze Star during World War II. Gen. Whaling was assistant commander of the 1st Marine Division during the latter part of the Korean War.

Lt. Gen. Reginald H. Ridgely, Jr.

Commanding General, MCRD — Dec. 1, 1951 - April 21, 1952

Born Aug. 18, 1902, in Lexington, Va. Died June 28, 1979 in Kilmarnock, Va.

Gen. Ridgely was commissioned a second lieutenant in July 1923 and was promoted to brigadier general in September 1951, major general in August 1954 and lieutenant general on retirement Oct. 31, 1959, for performance of duty during combat.

He fought on Bataan and Corregidor at the outbreak of World War II with the 4th Marines, and was taken prisoner by the Japanese. He was one of the few surivors of the Japanese "Hell Ship," in which 800 POWs starved to death. He was awarded the Purple Heart for his wounds, and the Bronze Star and a gold star in lieu of a second Bronze Star for "heroic conduct and gallantry in action." After the war, he was commanding officer, Fleet Marine Force, Mediterranean, and of the 8th Marines. In 1955, he was appointed Commanding General of the 2nd Marine Division at Camp Lejeune, N.C. From June 1957 until his retirement, he was Commanding General of Marine Corps Base, Camp Pendleton, Calif.

Lt. Gen. John T. Walker

Commanding General, MCRD — Sept. 13, 1952 - Jan. 30, 1954

Born Sept. 15, 1893 in Azle, Texas. Died Feb. 27, 1955, in La Jolla, Calif.

Gen. Walker reported for active duty as a second lieutenant in May 1917. He was listed as brigadier general in 1945, and major general from 1948 to 1954. Upon retirement July 1, 1954, he was listed as lieutenant general.

He fought in France with the 5th Marines during World War I. He served in the Dominican Republic during the early 1920s and in Haiti during the early 1930s. He took command of the 22nd Marines in June 1942 during World War II, and sailed with the regiment to Samoa. In 1944, he led the regiment in the capture of Engebi in the Eniwetok Atoll. He was assistant commander of the 2nd Division from June 1945 to April 1946. He was then stationed at Marine Corps Base, Camp Pendleton, Calif., in various posts, including assistant commander of the 1st Marine Division, until February 1948. He spent the next 18 months as Commanding General of Troop Training, Amphibious Training Command, Pacific Fleet, Coronado, Calif. His decorations include the Navy Cross, Legion of Merit, and Bronze Star.

Lt. Gen. John C. McQueen

Commanding General, MCRD — Jan. 31,1954 - July 25, 1956

Born July 5, 1899, at Carrollton, Mo. Died Dec. 7, 1985, in Menlo Park, Calif.

He was commissioned a second lieutenant in June 1921 and was promoted to brigadier general in Jaunary 1950, major general in August 1953 and lieutenant general upon his retirement July 1, 1958.

In 1936, as commander of the Marine detachment aboard the heavy cruiser USS *Quincy*, Gen. McQueen planned and carried out the evacuation of refugees from Spain during the Spanish Civil War. As chief of intelligence on the staff of commander, Amphibious Forces, Pacific Fleet during World War II, he participated in planning, seizure and occupation of Attu and Kiska in the Aleutian Islands. He became operations officer for the 5th Amphibious Corps, Pearl Harbor, and later the Fleet Marine Force, participating in the Marshall and Marianas Islands campaigns. In November 1944, he was named Chief of Staff for the 6th Marine Division, participating in the Okinawa campaign and the occupation of China. His decorations include the Legion of Merit with Combat "V" with two gold stars, and Bronze Star.

Lt. Gen. Thomas A. Wornham

Commanding General, MCRD — July 26, 1956 - Oct. 26, 1959

Born Dec. 12, 1903, at Rensselaer, N.Y. Died Dec. 17, 1984, in San Diego.

Gen. Wornham was commissioned a second lieutenant in June 1926. He was promoted to brigadier general in July 1952, major general in May 1955, and lieutenant general in November 1959.

He served in China during the late 1920s and Haiti in the early 1930s. He was appointed commander of the 27th Marines at Marine Corps Base, Camp Pendleton, Calif., in January 1944 during World War II. The regiment participated in the landing at Iwo Jima, where Gen. Wornham earned the Navy Cross. He graduated from the National War College in 1949 and was named director of the Senior School at Quantico. He commanded the 1st Marines during the Korean War, and was awarded the Legion of Merit with Combat "V" for fighting at Inje. He was named Commanding General of the 3rd Marine Division in July 1955. He was appointed Commanding General, Fleet Marine Force, Pacific, in November 1959, and received the Distinguished Service Medal for that service. He retired April 1, 1961.

Maj. Gen. Bruno A. Hochmuth

Commanding General, MCRD — Oct. 27 - Nov. 30, 1959; Nov. 1, 1963 - Feb. 1, 1967.

Born May, 1911, in Houston, Texas. Died Nov. 14, 1967, in Vietnam and buried at Fort Rosecrans National Cemetery, Pt. Loma, Calif.

Gen. Hochmuth was commissioned a second lieutenant in July 1935, and was promoted to brigadier general in November 1959 and to major general in August 1963.

During World War II, he participated in campaigns at Saipan and Tinian as assistant operations officer with the III Marine Amphibious Corps. Then, he served as commanding officer of the 3rd Battalion, 4th Marines in the Okinawa campaign, for which he received a Legion of Merit with Combat "V". As executive officer of the 4th Marines, he made the initial landing on Japan on Aug. 29, 1945. For his service as commanding general of MCRD, he received a Gold Star in lieu of a second Navy Commendation Medal. While on an inspection tour in Vietnam on Nov. 14, 1967, he was killed when the helicopter he was riding exploded in mid-air and crashed. He was posthumously decorated with the Distinguished Service Medal.

Lt. Gen. Victor H. Krulak

Commanding General, MCRD — Dec. 1, 1959 - Feb. 14, 1962

Born Jan. 7, 1913, in Denver, Colo. He resides in San Diego.

Gen. Krulak was commissioned a second lieutenant in May 1934, after graduating from the U.S. Naval Academy. He was promoted to brigadier general in July 1956, major general in November 1959 and lieutenant general in March 1964.

He was awarded the Navy Cross and Purple Heart after joining the 2nd Marine Parachute Battalion, I Marine Amphibious Corps in its week-long diversionary raid in 1943 on Choiseul Island to cover the Bougainville invasion. Then he joined the 6th Marine Division and took part in the Okinawa campaign and the surrender of Japanese forces in the China area, earning the Legion of Merit with Combat "V" and the Bronze Star. During the Korean War, he was operations officer, Fleet Marine Force, Pacific and later served as chief of staff, 1st Marine Division. During the latter period, he earned a second Legion of Merit with Combat "V" and Air Medal. He was decorated with a third Legion of Merit for service from 1962 to 1964 as special assistant for counterinsurgency activities for the Joint Chiefs of Staff. In March 1964, he was designated Commanding General of the Fleet Marine Force, Pacific. He retired May 31, 1968.

Maj. Gen. Sidney S. Wade

Commanding General, MCRD — Feb. 15, 1962 - Oct. 31, 1963

Born Sept. 30, 1909, in Bloomington, Ill. He resides in Albuquerque, N.M.

He was commissioned a second lieutenant in June 1933 and was promoted to brigadier general in May 1957 and major general in July 1960.

During World War II, Gen. Wade participated in raids on the Gilbert and Marshall Islands, New Guinea, the Bismarck Archipelago, and the Solomon Islands. He was awarded his first Legion of Merit with Combat "V" for service from December 1942 to May 1945 on the staff of the III Amphibious Corps during assaults on Bougainville, Emirau, Guam, Palau, and Okinawa. During the Korean War, he earned a second Legion of Merit and an Air Medal for service as commander of the 1st Marines, 1st Marine Division. He graduated from the National War College in 1953. He commanded the 2nd Provisional Marine Force in Lebanon during the 1958 crisis, and was decorated with the Navy Distinguished Service Medal. He served in Hawaii and on Okinawa during the mid-1960s as deputy commander, Fleet Marine Force, and was awarded his third Legion of Merit for those services. He retired Nov. 3, 1967.

Maj. Gen. Lowell E. English

Commanding General, MCRD — Feb. 2, 1967 - Sept. 1, 1969

Born July 8, 1915 in Fairbury, Neb. He resides in San Diego.

He was appointed a second lieutenant in July 1938, and was promoted to brigadier general in August 1963 and major general in January 1967.

Gen. English was a member of the 2nd Battalion, 21st Marines, 3rd Marine Division during World War II, taking part in combat on Guadalcanal and Bougainville. On Guam— as battalion executive officer — he earned the Bronze Star with Combat "V." On Iwo Jima — as battalion commander — he earned the Legion of Merit with Combat "V" and the Purple Heart. He earned a second Bronze Star and a second Legion of Merit with Combat "V" during the Korean War for service as commander of the 3rd Battalion, 1st Marines, and as executive officer of the 1st Marines. He was decorated with the Distinguished Service Medal for his work from 1965 to 1967 as assistant commander of the 3rd Marine Division in Vietnam. He retired in September 1969.

Lt. Gen. John N. McLaughlin

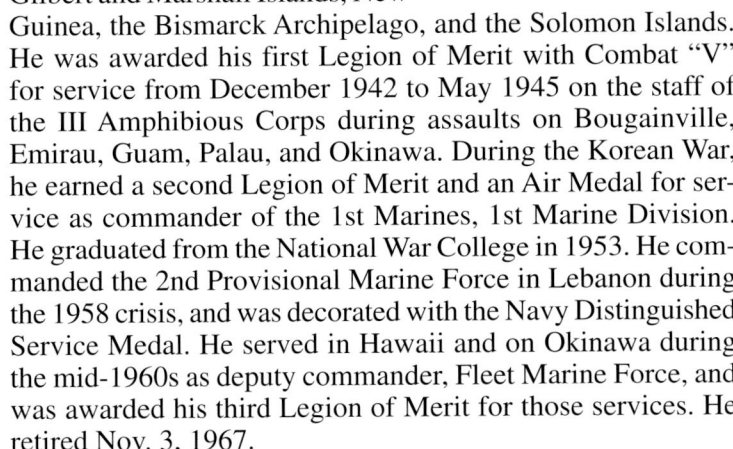

Commanding General, MCRD — Sept. 2, 1969 - Feb. 7, 1973

Born Sept. 21, 1918, in Charleston, S.C. Resides in Savannah, Ga.

Gen. McLaughlin was appointed a second lieutenant in November 1941, and was promoted to brigadier general in January 1967, major general in September 1969 and lieutenant general in September 1974.

During World War II, he took part in operations at Guadalcanal, New Britain, and the Palau Islands with the 1st Battalion, 5th Marines, 1st Marine Division. He was awarded a Silver Star for gallantry while leading an assault company ashore at Peleliu in September 1944. He was captured during the Korean War by the Chinese at the Chosin Reservoir, North Korea. He was liberated nearly three years later in September 1953, and was awarded the Legion of Merit. He was assigned to the U.S. Strike Command in 1967, earning a gold star in lieu of a second Legion of Merit. He filled several posts in 1968 and 1969 in Vietnam during the war, and was decorated with the Distinguished Service Medal. He was Commanding General, Fleet Marine Force, Pacific, when he retired July 1, 1977. His decorations include a second Distinguished Service Medal and the Bronze Star with Combat "V".

Lt. Gen. Joseph C. Fegan, Jr.

Commanding General, MCRD — Feb. 8, 1973 - Aug. 18, 1975

Born Dec. 21, 1920, in Los Angeles, Calif. Died Jan. 2, 1991, in San Diego and was buried at Fort Rosecrans National Cemetery, Pt. Loma, Calif.

Gen. Fegan was commissioned a second lieutenant in the Marine Corps Reserve in July 1942 and integrated into the regular Corps in 1943. He advanced to brigadier general in September 1968, major general in December 1971 and lieutenant general in August 1975.

He saw combat as an artillery battery commander during World War II with the 4th Battalion, 14th Marines, 4th Marine Division in the Marshall and Marianas Islands and on Iwo Jima. He earned the Silver Star during the capture of Saipan. During the Korean War, he was a company commander with the 3rd Battalion, 5th Marines, 1st Provisional Marine Brigade, until he was wounded in August 1950. His conduct in this action earned a second Silver Star. He went to Vietnam in 1966 as deputy, Combat Operations Center, U.S. Military Assistance Command, and received the Legion of Merit. From 1968 to 1971, he was Commanding General, Force Troops, Fleet Marine Force, Atlantic. In 1972, he commanded the 3rd Marine Division in Vietnam, which took part in the Easter Offensive alert. He retired May 1, 1978.

Maj. Gen. Kenneth J. Houghton

Commanding General, MCRD — Aug. 19, 1975 - Oct. 31, 1977

Born Oct. 17, 1920, in San Francisco, Calif. He resides in La Jolla, Calif.

Commissioned a second lieutenant in September 1942, he was promoted to brigadier general in August 1968 and major general in April 1973.

Gen. Houghton saw action during World War II at Tarawa, in the Marshall Islands and Saipan. For his service in reconnaissance during the Korean War, he received his first Silver Star and Bronze Star with Combat "V" and gold star in lieu of a second Bronze Star. He was featured on the cover of the Sept. 4, 1950, issue of *Life* magazine. He was wounded in action the next month. From April 1964 to February 1967, he was action officer, J-3 Division, Joint Chiefs of Staff and was awarded the Legion of Merit. He then took command of the 5th Marines in Vietnam, and for his service received the Navy Cross, a gold star in lieu of a second Silver Star and two gold stars in lieu of second and third Purple Hearts. From August 1967 to February 1968, he was assistant chief of staff with the III Amphibious Force. He retired Oct. 31, 1977 at MCRD, San Diego.

Maj. Gen. Richard C. Schulze

Commanding General, MCRD — Feb. 1, 1978 - Aug. 10, 1979

Born May 7, 1929, in Oakland, Calif. He died Nov. 10, 1983, in Boca Raton, Fla.

Gen. Schulze enlisted in November 1950, was commissioned a second lieutenant in the Reserve in May 1951 and completed the Basic School in Quantico, Va., in September 1951. He was promoted to brigadier general in July 1975 and to major general in January 1978.

He was ordered to Korea in 1951 and participated in combat as a mortar section leader and later as operations and training officer with the 1st Marines, 1st Marine Division. He was released from active duty in July 1953, but served in the Reserve while attending Stanford University. He integrated into the regular Corps in 1955. From July 1968 to September 1969, he served in Vietnam as operations officer, 3rd Marine Dvision and later commander of the 3rd Battalion, 3rd Marines, 3rd Marine Division. He was awarded the Silver Star and the Legion of Merit with Combat "V." He became director of the Personnel Management Division in June 1980. He retired Oct. 1, 1981. His decorations include a gold star in lieu of a second Legion of Merit and the Navy Commendation Medal.

Maj. Gen. James L. Day

Commanding General, MCRD — Nov. 1, 1977 - Jan. 31, 1978

Born Oct. 5, 1925, in East St. Louis, Ill. He resides in Southern California.

He enlisted in 1943. He was commissioned a second lieutenant and completed the Basic School at Quantico, Va., in September 1952. He was promoted to brigadier general in April 1976 and to major general in August 1980.

Gen. Day is believed to be the only Marine to fight as an infantryman, be wounded and decorated for valor in three wars. He saw combat as an enlisted man during World War II on Guam and Okinawa. He served with the 1st Battalion, 7th Marines and the 1st Reconnaissance Company during the Korean War. He completed two tours in Vietnam — in 1966 and 1972 — as commander of the 1st Battalion, 9th Marines, 3rd Marine Division and then as operations officer with the 9th Marine Amphibious Brigade, III Marine Amphibious Force. He was named Commanding General of the 1st Marine Division in August 1980, and a year later assumed the added responsibility of the I Marine Amphibious Force. He retired Dec. 1, 1986. His decorations include: the Distinguished Service Medal, three Silver Stars; Defense Superior Service Medal; Legion of Merit with Combat "V"; Bronze Star with Combat "V"; two Navy Commendation Medals with Combat "V"; and six Purple Hearts.

Lt. Gen. Charles G. Cooper

Commanding General, MCRD — Aug. 11, 1979 - May 14, 1981

Born Dec. 24, 1927, in Clarksdale, Miss. He resides in Falls Church, Va.

He was commissioned a second lieutenant in June 1950 and was promoted to brigadier general in June 1975, major general in July 1977 and lieutenant general in August 1982.

Gen. Cooper joined the 1st Battalion, 5th Marines, 1st Marine Division in Korea in 1951, taking part in combat as a rifle platoon commander, and was seriously wounded. He was awarded the Silver Star and two Purple Hearts. He helped plan and test amphibious helicopter-infantry operations and counter-armor tactics during the late 1950s. As commander of the 1st Battalion, 7th Marines, 1st Marine Division, he participated in a series of heavy-action operations in Vietnam during 1970, and was awarded the Legion of Merit with Combat "V". In August 1977, he was named Commanding General of the 1st Marine Division at Camp Pendleton and the I Marine Amphibious Force. He was named Commanding General of Fleet Marine Force, Pacific/Commander, Marine Corps Bases, Pacific, in 1983. He retired July 31, 1985.

Maj. Gen. W.H. Rice

Commanding General, MCRD — May 15, 1981 - Feb. 9, 1984

Born Feb. 7, 1932, in Baltimore, Md. He resides in Falls Church, Va.

Gen. Rice enlisted in 1951, attaining the rank of sergeant, and was selected for officer training. He was commissioned a second lieutenant in October 1952. He was promoted to brigadier general in March 1978 and to major general in May 1981.

He served as a platoon and company commander with the 1st and 3rd Marine Divisions at Marine Corps Base, Camp Pendleton, Calif., and in Japan and Korea. In July 1967, he served in Vietnam as deputy commander/chief of operations and training, Naval Advisory Detachment. He was assistant commander of the 3rd Marine Division, Fleet Marine Force, Pacific, in 1978, and a year later was deputy commander, Fleet Marine Force, Pacific. He was then named Commanding General, 1st Marine Brigade, Fleet Marine Force, Hawaii. His last posting was as Inspector General of the Marine Corps at Marine Corps Headquarters. He retired Jan. 31, 1988. His decorations include the Legion of Merit with Combat "V" and the Bronze Star with Combat "V."

Lt. Gen. Anthony Lukeman

Commanding General, MCRD — July 10, 1984 - June 23, 1986

Born March 24, 1933, in Jamaica, N.Y. He resides in Nokesville, Va.

Gen. Lukeman was commissioned a second lieutenant in 1954, and promoted to brigadier general in April 1980, major general in May 1983, and lieutenant general in March 1987.

He served in three active divisions and commanded infantry organizations from platoon to regimental levels. He served in Vietnam with the 3rd Marine Division in 1966 and 1967. He also served with the Vietnamese Marine Corps in 1974 and 1975, helping to evacuate Saigon in 1975. He was director of Manpower Plans and Policy Division at Headquarters Marine Corps and commanding general of Marine Corps Base, Camp Pendleton, Calif. He was named deputy assistant secretary of defense for manpower and personnel policy in the office of the Secretary of Defense in Washington, D.C., in August 1986. His decorations include the Bronze Star with Combat "V", Meritorious Service Medal with two gold stars in lieu of second and third awards, and Joint Service Commendation Medal. He retired Jan. 1, 1989.

Brig. Gen. Hugh T. Kerr

Commanding General, MCRD — Feb. 10 - July 9, 1984

Born Dec. 19, 1933, and raised in Philadelphia, Pa. He resides in Oregon.

Gen. Kerr was commissioned a second lieutenant in June 1955. He was promoted to brigadier general in April 1981.

During May 1965, he was serving in the 3rd Battalion, 1st Marines when it landed at Chu Lai in Vietnam. He was battalion logistics officer and later commander of Company K. He returned to the United States in January 1966, serving as assistant operations officer of the Recruit Training Regiment at MCRD, San Diego. In July 1969, he was again in Vietnam, this time as the Manpower Plans Officer with Headquarters, III Marine Amphibious Force. From 1972 to 1975, he again served at MCRD, San Diego, where he was commanding officer, 3rd Recruit Training Battalion. He was ordered to Marine Corps Base, Camp Pendleton, Calif., in July 1975, and served as executive officer of the 5th Marines, 1st Marine Division. He assumed command of the 9th Marines, 3rd Marine Division and Camp Hansen, Okinawa, in June 1980. He retired Dec. 31, 1984. His decorations include the Bronze Star with Combat "V," gold star in lieu of a second award, and Navy Commendation Medal.

Maj. Gen. Donald J. Fulham

Commanding General, MCRD — June 24, 1986 - Sept. 26, 1988

Born July 4, 1928, in McMinnville, Ore. He resides in San Diego.

Gen. Fulham enlisted in August 1946 and was discharged in 1948. He was commissioned a second lieutenant in November 1952, and was promoted to brigadier general in April 1980 and major general in April 1983.

He deployed with the 3rd Marine Division from Marine Corps Base, Camp Pendleton, Calif., to Japan in 1953 and then was company executive officer with the 1st Marine Division in Korea in 1954. In the mid-1950s, he was executive officer of the Marine detachment aboard the carrier USS *Intrepid*. In 1963, he graduated from the Amphibious Warfare School and returned four years later as an instructor. In July 1971, he was posted for a year to Vietnam as team chief, Command Center, Military Assistance Command in Saigon. In the mid- and late-1970s he was deputy director and then director of the Personnel Procurement Division at Marine Corps Headquarters. In 1982-83 he was Commanding General of Marine Corps Base, Camp Lejeune, N.C. He retired Sept. 30, 1988. His decorations include the Legion of Merit with Combat "V", Bronze Star with Combat "V", and Navy Commendation Medal.

Brig. Gen. Frank J. Breth

Commanding General, MCRD — Sept. 27, 1988 - Aug. 21, 1989

Born Oct. 12, 1937, in Fairmont, W. Va. He resides in Kansas City, Mo.

Gen. Breth was commissioned a second lieutenant in 1959, and was promoted to brigadier general in June 1985.

In the early 1960s, he completed two Western Pacific tours, including one as executive officer of the Marine detachment aboard the light cruiser USS *Galveston*. In August 1967, he was assigned to the 3rd Battalion, 9th Marines, 3rd Marine Division in Vietnam, serving as a rifle company commander and operations officer, and later as the division liaison officer to the 1st South Vietnamese Army Division in Hue. In 1975, he was liaison officer between the Korean Marine Corps and the U.S. Navy. In 1979 he returned to Korea as chief of the Contingency Plans Branch of the Combined Forces Command. In 1984, he was posted to Marine Corps Base, Camp Pendleton, Calif., as assistant chief of staff for the 1st Amphibious Force, and a year later was named director of intelligence at Marine Corps Headquarters. He retired in August 1989. His decorations include the Legion of Merit, Bronze Star with Combat "V", and two Purple Hearts.

Maj. Gen. J.A. Studds

Commanding General, MCRD — Aug. 22, 1991 - Sept. 19, 1993

Born March 31, 1937 in Evanston, Ill. He resides in Melbourne, Fla.

Gen. Studds was commissioned a second lieutenant and completed the Basic School at Quantico, Va., in January 1961. He was promoted to brigadier general in July 1986 and major general in March 1989.

He reported to the 3rd Marine Division, Fleet Marine Force in Vietnam, serving in 1965-66 as commander of a service company and then a reconnaissance company. From 1977 to 1979, he commanded the Marine Barracks, Naval Weapons Station, Yorktown, Va. He was assistant chief of staff of the 1st Marine Division, Fleet Marine Force, at Marine Corps Base, Camp Pendleton, Calif., from 1981 to 1982, then became commander of the 1st Marines until April 1984. He served from 1989 to 1991 as assistant chief of staff, Command, Control, Communications and Computer, Intelligence and Interopability/Director of Intelligence at Marine Corps Headquarters. He retired Sept. 20, 1993. His decorations include the Defense Superior Service Medal, Legion of Merit, and Bronze Star with Combat "V."

Maj. Gen. John S. Grinalds

Commanding General, MCRD — Aug. 22, 1989 - Aug. 21, 1991

Born Jan. 5, 1938, in Baltimore, Md. He resides in Woodbery Forest, Va.

In June 1959, Gen. Grinalds became the first West Point Cadet to be commissioned a second lieutenant in the Marine Corps since 1814. He was promoted to brigadier general in June 1986 and to major general in May 1988.

He was ordered to Vietnam in March 1966 as an advisor to the 4th Battalion, Vietnamese Marine Corps, serving for a year. He returned to Vietnam in June 1970, serving as operations officer, 2nd Battalion, 1st Marines, and as intelligence officer for the 1st Marines. He graduated from the National War College in June 1978. Subsequently, he assumed command of the 9th Marines and Camp Hansen with the 3rd Marine Division on Okinawa in May 1981. From 1986 to 1989, he served with the Joint Chiefs of Staff, advancing to director of Force Structure, Resource and Assessment. He retired in August 1991. His decorations include the Defense Distinguished Service Medal, Silver Star, Defense Superior Service Medal, and two Bronze Stars with Combat "V."

Brig. Gen. Edwin C. Kelley, Jr.

Commanding General, MCRD — Sept. 20, 1993 - May 24, 1995

Born Dec. 14, 1943, in Reading, Pa. He is presently Commanding General, Marine Corps Base, Quantico, Va.

Gen. Kelley was commissioned a second lieutenant and completed the Basic School at Quantico, Va., in April 1968. He was promoted to brigadier general in March 1993.

He reported to the 3rd Battalion, 4th Marines, 3rd Marine Division in Vietnam in 1968 as a rifle platoon commander, earning the Navy Cross for extraordinary heroism on March 13, 1969. Then-1st Lt. Kelley led reconnaissance of enemy bunkers and formulated and led an attack, destroying four bunkers without air support and with only limited artillery fire. His award cites his "courage, superb tactical skill and unwavering devotion to duty in the face of grave personal danger." He graduated from the Amphibious Warfare School, Quantico, Va., in 1973; the Armed Forces Staff College in 1980; and the Naval War College, Newport, R.I., in 1986. During 1986-89, he was section head of the Officer Plans Section in the Manpower Plans and Policy Division at Marine Corps Headquarters, Washington, D.C. His decorations also include the Legion of Merit, Bronze Star with Combat "V", Purple Heart, and Defense Meritorious Service Medal.

Brig. Gen. Garry L. Parks

Commanding General, MCRD, May 25, 1995 -

Born March 9, 1947, in Huntington, Pa.

Gen. Parks was commissioned a second lieutenant in 1969. He was promoted to brigadier general Sept. 1, 1996.

His first tour was with the 1st Reconnaissance Battalion, 1st Marine Division in the Republic of Vietnam, where he served as a platoon commander and company executive officer. He then served as a company commander with the 2nd Battalion, 3rd Marines, and as aide-de-camp to the Commanding General, 1st Marine Brigade. His next assignment was as a company commander at MCRD, Parris Island, S.C., followed by attendance at The Infantry Officer Advanced Course at Fort Benning, Ga., where he graduated on the Commandant's List. Subsequent tours included assignments to the 2nd Battalion, 9th Marines, where he served as a company commander and later as battalion logistics officer, and a tour at the U.S. Naval Academy where he was a company officer. From 1982 to 1985, he was the commanding officer of the Recruiting Station, Raleigh, N.C., followed by a tour at Marine Corps Headquarters. Graduating from the Naval War College in 1987, he was assigned as executive officer, 5th Marines, and later as commanding officer, 2nd Battalion, 5th Marines. In 1990, he served as officer in charge, III Marine Expeditionary Force, Special Operations and Training Group. He became commanding officer of the 9th Marines and commander of Camp Hansen, Okinawa, in 1991. While serving as Chief of Staff, Marine Forces Pacific, he was selected for promotion to brigadier general. His decorations include the Legion of Merit, Bronze Star with Combat "V", Meritorious Service Medal and Navy Commendation Medal.

Additional base commanders

The following officers commanded the base when there was no Commanding General.

Lt. Col. James McE. Huey — Dec. 1, 1921 - Jan. 3, 1922
Maj. Eugene P. Fortson — Jan. 4 - March 7, 1922
Lt. Col. Giles Bishop, Jr. — March 8, 1922 - Feb. 29, 1924
Col. John T. Myers — June, 2, 1924 - Oct. 31, 1925
Col. Alexander S. Williams — Nov. 1, 1925 - Feb. 24, 1926
Lt. Col. William H. Pritchett — April 1 - Aug. 8, 1927
Col. Charles H. Lyman — Aug. 9, 1927 - June, 24, 1928; Nov. 23 - Dec. 6, 1931

Col. Harry R. Lay — April 5, 1929 - Jan. 30, 1930
Col. William H. Rupertus — Dec. 8, 1941 - March 18, 1942
Col. William C. James — April 1, 1943 - April 16, 1944
Col. Roswell Winans — April 17-26, 1944
Col. John Groff — June 13 - July 12, 1945
Col. Miles R. Thacker — Jan. 24 - April 25, 1946
Col. Harry B. Liversedge — April 26 - June 2, 1946
Col. Gilder D. Jackson, Jr. — June 3 - July 28, 1946

Commanding Officers Recruit Training Regiment 1956-1997

Brig. Gen. A. Shapley	May 1956-September 1956
Brig. Gen. A.L. Bowser	July 1957-June 1958
Brig. Gen. R.G. Weede	June 1958-October 1959
Col. R.W. Boyd	October 1959-December 1959
Brig. Gen. B.A. Hochmuth	December 1959
Col. G.R. Newton	January 1960-March 1962
Col. M.E. Day	March 1962-January 1964
Col. G.T. Fowler	January 1964-September 1964
Col. J.O. Bell	September 1964-September 1965
Col. W.L. Dick	September 1965-September 1966
Col. B.M. Boress	September 1966-August 1968
Col. J.W. Donnell	August 1968-August 1969
Col. W.G. Joslyn	August 1969-July 1970
Lt. Col. J.H.A. Flood	July 1970-September 1970
Col. E.G. Derning	September 1970-September 1972
Col. R.P. Coffman	September 1972-June 1973
Col. G.W. Rodney	June 1973-July 1974
Col. D.M. Twomey	July 1974-July 1975
Col. R.A. Seymour	July 1975-February 1976
Col. W.J. Woodring, Jr.	February 1976-July 1976
Col. E.R. Savoy	July 1976-September 1978
Col. J.W. Abraham	September 1978-May 1980
Col. H.C. Stackpole, III	May 1980-May 1981
Col. H.J. Gibson	May 1981-May 1983
Col. R.J. Graham	May 1983-May 1984
Col. K.D. Jordan	May 1984-May 1986
Col. J.R. Davis	May 1986-January 1988
Col. M.C. Bell	January 1988-December 1989
Col. W.P. Symolon	December 1989-June 1991
Col. J.M.D. Holladay	June 1991-June 1993
Col. J.M. Guerin	June 1993-June 1995
Col. S.A. Cheney	June 1995-

Sergeants Major
Marine Corps Recruit Depot, San Diego
1920-1997 *

Sgt. Maj. Lloyd B. Rice, August 1920-March 1922
Sgt. Maj. Edward Wilcox, March-May 1922
Records Unavailable, May-July 1922
Sgt. Maj. James L. Feeney, July-August 1922
Records Unavailable, August-November 1922
Sgt. Maj. Olaf J. Christiansen, November 1922-March 1923
Sgt. Maj. Lacey Moore, April 1923-May 1924
Sgt. Maj. Edward Wilcox, May-October 1924
Sgt. Maj. Oscar J. Little, October-December 1924
Sgt. Maj. Horace Larn, December 1924-January 1929
Sgt. Maj. Henry Cummins, January-March 1929
Sgt. Maj. Eugene Smith, March-April 1929
Sgt. Maj. Oliver H. Schneider, April-June 1929
Sgt. Maj. Lloyd B. Rice, June 1929- February 1930
Sgt. Maj. Bennie C. Atkinson, February 1930-December 1932
Sgt. Maj. Loyd B. Rice, December 1932-June 1937
Sgt. Maj. Horace Larn, June-August 1937
Records Unavailable, August-September 1937
Sgt. Maj. Ira Ward, September 1937- February 1939
Sgt. Maj. Ford E. Wilkens, February 1939-March 1942
Sgt. Maj. George T. Green, March-May 1942
Sgt. Maj. Joseph A. Inferra, May-August 1942
Sgt. Maj. Joseph A. Plumadore, August 1942-August 1943
Sgt. Maj. Charles S. Cram, September 1943-January 1944
Sgt. Maj. Plummer W. King, January 1944-August 1945
Sgt. Maj. Ralph L. Minkler, August-October 1945
Sgt. Maj. Hugo H. Fromman, October-December 1945
Sgt. Maj. Joel R. Evans, December 1945-June 1946
Sgt. Maj. Garland B. Respese, June 1946-April 1947
MSgt. Stanley J. Wood, April 1947-October 1948
MSgt. William B. Ehlen, October 1948-September 1950

MSgt. Earl C. Weir, September 1950-March 1951
MSgt. Harry E. Bryan, March-October 1951
Records Unavailable, October 1951-July 1958
Sgt. Maj. Ross J. Heikes, July 1958-November 1959
Sgt. Maj. George H. Rose, December 1959-April 1961
Sgt. Maj. Delmas L. Bryant, April 1961-April 1962
Record Unavailable, May-July 1962
Sgt. Maj. Levy A. Switzer, July 1962-August 1964
Sgt. Maj. Maurice A. Ledbetter, August 1964-February 1965
Sgt. Maj. Bud H. Le Grand, March 1965-August 1966
Sgt. Maj. N. D. Parice, August 1966-July 1967
Sgt. Maj. E. J. Catallo, August 1967-February 1968
Sgt. Maj. J. A. Nastasi, Jr., February 1968-July 1969
Sgt. Maj. Kenneth Chase, July 1969-September 1970
Sgt. Maj. Milton B. Gardner, September 1970-February 1972
Sgt. Maj. Charles W. Skinner, February 1972-August 1973
Sgt. Maj. Robert E. Burnett, August 1973-July 1975
Sgt. Maj. Guadalupe Gusman, July 1975-December 1975
Sgt. Maj. Edward R. Kubow, December 1975-August 1977
Sgt. Maj. Samuel H. Pierce, Jr., August 1977-March 1980
Sgt. Maj. Lee M. Bradley, March 1980-December 1981
Sgt. Maj. Theodore W. Kennedy, December 1981-January 1984
Sgt. Maj. Joseph J. Johnson, January 1984-December 1985
Sgt. Maj. James P. Henderson, December 1985-July 1987
Sgt. Maj. Armando R. Aguilar, August 1987-September 1988
Sgt. Maj. Alexander Robinson, October 1988-April 1990
Sgt. Maj. Harold G. Overstreet, April 1990-June 1991
Sgt. Maj. Michael S. McGraw, June 1991-February 1994
Sgt. Maj. Anthony Reese, February 1994-September 1995
Sgt. Maj. Charles L. Brown, III, September 1995-

* List compiled by Professor John Hancock, University of Washington, from: Marine Corps monthly Muster Rolls (1914-1950)/Bound Diaries (1951-1964), and MCRD, San Diego Command Chronology annual since 1965, Reference and Archives Sections respectively, Headquarters, Marine Corps, Washington, D.C.; Chevron, and names on wall plaque mid-1959-today in Depot Sergeant Major's Office, MCRD, San Diego.

Preserving History

MSgt. Dave Dendy discusses an acrylic painting by Col. Charles Waterhouse with recruits at the MCRD Command Museum in 1989.

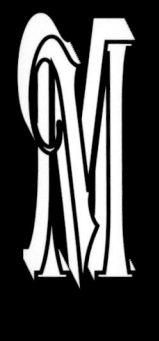ore than one million visitors from 1987 to 1996 have stepped into a time tunnel at the Marine Corps Recruit Depot and learned

about sacrifice, leadership, and war.

The Depot's two-story Command Museum resurrects Marine Corps heroism through exhibits of thousands of artifacts, photographs, and documents. Visitors learning from this vivid history lesson include: recruits complementing their classroom instruction in the history of the Marine Corps; family and friends enriching their understanding of the Marine Corps culture; veterans reliving memories; and civilians of all stripes learning about the Depot's place in San Diego history and the place Marines have made for themselves around the world.

The Museum's civilian support group — the MCRD Museum Historical Society — backs the Museum's mission and also offers living history lessons through regular seminars led by veterans whose experience of historical events provides insight into warfare and leadership.

Long before the Museum was established, the Depot was the recipient of historical artifacts. At the suggestion of now-retired Maj. Jack Buck in 1956, Lt. Gen. Edward A. Craig donated a pair of Japanese mountain howitzers that now sit in the Museum courtyard. In 1972, Maj. Buck helped bring more of the general's collection onto the base via display cases in the Depot's Memorabilia Room. The donation included World War I and World War II equipment such as a clothing roll, canteen cover for mounted Marines, field rations, a seabag, a marching compass and a Japanese knee mortar.

Officials on the base noted the increasing number of donations from veterans. Equipment and artwork were coming into the Depot and decorating command offices or sitting in storage for lack of proper display space. A museum seemed the natural solution. Retired Col. Richard D. "Mick" Mickelson recalls discussions of starting one when he was the Depot's chief of staff to the Commanding General, Maj. Gen. Kenneth J. Houghton, in 1975. Retired Maj. Gen. Marc Moore, a long-time friend of Col. Mickelson's, recalls talk of placing memorabilia in the base reception center. Back then, the reception area was at a Quonset Hut with a "geedunk stand" — Marine Corps slang for snack bar.

But funding and support would have to wait until the mid-1980s when the Reagan administration infused new funds into the military, and Brig. Gen. Edward Simmons, in charge of the Marine Corps History and Museums Division, initiated new support for historical preservation at the local level.

In 1984, under Gen. Simmons' direction, the Marine Corps published guidelines for command museums. Gen. Simmons wrote that collection of Marine Corps and military history were "a vital part of any approach toward meeting current operational or institutional problems." But the mission of the historical division did not stop at the big picture. "In addition, tangible evidence of unit and individual achievement complements written history by fostering high standards of military virtue. This requires a comprehensive program that honors tradition and builds

The courtyard of Building 26, with its Spanish revival architecture, provides a graceful entrance to the MCRD Command Museum, which opened its doors in 1987.

esprit through display of awards, battle honors, historical flags and other objects of historical and sentimental significance." Fulfilling the mission of collecting and preserving this vast body of data and artifacts, he wrote, was not solely laid on the History and Museums Division in Washington, D.C. "Commanders have the responsibility of conducting adequate command historical programs."

The division published a manual outlining the concept and implementation of a command museum. It stated:

"Knowledge of the sacrifice, dedication, skill, physical and spiritual endurance, resilience, and courage of Marines of the past is essential to the individual and group morale of today's Marine in order to establish a framework and sense of mission to daily responsibilities. Consequently, the study of military history is a key to professional growth. One effective means of heightening interest in history and fostering esprit de corps is through the exhibition of historical material. Since exhibition exposure should not be limited only to Marines able to visit the museums in the Washington area, it is important that all major posts and stations establish command museums, exhibits and historic displays."

It continued, "Each command museum should have a theme which will center on local military, Marine Corps history, and the current and past missions of the hosting post or station."

But it was not simply a matter of opening the doors to Building 26, where the Museum is housed today. Retired and active duty officers worked together for four years — from 1984 to 1987 — to take the Museum from concept to reality, and it would be another four years before

Retired Maj. Gen. Marc Moore, right, visits retired Brig. Gen. Edward Simmons at his office at the Marine Corps History and Museums Division, Washington, D.C., to discuss setting up the MCRD museum.

final certification was awarded.

The process got its start with a small group of dedicated Marines led by retired Maj. Gen. Marc Moore. His career began as a boot at MCRD and included a stint there as a drill instructor. He returned to retire in 1982 and with a desire to give something back to the Corps.

Moore had set up small museums during his active duty career, including one while he was Commanding General of the 4th Marine Division in New Orleans. In late 1983, he approached MCRD, San Diego's Commanding General, Maj. Gen. Wesley H. "Duff" Rice, and broached the subject that had first been discussed nearly a decade earlier — starting a museum.

On Jan. 30, 1984, Gen. Rice formally requested that Gen. Moore chair a committee "to study facility requirements, resource requirements (memorabilia and displays) and, last but certainly not least, funds required to support a first-class West Coast Marine Museum." Gen. Rice noted in his letter to Gen. Moore, "I have spoken to (Gen.) Ed Simmons regarding such a committee and project, and we have his endorsement."

The committee also got Gen. Simmons' support, including a how-to guide that would generate staff support from Washington, D.C., visits to MCRD, critiques of planning documents, and — eventually — artwork and artifacts for display.

But first there were monthly meetings of an advisory board that included

Donations, such as this World War I Ford Model T ambulance, have enriched the museum's exhibits. The ambulance was donated in 1990.

Gen. Moore and Col. Mickelson. Other early members of the advisory board included the following retired Marines: Lt. Col. Robert M. Calland, Lt. Col. Tom Edwards, Maj. Arthur Weiss, Maj. Jack Buck, Sgt. Maj. Leland D. Crawford and Sgt. Maj. Bill Paxton.

That first meeting, March 21, 1984, established a firm groundwork.

The deputy director of Marine Corps Museums, Col. Brooke Nihart, was also in attendance along with assistant facilities officer Maj. D.O. Hendricks, setting a precedent for staff support from Washington, D.C., as well as from MCRD.

One of the museum's earliest exhibits, situated on the second floor, is of a "horse Marine" circa 1927. These Marines were sent to Nicaragua on expeditionary duty.

The board identified Building 26, then used for recruit processing and the Family Service Center, as the site for the Museum. Historically, Building 26 was a barracks and was later used as a dispensary and the Communication and Electronics School. The Corps planned to renovate it in fiscal year 1989 for use as a reception center and the Family Service Center.

Maj. Hendricks told the board the construction project might be moved up if it could be justified to Headquarters. Board members quickly began digging into the nuts and bolts of the project: establishing a mission, and determining the scope, content and structure of exhibits.

Their work apparently impressed Headquarters. In October 1984, the construction project was moved up to fiscal year 1986. Two months later, Gen. Moore brought word back from Washington that Gen. Simmons would visit MCRD in February 1985. Other meetings with Gen. Simmons would follow.

In July 1985, Gen. Simmons provided the board with a written scenario for a museum along with ideas on the construction and flow of exhibits. The board began adapting these documents and ideas to MCRD.

And the following month, board members set about tracking down the many items that had been donated over the years to the base. Gen. Craig's World War I and World War II donations, for example, had migrated from the base library to the office of Headquarters and Service Battalion. Also in August, the first steps were taken toward establishing a civilian position for a curator.

In September the board met with representatives from the architects for the Museum — Salerno-Livingston and Partners of San Diego — and in October Carl. M. Devere Sr., chief of exhibits for the museums branch at the History and Museums Division, discussed construction and traffic flow.

Several commanding generals helped shepherd through plans and provided staff support including Gen. Rice, Brig. Gen. Hugh Kerr, and Lt. Gen. (then-Maj. Gen.) Anthony Lukeman.

There was discussion and planning early on for an interim museum at the reception center that could be used to help generate enthusiasm for the permanent Museum. But the board — concerned about security, quality and possibly finding their temporary solution adopted as permanent — opted to wait for renovations at Building 26.

In the summer of 1986, Maj. Gen. Donald J. Fulham pushed through funding $850,000 for construction as part of a $100 million 10-year restoration project for the base that was allocated in 1984.

The building was dedicated in 1986 with a flourish with dignitaries including then-California Sen. Pete Wilson in front of television cameras. (Wilson, now governor of California, reportedly promised to donate a pair of his own Marine-green skivvies for posterity, but they have yet to arrive.)

The first Museum curator — George Kordela — was appointed that year to begin setting up in 11,000 square feet of space.

The Museum officially opened its doors Nov. 10, 1987, approximately 18 months after the dedication. On the second floor, one gallery focused on the history of the Depot and the activities that took place on the base, such as Sea School and the Drill Instructors School. Another gallery dramatized Marine Corps history with costumed mannequins and artifacts from various eras, such as the Banana Wars of the 1920s. On the first floor, the MCRD Command Museum also proudly displays a collection of 12 original 7-foot-by-5-foot acrylic paintings by Marine Reserve Col. Charles M. Waterhouse showing Marine Corps history in California. These were brought together from various locations by Gen. Simmons.

These efforts did not go unnoticed by civilians dedicated to preserving history. The California Congress of History in July 1989 recognized MCRD Command Museum as the "Most Outstanding New History Museum of the Year."

Seeing the Museum open, and recruits and their families walk through gave its founders tremendous satisfaction, but they recognized that if the Museum were to expand and not be left to the whim of sometimes uncertain government funding, it would need on-going civilian support. The MCRD Museum Historical Society was formed April 29, 1988, with $300 and three members: Lt. Col. Robert M. Calland, president; Col. Richard D. Mickelson, secretary; and Maj. Arthur Weiss, treasurer. The Society applied for tax-exempt status in August, and on Jan. 19, 1989, became a nonprofit organization.

The Society's first volunteer executive director was Col. Mickelson.

Gradually, the duties of the advisory board to the Commanding General were transferred to active duty officers, and the Historical Society became the volunteer civilian vehicle to support the Museum's activities.

Since its inception, the Society has contributed to the Museum in a variety of ways, beginning with fund raising through membership drives and fund-raisers.

The Society's first charter member was a distinguished one: former Marine Corps Commandant, Gen. Lemuel C. Shepherd Jr., who had retired to San Diego after 42 years of service. Its first sustaining member — with a $1,000 donation — was retired Sgt. David V. Enter, whose career from 1963 to 1967 began with boot camp at the Depot and included stints in electronics and ground radar schools.

By the end of 1989, the Society had 300 members, including 23 sustaining members and 83 charter members such as former commanding generals Maj. Gen. Fulham, Lt. Gen. Victor Krulak, Lt. Gen. Joseph C. Fegan Jr., Maj. Gen. Houghton and Lt. Gen. Lukeman.

Following are some of the Marine and Navy organizations that have provided valuable support to the Museum: San Diego Council of the Navy League; the Third Marine Division Association, Southern California Chapter; the Orders and Medal Society of America; the Fourth Marine Division Association and its Chapter Seven; the North China Marine POW Memorial; and the 7th Marine Reserve Officer Class Association.

The Society also brings in corporate support for the Museum, including American Television and Communications Corp., and BankAmerica Foundation.

And the organization funnels volunteers into the Museum. In 1996, there were more than 60 regular Historical Society volunteers putting in time with the Society and at the Museum.

The Society's first "volunteer of the quarter" in March 1989 was retired Col. Nathan R. Smith, who seven years later can still be found working in the Museum's archive on a regular basis.

The Society's programs in reaching military and civilian communities have brought them closer together.

In January 1990, Gen. Moore led the Historical Society in establishing the Warfare Leadership Center at the Museum. The Center's mission is to pursue the study of leadership in war through military and historical models, and thereby enhance the leadership capabilities of officers and noncommissioned officers. The Center provides a research facility and seminar rooms, and quarterly invites retired and active duty officers to discuss their wartime experiences.

The Society sponsors a quarterly "Breakfast With The Commanding General" to keep its membership advised about military issues and the Depot.

Beyond these services, the Society provides an expeditious way for Museum donors to receive tax benefits. Without the Society as an intermediary, donors would have to wait as much as two years for the wheels of govern-

Veterans visit the museum in 1995 to commemorate the 50th anniversary of the battle of Iwo Jima. The museum often hosts veterans groups.

ment to process and accept their donation. When the Society accepts a cash or artifacts, it can provide an immediate tax writeoff.

Contributions to the Museum have helped build a remarkable memorial to Marines' role in history.

For example, Maj. Weiss contributed the "Vouza of the Solomons" display — a collection of medals awarded to Guadalcanal native Jacob Charles Vouza, who supported the American invasion of his homeland against the Japanese during World War II. For his courage, Vouza was named an honorary Sergeant Major of Marines.

Donations such as these complement contributions that capture changes in military technology. A $12,000 World War I Ford Model T ambulance that was donated in 1990 by Society charter member Gordon W. Bartow is a good example.

Moreover, the Society, with its members' widespread contacts in the retired community, brings in rare displays enriched by heroic sentiment. "Old Blue," the color of the 4th Marine Regiment, is prominently displayed in the Museum thanks to one of the Museum's first supporters — Lt. Col. Calland. The 4th Marine Regiment established its first base in San Diego in 1911 and came to be known as "San Diego's Own." In 1937, the regiment's color — with the original blue — was retired and replaced with the Marine Corps scarlet and gold.

Despite orders to have the color "destroyed by burning," the flag was preserved clandestinely by sentimental Marines. Lt. Col. Calland met one of these Marines in the 1960s, while he was working at the Smithsonian in Washington, D.C. He arranged for its donation to the Marine Corps Museum in Washington, D.C., which in turn stored it at Quantico, Va. Lt. Col. Calland didn't forget "Old Blue" and raised $3,000 to have the deteriorating flag restored and, finally, brought home in February 1991.

Today, the Society is operating on an annual budget of $193,600 and has three half-time employees: an executive director an assistant and a gift shop manager. And with more than 700 members, the Society boasts a 91 percent renewal rate. Thanks to this kind of dedication, the Museum continues to grow. It has tripled in space, going from its original 11,000 square feet to 32,000 square feet. Its goal is eventually to take over the entire 50,000-square-foot building.

The first floor includes the California Room with the Waterhouse paintings, a workshop for restoration, a theater and reception center. Family Service Center presently utilizes 18,000 square feet on the first floor.

Topside, in the east wing, the main gallery tells the Marine Corps story in conjunction with MCRD history and activities. There is also a room devoted to displaying, on a rotating basis, the histories of various Marine Corps organizations. Currently displayed is the history of the

Marines pose in period costumes in December 1994 for the Tun Tavern Tea, an Historical Society volunteer recognition event at Christmas time.

6th Marine Division, the only division to be formed and deactivated outside the United States. In addition, the second story houses the archives, the gift shop, and office space. In the west wing is the Boxer Rebellion Room, lecture and conference rooms, an audio video room for filming oral histories, and a weapons display room.

Visitor attendance has expanded exponentially. In 1988, the Museum's first full year, 68,341 recruits and civilians saw the displays. In 1989, that number jumped to 82,420; and in 1990 there were 102,598 visitors. Interest in the military increased with the war in the Persian Gulf in 1991, and the Museum was there to help civilians understand the mission of the Corps, serving 172,036 visitors. By the end of 1995, the Museum could boast a total of 836,772 visitors since its opening.

Of the 28 museums in San Diego County, the MCRD Museum is seventh in total attendance. The Marine Corps Recruit Depot public affairs office estimated in 1993 that 70 percent of the museum's civilian visitors come from outside the county, and they stay three to five days, spending $50 million a year in San Diego County. Thus, the Command Museum contributes substantially to the civilian community's economic and civic vitality.

MCRD Museum Historical Society 1997 Board of Directors

At right, President Patrick Ryan.

Above:
Front row, from left: Charles A. Pinney, III; Jeannette S. Maxwell; Paul T. Petit, Jr; Patrick O. Maloy; Edward L. Fike.

Second row, from left: Thomas A. Richards; George L. Lefferts; Donald E. Wilson; Thomas G. Johnson; Michael G. Zacker; Charles A. Cheatham.

Back row, from left: John A. Buck; Charles L. Zangas; James W. Gleave; Allan J. Rappoport.

Not pictured: Gordon W. Bartow, Victor E. Bianchini, Mary Kay Forsyth and Gerald A. Fulk.

The Crucible

At a press conference in July 1996, Gen. Charles C. Krulak, Commandant of the Marine Corps, outlined a formula for what he called, "building Marines for the 21st century." His blueprint promoted recruit training methods aimed at making Leathernecks "tougher physically, mentally and morally." The cornerstone of his plan: the Crucible.

"He wanted to make boot camp harder and to teach recruits to rely on each other," said Col. S.A. Cheney, commanding officer of Recruit Training Regiment at MCRD, San Diego.

The Crucible is modeled on the rigorous training special forces receive, according to Col. Cheney. The Marines looked at the training Navy SEALS received on the West Coast and Army Rangers went through on the East Coast. "Gen. Krulak wanted an event that would really put the boot through the wringer," said Col. Cheney. "But unlike the SEAL's hell-week, we're not looking to weed people out."

The Crucible is a grueling 54-hour final examination the recruits take on their 11th week of boot camp. It consists of eight major events with 32 obstacles intended to promote teamwork. "It's designed so that recruits have to work together," said Col. Cheney. They're given problems to solve that they can't possibly do by themselves. A squad might have to go through an obstacle course carrying ammunition boxes."

Although the course is spread out over four miles, re-

cruits actually cover about 40 miles, counting the required hikes. It's accomplished on four hours of sleep each night and only one Meal Ready To Eat (MRE) each day.

Company C, under the command of Capt. M.A. Buck, completed the first official West Coast Crucible in December 1996. Drill instructors join recruits, but they take on a different persona.

"They (DIs) are not in their traditional roles," said Col. Cheney. "Everyone wears helmets, so everyone looks the same. "The DI is there to help them through problems if they (recruits) are off the mark."

The West Coast Crucible is mirrored at Parris Island, S.C. "It's the same event, but space is more critical at Parris Island. They're not as spread out as we are. However, the East Coast Crucible opened a few weeks earlier because a rodent on the Endangered Species List delayed construction at Camp Pendleton. That area has the world's largest concentration of the Pacific Pocket Mouse," said Col. Cheney.

As a result, the "warrior stations" that house the obstacles throughout the course had to be built at least three inches off the ground to allow the mice to move freely through their habitat.

Construction of the $250,000 course started Aug. 21, 1996. More than 200 Marines and Navy Seabees worked six-day weeks to complete the project by October. The up-keep and maintenance of the course is the responsibility of personnel from Edson Range Facility Maintenance.

Most stations are named for Marine recipients of the Medal of Honor. For example, the Crucible begins with a trapeze-like warrior station called Garcia's Leap, named for Pfc. Fernando L. Garcia of San Juan, Puerto Rico. On Sept. 5, 1952, during the Korean War, Pfc. Garcia threw himself on a grenade to save his platoon sergeant's life. He was awarded the Medal of Honor posthumously.

Col. S.A. Cheney

Col. J.M. Guerin

The last — and biggest challenge — is one the Marines didn't have to build. Called the Grim Reaper, it is a giant hill the entire company must conquer as a team.

"So far we've had a few injuries and only two recruits quit," said Col Cheney.

The Crucible is the newest innovation in the Marine Corps. The event has expanded recruit training from 11 to 12 weeks. The Crucible is already deemed indispensable. Even if boot camp were reduced in length — as it was during past wars — the Crucible would be retained, said Col. Cheney. "In the short time we have been running this event," Col. Cheney said, "the Crucible has become part of Marine Corps tradition. We have Marines who are now boasting about the fact that they made it

through the Crucible."

Col. Jim Guerin, who was the commanding officer of Recruit Training Regiment from June 1993 to June 1995, contends there has been an overall shift in the philosophical approach to training recruits. "We rekindled Gen. Lejeune's charge to all leaders and began training as we would want to be trained. The DIs responed magnificently and excelled as leaders. Equally important has been the enhancement to teaching core values. Col. (J.M.D.) 'Doc' Holladay, Col. Steve Cheney and I have been fortunate to be involved in changes and enhancements to recruit training that will positively impact on the Corps well into the next century."

Second from left, Brig. Gen. Garry Parks, MCRD's Commanding General, leads recruits in a pre-graduation motivational run in 1996. Accompanying him, from left, are: Col. Steven A. Cheney, commanding officer of the Recruit Training Regiment; Lt. Col. John J. Hogan III, commanding officer of the 2nd Recruit Training Battalion; Lt. Gen. Paul K. Van Riper, Commanding General, Marine Corps Combat Development Command; Capt. Michael R. Pfister; and Sgt. Maj. Charles Brown II, Depot Sergeant Major.

The Tradition Continues

Uniform Code of Military Justice

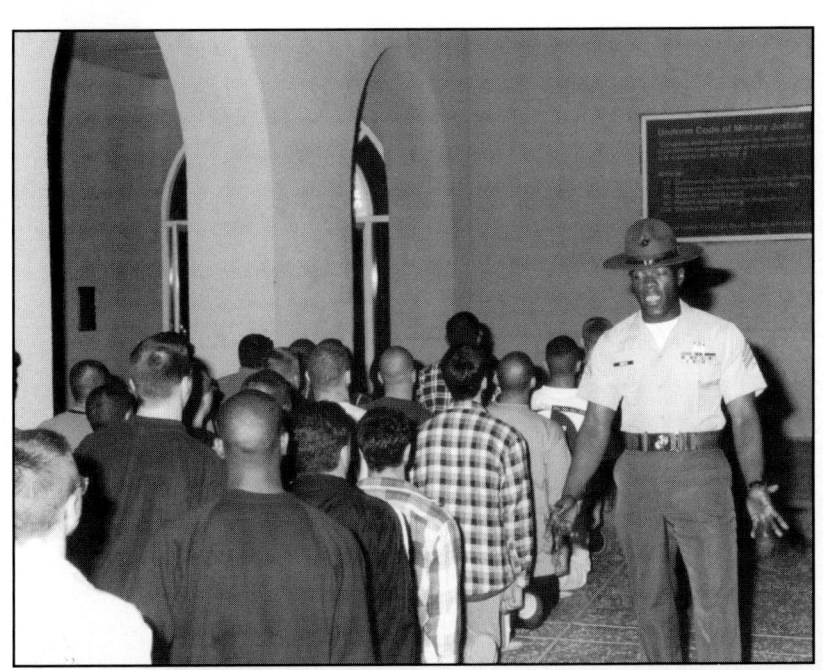

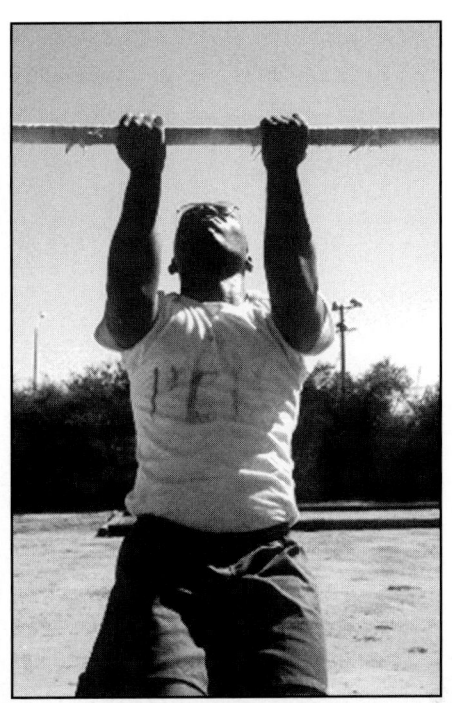

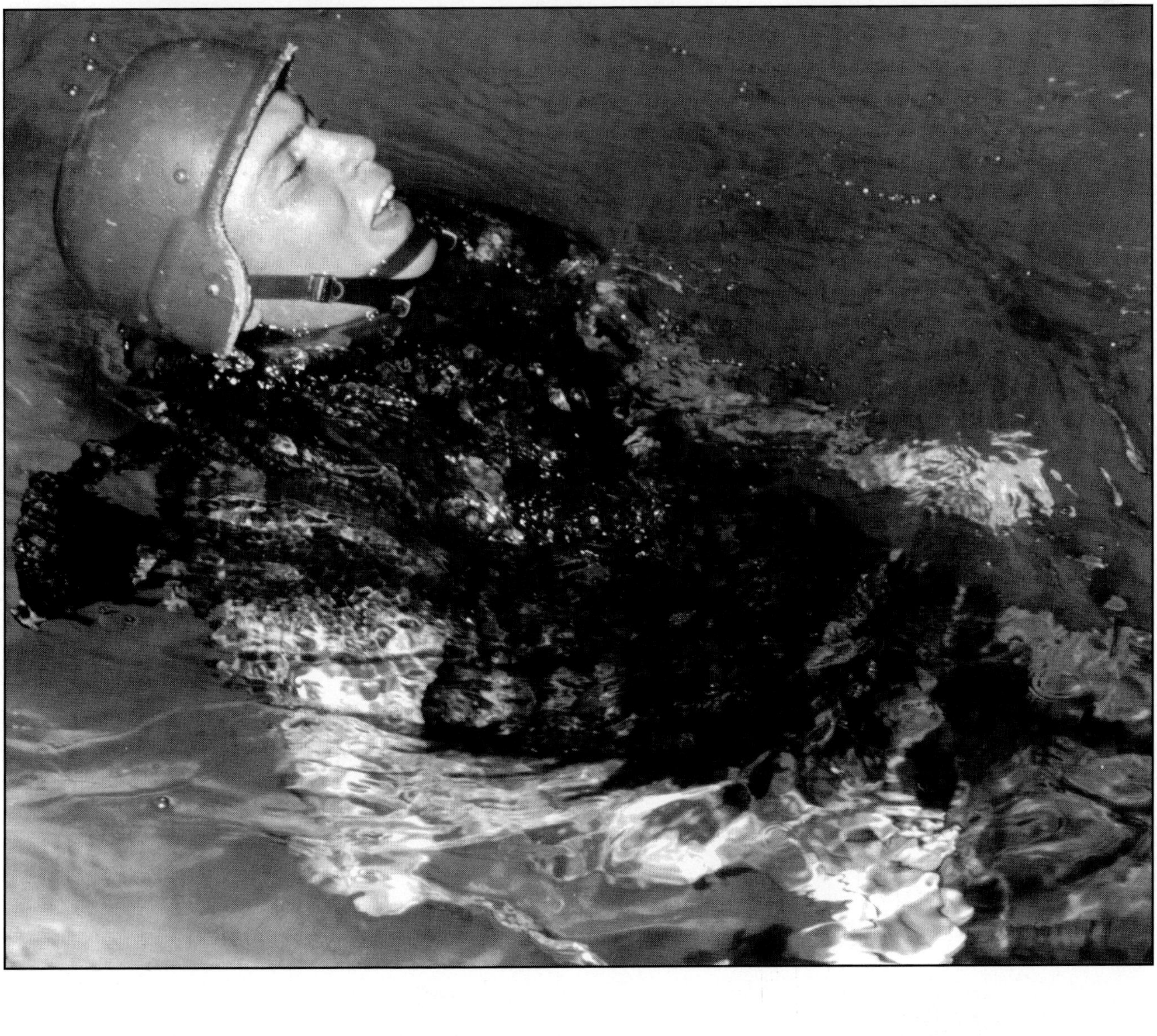

Dedications

Corporate Sponsors

Grosvenor Hospitality Group
Dr. Seuss Foundation
Charles A. Pinney III
Helen K. Copley
The Hon. Ross G. Tharp
in Honor of Colonel Raymond M. Ryan, USMC "A Marine's Marine"
Thomas G. Johnson   Western Scientific
Stephen Elms-Officers' Equipment Company

Patrons

Patrick J. & Terry E. Ryan
Allan J. Rappoport, Sergeant, USMC
Dr. Doyle D. Hansen-In Memory of Doyle Henry Hansen
Sgt. D.V. Enter, USMC
Paul T. Petit, Jr.-Dedicated to two fine Marines:
    Capt Paul T. Petit III & 1st Lt Kemper Petit
Everett L. Bobbitt
Major Keith M. Rice - In Memory of Colonel Arthur J. Noonan, USMC
Mary Lee Worneski-In Memory of Sgt. Leon A. Worneski,
    3d Division Ordnance Company
Ralph Feeley
Lieut. Steven Briggs McNicol, USMCR
Col E. S. Schick Jr USMC (Ret)
John G. Moore
Col S.A. and LtCol R.W. Cheney, USMC
Major F.A. Waters USMC (Ret)
C. L. Zangas
MGen. Marc A. Moore USMC (Ret)
Col Robert D. White USMC (Ret)
Major Bruce H. "Doc" Norton, USMC
George L. Lefferts
E.H. "Obie" O'Bryant
Sergeant Oliver G. Wiley III
William M. Coats VMF 224 MAG 11 SGT
Philip M. Klauber
Colonel John W. Guy-In Memory of
    LtCol Thomas H. Garity USMC - My Mentor
Richard C. & Marjorie H. Mitchell
John C. Binder-Philippe The Original
James W. Gleave-In Memory of Fred G. O'Malley
Gil L. Bauer USMC Platoon 2214   2 Jan 1969
LtCol. Johann Haferkamp USMC Ret
In Memory of Captain Paul George Lopez, USMC
In Memory of Captain David R. Herr, Jr, USMC
R. D. Wickwire
Captain and Mrs. Michael J. Gann II
Colonel George T. Fowler
LtCol Rudolf S. Sutter-In Memory of: Mr. and Mrs. R.K. Sutter

MGySgt Floyd W. Danley, USMC (Ret)
Roger Thomas Dooley
Mark A. Cunningham
John R. (Jack) Kessler
C. J. Busick
Kenneth R. Stephens-In Memory of Roy L. Stephens
Kent P. Tupper
Ronald Tribble MCRD Plt. 3072 3rd Battalion
Cpl. John C. Lacny "The Best of the Best Seagoing Marines"
George N. Coleman
Colonel Stormy Sexton, USMC (Ret)
Melvin D. Heckt
William J. Dickerson
Albert P. Pagoaga/Platoon 964/October, 1943
Michael C. Clark
Kenneth D. McGill
1stSgt. John Harvey Hood - USMCR (Ret)
Cpl Michael G. Stamenson
Walter C. Hay - Co "A" 1st Bn. 6th Marines
Thomas Frederick Elliott - 1052787
John J. Doherty-In Loving Memory of Pfc Helen L. Doherty USMC WWII
Dan P. Dollison, Capt. USMC (Ret)
Val R. Schiele USMC 1962-1966
MSgt. Ronald A. Bruchhauser - 1959819/USMC 1st RTBn. "Plt. 124 - God,
    Country, Corps!" Dedicated To My Wife-Phyllis J.
Harry W. Leeds Jr
Sgt.Maj. Stanley Cheslock, Retired
James M. McMenemy, 750th Plt.,11,1943. 16thDefBnSpcWpns 1943.
1stAAA&ReconBn 2/1944. 4th Div, 3/G/14, 7/1944.
Paul S. Rubera, Cpl USMC 1968-1972
Herb List, CEO, List Industries Inc.
Pierre F. Meunier
San Diego Bulldog Detachment 835
Thomas Curry Roberts, India Company
Lawrence G. Ward-To All Marines Who Have Been or Ever Will Be
Martin K. Leppo Former Marine
James Talbot Smith
J. E. (Jim) Hulgan

Sponsors

Scott James Larson
Col. Werner Hellmer, USMC
Brigadier General Garry L. Parks, USMC
Colonel Nate Smith, USMC (Ret.)
Commissioner Clinton G. Brame, Ret.
Colonel Jacques W. Carter, USMC (Ret.)
Dan Poukkula
Presented to Colonel Harry W. Peterson from I MEF G-3 SNCO's
Bill James
Dedicated to all GRUNTS of G-3-5 who participated in the Pusan Perimeter through the Chosin Reservoir campaigns Aug-Dec, 1950, Korea. Bob Snyder
Alexandra Downen-In Memory of Major Robert E. Downen, USMC (Ret.).
Sergeant Major Charles L. Brown III
To The Drill Instructors, From Whom All Things "Marine" Begin. Capt Ron Burton, USMC (Ret).
Colonel and Mrs. James M. Guerin
Colonel Richard D. Mickelson- In Memory of Carlan F. Mickelson
Maj. Earl R. Gimpel, USMC
Leonard V. Smith
Bert D. Mullins
SSgt Harold E. Rogers, USMC (Ret)
Joseph & Susan Ryan
Irwin F. "Ike" Waldvogel
Colonel Gerald D. Schmidt, USMC (Ret) Dedicated to: Gerald D. Schmidt III
Colonel Miller M. Blue
Frances L. Bott-In Memory of Major James J. Bott
Norman Dores-In Memory of Pappy, Dick and Dad
CWO 4 Andy Olesak, USMC (Ret.)
1st Lt. William G. Metzler, USMC (Ret)
Maximilian Berktold
Rebecca Kmet-In Memory of General Lemuel C. Shepherd, Jr. USMC
S/Sgt Harry R. Hoover 1347661 1952-1960
Norvyn J. Krager-Dedicated to My Wife Annelise
Robert J. Cruce
Douglas Edward Snarski 6-20-60 7-20-64
GySgt. J. B. Geggie
Jean P. White, LtCol, USMC (Ret). Platoon 56, 1945
Buford E. Thurmon Co. B, 4th Marines, Shanghai, China
Colonel William F. Pulver, USMC (Ret)
Sgt Maj. Michael G. Zacker, USMC (Ret)
Jerry Stadtmiller
CAPT Gerald A. Fulk-In Memory of Master Sergeant Oliver Jul Vanderbilt, USMC
Colonel Byron T. Schenn, USMC
Clarence E. Gibson Jr.
Donald W. Carlson, Platoon 561,1952
Catharine J. Miller, USMCWR
Scott Gregory Quinn
Roland C. Beisenstein
GySgt William F. Freestone
LtGen John N. McLaughlin
John L. Hancock
Pfc. Peder Gustawson
SgtMaj. Robert F. Singer USMC
Major General W.H. Rice, USMC Commanding General, MCRD 1981-1984
Eve Murphy-In Memory of Master Sergeant Stephen E. Murphy, USMC (Ret) 287485
1st Sgt James N. Anderson Jr USMC (Ret)
June Davis-In Memory of Lt. Col Howard L. Davis
CDR Ernest J. Irvin, MSC, USN
T.K. Versaw Plt. 154 Winter 1945
Borghild and Bob De Villiers
SgtMaj Marvin A. Delgado USMC (Ret)
W.R. Crim
Nick Bacile
Delbert Sumner Westling
Lt Stan Kloss, US Navy
Charles L. Henry, Jr. Class of '42
Ashley W. Fisher, III Class of '42
Walt Sandberg

Major General J.A. Studds, USMC (Ret) CG '91-'93. Dedicated to my wife Sybil E. Studds.
Sharon L. Smith
Edward L. Fike
Warren William Hanson
John J. Leonard
Frank A. Turiace, Jr. S/Sgt USMC 1950-1954
Mrs. E.T. Guymon, Jr.
Patricia & Peter A. Love
Robert E. Melbourne
C. Neil Ash
S/Sgt Kenneth D. Tomlinson USMC (Ret) PLT 2007 1956
Kevin R. Rounsavelle
E.L. Waldron-This book is dedicated to: GySgt E. L. Waldron, USMC, Co M, 3d Bn, 6th Marines,2nd Marine Division. Served: 1938-1945.
David A. Zeferjohn Captain USMC (Ret)
Wesley E. Henry MSgt Ret.
Colonel Vaughn L. DeBoever, USMC (Ret)
Manuel Mancillas Jr. MSgt USMC (Ret) Recruit Plt #62 2/13/48 MCRD San Diego, CA.
Harold Brooks - First Battalion, Platoon 196
E. Boyce Clark - E Co. 7th Marines - 1st Marine Division
LtCol Joseph N. Mueller USMCR
Don Cummins-Marine Corps League San Diego Bulldog Detachment
J. Mitchell Bloom
James H. Parish GySgt (Ret) USMC
Robert D. Pitts Maj/USMC (Ret)
Captain and Mrs. J.V. Larkin
Jack P. Garland & Garland Insurance Group
H "K" Throneson   1st Recruit Training Battalion 1952
Patricia Wernet-To Bob Friend, Happy Birthday!
Louis Misko
Clara Duncan-In Memory of Captain Louis E. Duncan, USMC (Ret)
James W. Kovar
Ray and Lillian Hicks
Colonel John A. White-In Honor of Pennie White - "Optimist of the Year"
Kenneth L. Pyle (CWO-3, USMC, Ret.)
Meredith Vezina
LtCol Bill Dollard   USMC (Ret)
Larry F. Buckeye, Plt. #392, 3rd Btn., RTR (1961)
George Butela Jr.
Kenneth J. Idol-In Memory of Dottie Idol
GySgt. Macario Domingo USMC (Ret)
J. Harrington Cahoon "49th Platoon - 1941"
General Kenneth McLennan USMC (Ret)
Mr. and Mrs. Robert Adelizzi
Capt. Harvey Tennant, USMC (Ret)
Major Clifford C. Doughty
Robert C. Schlein-In Memoriam Sgt. Louis B. Schlein, USMC
Steve Newton-In Memory of: Lance Corporal Ralph Meaney, 4/27/40 - 1/16/87
James W. Street, Major, USMCR
LtGen & Mrs. Victor H. Krulak
LtCol Guy O. Badger, USMC (Ret)
Mr. Hector Pena, Former Marine
Capt. Thomas E. Bickford
Captain Joseph F. Suddith, USMC
A. T. Hornbeak
Willie Leon Johnson
Alan M. Miller
LtCol Edwin W. Allard-Dedicated to: Joseph Abel
Pfc. Bill Nicholson Ret.
SSgt Walter J. O'Neil Jr USMC (Ret) Plt 395 1951
Thomas M. Sagar - Captain, USMC 1942-1952
Leland H. Montgomery
Jim & Maria Taggart
Dedicated to CWO Henry Bianchini, USN, by his son, Judge Victor E. Bianchini
Major John A. Buck, USMC (Ret) World War II, Korea and Vietnam
Robert B. Layton

Jim Lorenz
MGySgt William J. Countryman-Amphibious Reconnaissance Bn. FMF PAC
LtCol and Mrs. Russell E. McCreery
Sgt. George Steve Hilliard 1967 - 1973 Vietnam Veteran
M/Sgt Steve Spanovich Ret. USMC 295576
Richard D. Scannell
Col. W. J. Harnden, USMC (Ret)
Dale & Stephanie Marsh
Pvt. Harvey Cash Plt 258 10/1963
Dick Murphy
Maurice Kollasch
Gordon W. Bartow
Thomas M. Bruno
Law Office of James Winston Gleave
Eugene K. Hamilton
Don E. Wilson, M.D.
Arthur L. Anderson 1-C+H+S-14 4MARDIV
Patrick Nonnatus D. Ignacio
The Ballarin Family
Horst Molter
In Dedication to Brigadier General Jim Lawrence USMC (Ret)-Old Shipmate Nate
Dywane E. Calapp - Love, Jonnie
J.A. Dickison
MSgt. Gregory S. Domasig, Marine Band SNCOIC
Gerald J. Rappoport USMC 2-3-8 1943-1946
Elbert C. Whitaker-Memory of 4th Raider Battalion
Lieutenant Colonel William Odell Wagoner
William A. High
Mr. and Mrs. John Rey-In Memory of: Mr. Ed Schoenbart
Andrew G. Comer USMC (Ret)
Leonard Hancock-In Dedication To: Sgt. Roland Demers
MGySgt Norberto Martinez, Jr
Lon V. White, SgtMaj USMC Ret
Major Richard A. Barfield, USMC
Jeannette S. Maxwell
Bronson C. Jacoway, Sr.
Larry Manuel (Captain 0802)
CWO-4 George J. Green USMC (Ret) WWII
Cpl Vinh H. Nguyen, USMC
Paul Recasner-Plt 178 1st Recruit Training Battalion, San Diego MCRD 1951
Henry S. Lambert, Plt 2002 13 January - 4 April 1986
Conrad E. Nilsson G-3-5 1st MARDIV
Robert E. Sabisch
Patrick O. Maloy, Captain USMC
J.M.D. Holladay, Colonel USMC Retired
Patrick O. Maloy-In Memory of Eugene F. Maloy, Sergeant Major USMCR
Patrick O. Maloy-In Memory of Jack L. Adams, Commander USNR
Capt. Art DeFever Vietnam Veterans of San Diego
David C. Yorck-Feld Marschall Graf Yorck von Wartenburg
Tom Laskoski
Steve J. Zupanovich G-3-5 1st Provisional Brigade
William B. Adams-In Memory of Miles E. White
Brigadier General Frank J. Breth USMC
Richard J. Floyd-District Lodge 94
Ronald W. Sadewater
Lieutenant General and Mrs. H.C. Stackpole, III
Don Oliphant
Dearl A. Glenn
Fred Gil
Major David R. Musgrave
Captain Dan Oliphant
Keith Christie
1st Sgt and Mrs. R.A. Payson
George J. Weiss, Jr.
Edward F. and Daniel C. Jallits
Leonard G. Peterson Platoon #452-1944
Edward J. Harloff Always A Marine
Chris Harloff
Charles "Chilly" Newman A True Marine
Maida M. Masterpool-In Memory of William J. Masterpool
Michael J. Brotsis

Lyle Harris
San Diego Council United States Navy League
Lewis E. Wood, 2107662 Plt 137, May 1964
Leonard Moore
Don Moore, Illustrator
William G. Spraker
Cpl. Stephen Melinder Sr. 2329939 U.S.M.C.
Sgt. Vetula, James J. Semper Fidelis
Stanley Smulski Family
Louis W. Balog 554271 U.S.M.C.R. D Co. 2nd Bn. 27th Marines
        5th Div. Iwo Jima 2-19-45
William D. Chandler
Richard E. Southern II
James M. Barger USMC (Ret)
Victor Tolley Platoon 587
George Peterson "In Memory of Howard Vaugh, A Khe Sanh Vet"
James H. Shultz
Cpl. S.J. Kopec I-3-1 Korea
Dale G. Jenkins
T/Sgt. Magness F. Hyles USMC (Ret) 2nd Pt 1938 D-1-7 1940-44
Sgt. Bruce L. Morton
G.R. "Ski" Piaskowski Plt 3008 MCRD 1956
Cpl. William P. Crowley Fox Co. 2nd Bn. 23rd Reg. 4th MARDIV
Lt.Col. Byron F. Brady USMC (Ret)
Eric E. Gillen-Leatherneck Barber Shop
Colonel Corbin J. Johnson (Plt No. 725, 1942)
LtCol Daniel B. Corts USMC Ret.
Reiss P. Tatum-In Memory of Major William M. Tatum, Jr. USMC Ret.
Charles W. Cummings
Sergeant Raul A. Martinez 1st Marine Division 5th Regiment
        3rd Battalion HOW Company
MGySgt Richard J. Fowler
Don C. Gibson "Thanks For The Memories"
Dixon L. Poole, Plt. 379, 22 August 1954
Robert T. Donald-Platoon 1001, 15 Nov 1955 - 6 Feb 1956 Sr. DI: SSgt. G.E. Schlecht
MSgt Donald G. Barker USMC (Ret)
Sgt. Richard J. Burbine, Plt. 1095, 1981
Robert R. Meadows H&S Co. 3/1 1st MARDIV, RVN
Colonel Paul E. Pruett USMCR
"In honor of all my Marine friends." Major Gunnar A. Johnson, USMC Retired
Cpl Shawn A. Miller-Marines of Force Maintenance 24 MEU
David L. Gally
Joseph F. Brittain
LCpl Justin S. Garcia
Melvin A. Traylor, Jr. Platoon 138, 1941
Major Scott S. Smith-In Memory of:
        "Second Marine Division" (All the Fallen Heroes of WWII 1941-1945)
J. Craig Bird-In Memory of the Grunts
Geraldine Kienly
Larry G. Carmon
Captain Frank M. Porpotage II USMC
Gary W. Lee, Platoon 3052, Mike Company, 3rd Battalion, RTR
1st Lt. David E. Baker-In Honor of the
        Steadfast Dedication of Those Serving in Headquarters Company, HSBN, DB
Cpl William F. Gavin-Plt. 3027, Graduated 7/29/66-Cpl. M.J. Dingus, Cpl. G.R. Gallion,
Cpl. B.W. Grunewald, Cpl. G.D. Kemski, L/Cpl. W.Z. Moore-KIA Vietnam "Warriors All"
Marvin E. Yoder
Colonel Bruce J. Matheson USMC (Ret)
A.J. Ramirez-Kilo Co 3-3 Marine Division
Mark Wm. Viles, L.A. Co. F.D.
Donald P. Lee
David W. Simpson-PLT 291, MCRD 1960
LtCol Thomas Kalus USMC (Ret)
Gene Dixon
Carroll W. Sprenger
Joe W. McHenry
James Q. Ferris Sr.
LtCol Rutilio R. Zuniga
Cpl M.T. Casebolt H & S Co. 2/4 2nd Bn.
Colonel John M. Keeley USMCR
P.F.C. Robert E. Galligan, U.S.M.C. 3rd Marine Division

MCRD San Diego
75th Anniversary Book

The soft cover edition of the MCRD 75th Anniversary Book is now on sale.

$19.95
+ $4.50 s&h

Makes a great gift!

Think you have it tough! You should read what boot camp was like when your father and grandfather were here.

Enclosed is my check for $19.95 plus $4.50 shipping and handling (CA residents add $1.55 state tax) for each book. Please send a copy (ies) of the MCRD soft cover edition to:

(1) name_____

address_____

city_____state_____zip_____

(2) name_____

address_____

city_____state_____zip_____

(3) name_____

address_____

city_____state_____zip_____

Please enclose a gift card from:

name_____

To order by credit card, call toll-free **1-800-277-1977**, or make check payable and send to:
Heritage Press
102 West 6th Ave
Escondido, California 92025

Please allow two weeks for delivery.
For priority mail (3 day) delivery add $7.50 for each book.

George Northrup Platoon 195 March 1943
GySgt John N. Manfredi Retired
Thomas A. Geise - Platoon 268
Robert J. Clay
Eugene Wilson Barnette
Donald Lee Montgomery
Terrence O. Quong
Dedicated To: S/Sgt W. Salmond Platoon 2207 From J. Lopez Graduate - Oct 31, 1966
Huell Howser
Paul T. Mondry
Sharon Leal-In Honor of John F. Leal for Service in The U.S. Marine Corps
James Franchetti Plt. 241 MCRD 1965
Pvt. Johnson, Robert G. Plt. 1016 Nov 1957-Jan 1958
William J. Timper III-In Memory Cpl. William J. Timper Jr. USA
M/Sgt O.E. Gilpin, C &E Bn.
Phil G. Foltz
Gy/Sgt James A. Rohloff, Retired 1953-1975
Robert Hartley Platoon 1-52 1950
Cpl. George H. Moffett - Marine Detachment U.S.S. Kearsarge 1951 to 1954
Sergeant Major Herbert L. White
Ron C. Deverick-Dedicated to
      the Brothers from 3rd Bn 12th Marines Killed in Vietnam 1965-1969
Cpl. R.R. Lemley Plt. 2028 1966
Marine Corps Historical Foundation
Gerald G. Crimmins
Mike McCullar, Plt 1115, MCRD - San Diego, June - August 1969
J. R. Martin - USMC - Retired
LtCol Arnold G. Whittelsey from the Marines of MCRD/WRR San Diego 1 July 1996
Charles H. Swindell
LtCol Edward A. Benes
B.J. Dinius
Ruth Sidders-In memory of CMSgt George E. Sidders 1920-1993
William A. Risen - 65th Platoon - July 1941 USMCRD San Diego, California
Corporal Christopher C. Mueller
Fred Miller-In Memory of Cpl Joseph W. Miller
Sgt Juan A. Marquez Jr RS-Albuquerque, NM RSS-Roswell, NM In Honor of
      Diligent Recruiting Efforts. 931129-961129
Childs, James E. MSgt USMC (RET)
GySgt. David R. Ayers
Sgt.Maj. Stanley J. Peloza, USMC RET'D.
James Richard Allriedge
John F. McCorkle-In Memory of Major Floyd M. "Mac" McCorkle
LCpl Richard Gross Platoon 278, 2nd Battalion (1958), HQ, FMFLANT
Clinton William Howe Sr.
Lawrence J. Kay, Platoon 2083, 1975
Edward Raymond Moore
Colonel Michael H. Smith, USMC
Colonel John P. Wright, USMC
Colonel John M. Studenka, USMC
Don L. Mallaghan
Cpl Erik Roed
David Redsun
Lieutenant Colonel & Mrs. D'Arcy Grisier
Charles L. Huestis - USMC - WW II (Ser. #329236)
Gerald E. Anderson 1st Sgt USMCR-Ret
John Wayne Texada
Michael B. Blackburn
Grace Fedor-In Memory of Dexter A. Fedor
Thomas J. Duffy III, MGySgt
Max R. Hembree
Randall Scott Lauer
Pfc. Paul E. Ison H.Q. Co. 3rd Bn. 5th Marines, 1st Marine Div. WWII
Sgt. Donald James Childs
Nancy and Robert Kelly
The Spruel Family
Senior Drill Instructor SSgt J.S. Vaughan
John J. Leonard #1825877 7th Comm Bn
MGySgt Jesus T. Galindo 2126385
Wayne E. Radetski, Sgt. "M" Co, 3rd Bn 4th Marines
Dean C. Ryalls
Dean C. Ryalls

Dr. Donald V. Healas, CWO3 - USMCR
L/Cpl Michael A. Machie KIA
Lieutenant Colonel Gerard J. Lyons USMC
Michael Torres
Donald J. Hughes
Rodger E. Wood Platoon 165 1958 1837586
Sgt. Ralph A. Ventura USMC (2/16/67 - 11/2/72)
R.A. Cruickshank
Phil Pincus-To Sgt. Dave Rose
"Dedicated to the service and sacrifices of our comrades-in-arms, past,
      present, and future. Semper fi!" Thomas A. Richards
Allan J. Rappoport-In Memory of Marjorie R. Weber, Cpl USMC
James L. Heron 3rd Raider Bn.
Gunnery Sgt. Jim Humason - All American POWS - MIAS
Will Bracken Evans
LCpl Kenneth C. Crosby USMC Tradition Continues
Joseph A. Musto
Sgt. Frank R. Chang
Colonel John J. Hogan
Robert O. Hunter, Major USMCR
Colonel George W. Houck USMC (Ret)
Pfc Brandon L. Williams
Donald R. Miller '43
Robert F. Samuel USMC
Norman Cabael Arias USMC
Rocklin Lyons
Del Treichler
Pfc Edgar Fulwider USMC
Victor B. Snider
Lewis E. Wood, 2107662 Plt. 137, May 1964
John F. Stofiel GySgt U.S.M.C. Ret. MCRD Recruit 1959 - MCRD DI 1965-1968
Bob Hanna #(281) 444-1941 Plt 372 August 1960 In honor of
      GySgt Charlie Soltiysiak, Senior Drill Instructor, MCRD, San Diego.
Wayne Cates First Shore Party Battalion Vietnam
Darrell Larson, Sgt. USMC 5711/0311 Platoon 3301 Oct. 1967
Dennis A. Davis
Sgt. Richard Boemer Baker Co. 1st Bn 7th Marines Korea

Index

1st Advanced Base Force 16
1st Air Naval Gunfire Liaison Company 63
1st Marine Brigade 139, 145, 147
1st Marine Depot Company 48
1st Marine Division 54, 101, 141-147, 167, 168
1st Marine Raider Battalion 94, 96
1st Marine Regiment 142-146
1st Recruit Training Btn. 55, 58
2nd Advanced Base Force 15, 23, 24, 28
2nd Marine Brigade 25, 35, 38, 40, 138, 139
2nd Marine Division 38, 43, 96, 139, 140, 167
2nd Marine Regiment 96
2nd Recruit Training Battalion 58, 63, 162
3rd Marine Division 142-146, 168
3rd Marine Regiment 144, 147
3rd Recruit Training Btn. 94, 145
4th Marine Regiment 1-4, 6-12, 24-27, 29, 33, 35, 78, 135, 141, 142, 146, 155
4th Prov. Marine Regiment 2, 3
4th Recruit Training Battalion 58
5th Marine Brigade 12, 24, 85
5th Marine Regiment 33, 96, 139, 141, 143-145, 147, 169
6th Marine Division 155
6th Marine Regiment 33, 35-39, 54, 140, 166, 167
7th Marine Regiment 24, 144, 167
7th Marine Reserve Officer Class Association 154
8th Marine Corps District 120
9th Marine Corps District 120
9th Marines 144-147
10th Marines 27, 33, 35, 38
11th Marines 96
11th Naval District 17, 24, 54, 124, 127, 130, 132, 133
11th Tank Battalion 55
12th Marine Corps District 68, 120
27th Marines 63
29 Palms, Calif. 116, 117
1916 Naval Appropriations Act 11

Abraham, Col. J.W. 148
Agony Hill 86
Alexander, Grover Cleveland 130
All-Marine Team 124-126, 133
Allen, Brig. Gen. Chester R. 59
Allermann, Sgt. Maj. Stephen D. 116, 117
American Television and Communications Corp. 154
Amphibian Tractors Mechanics School 115
Armed Forces softball championship 133
Army Rangers 158
Arneson, Arne 129
Attu, USS 54
Aviation 14, 29, 33, 34
Avila, D'Wayne 63

Balboa Park 6-8, 10-12, 16, 22, 24, 28, 88
Balboa Stadium 127, 128, 130
BankAmerica Foundation 154
Banker, Maj. Edward W. 18, 24
Barnes, MSgt. J.L. 118
Barnett, Maj. Gen. George 4, 5, 7, 9, 11, 17
Beaumont, Brig. Gen. John C. 35
Beckett, Capt. Johnny 124, 126
Beeson Field 133, 135
Beeson, Maj. Donald M. 123, 125, 127, 132, 133
Bell, Col. J.O. 148
Bell, Col. M.C. 148
Benny, Jack 45
Bickford, Charles 31
Biddle, Commandant, Maj. Gen. William P. 2, 74, 99
Bishop, Lt. Col. Giles Jr. 147
Blewett, Johnny 123-127, 130, 132
Blue Ridge, USS 113
Boathouse 38, 39, 68
Bonhomme Richard, USS 108
Boone, Cmdr. J.T. 38
Boot Bowl 128
Boress, Col. B.M. 148
Borrego Desert, Calif. 35
Bourke, Col. Thomas E. 35
Bowser, Brig. Gen. A.L. 101, 148
Boxer Rebellion Room 155
Boyd, Col. R.W. 148
Boyd, Scharod 63
Bradman, Brig. Gen. Frederic L. 138
Breth, Brig. Gen. Frank J. 146
Bridge Over Troubled Waters 80
Brown, Sgt. Maj. Charles II 162
Buck, Capt. M.A. 159
Buck, Maj. John 101, 151, 153, 156
Buffalo, USS 2
Bureau of Yards and Docks 15, 17, 20, 21, 23
Burnham, George 6, 10, 11
Butler, Maj. Gen. Smedley D. 27, 29, 34, 135, 137

California, USS 3, 6
Calland, Lt. Col. Robert 153-155
Camp C.J. Miller 44
Camp Del Mar 115
Camp Dunlap 44
Camp Elliott 43, 44, 46, 53, 72, 78, 89, 115, 139
Camp Gillespie 44
Camp Holcomb 43
Camp Howard 2, 3, 6
Camp Kearny 35, 43
Camp Lejeune, N.C. 64, 117, 130, 141, 145
Camp Linda Vista 89
Camp Margarita 95
Camp Matthews 43, 54, 55, 82-84, 86, 88-96
Camp Nimitz 35
Camp Pendleton 12, 48, 55, 62, 72, 80, 84, 94-96, 112-115, 137, 141, 142, 144-146, 159
Camp Stuart Mesa 94
Camp Thomas 2-4

Campbell, Maj. H.D. 38
Capps, Billy 134
Chaney, Lon Sr. 30
Chapman, Lt. Gen. Leonard F. 60, 61
Chappo Flats 95
Charleston, USS 130
Chaumont, USS 29
Cheatham, Charles A. 156
Cheney, Col. Steven A. 148, 158-160, 162
Cieslinski, MSgt. Raymond 80, 102
Clancy, Tom 118
Clark, Sgt. Linda N. 120
Clement, Lt. Gen. William T. 58, 135, 141
Clerical School 122
Cleveland, USS 63
Coats, 2nd Lt. Maxine E. 48
Coffman, Col. R.P. 148
Collier, D.C. 6, 10
Colorado, USS 7
Command Museum 101, 150-155
Communication and Electronics School 106, 107, 114, 115, 153
Communication-Electronics Schools Battalion 116, 117
Consolidated-Vultee Aircraft 39, 44, 48
Coontz, CNO, Adm. R.E. 24
Cooper, Lt. Gen. Charles G. 144
Coronado, Calif. 12, 21, 29, 34, 44, 65, 113, 137, 138, 140, 141
Cotten, Lenly Marvin 79
Cowie, Gay 129
Craig, Lt. Gen. Edward A. 36-38, 122, 151, 153
Cram, Ralph Adams 16
Crawford, Sgt. Maj. Leland D. 153
Curtis, Tony 30

"D.I., The" 30, 59
Dahms, Jerry 133
Dahne, Dr. Eugenio 6
Dalton, Capt. Ronald 122
Daniels, Secretary of the Navy Josephus 10
David S. McDougal Memorial Trophy 95
Davidson, G. Aubrey 6
Davies, Col. William W. 53
Davis, Col. J.R. 148
Davis, Mike 130
Dawson Construction Co. 15
Day, Col. M.E. 148
Day, Maj. Gen. James L. 144
Dawson MSgt. Dave 150
Dendy, MSgt. Dave 150
Derning, Col. Edmund G. 64, 148
Des Voignes, Clair 43
Destroyer Base, San Diego 33, 124, 130
Devere, Carl M. Sr. 153
Diamond, Cpl. Leroy P. 50
Diaz, President Porfirio 2, 4
Dick, Col. W.L. 148
Dickinson, Sgt. Lee 103
DiMaggio, Pfc. Joseph P. Jr. 60
Dix, Richard 30
Dolphin, USS 4
Donnell, Col. J.W. 148

Dorow, Al 134
Doyen, Col. Charles A. 2, 3
Drill Instructor School 68, 99, 100, 102, 104, 154
Drill Instructors Association, West Coast Chapter 80
Drum, Lt. Col. Andrew B. 33
Duffy 50, 135
Dunlap, Brig. Gen. Robert H. 33, 137
Dutch Flats 5, 6, 11, 12, 14

Edson, Maj. Gen. Merritt A. 94, 96
Edson Range 84, 94, 159
Edwards, Lt. Col. Tom 153
Elliott, Commandant, Maj. Gen. George F. 43
Ellis, Ted 134
English, Maj. Gen. Lowell E. 143
Enter, Sgt. David V. 154

Family Service Center 153, 155
Farragut, Adm. David G. 108
Faulconer, T.N. 8
FBI 122
Fegan, Lt. Gen. Joseph C. Jr. 143, 154
Field exercise training 122
Field Music School 108
Field Radio Operators Course 116, 117
Fighter Squadron Three 34
Fike, Edward L. 156
First Sergeants School 122
Fleet Marine Force (FMF) 25, 26, 33, 35-38, 40, 43, 44, 53, 54, 72, 78, 122, 138-146
Flood, Lt. Col. J.H.A. 148
Flores, Staff Sgt. Hector M. 113
Fortson, Maj. Eugene P. 147
Foster, Cpl. Claude E. 63
Fourth Marine Division Assn. 154
Fowler, Col. G.T. 148
Fox-West Coast Theater Corp. 45
Franciscus, James 30
Franklin, MGy. Sgt. Chauncey 122
Fulham, Maj. Gen. Donald J. 145, 153, 154

Games, 1st Lt. E.B. 38
Garcia, Pfc. Fernando L. 159
Garcia's Leap 159
Gen. William Weigel, USS 63
Gibson, Col. H.J. 148
Gleave, James W. 156
Gloeckner, Lt. G.L. 20
Goat Island, Calif. 21
Goodhue, Bertram G. 13-17, 21-23
Graham, Col. R.J. 148
Griffin, Cliff 129
Grim Reaper 159
Grinalds, Maj. Gen. John S. 146
Groff, Col. John 53, 78, 147
Gronke, MSgt. D.D. 122
Guerin, Col. James 148, 159, 160
"Gung Ho" 30

Haggert, Col. John W. 65
Haines, Brig. Gen. H.C. 24
Haines, William 30
Hale, 1st Lt. Mary Jane 54

170

Hall, Col. George T. 100
Hall Field 130
Hall, Gen. Elmer 44, 124, 129, 130
Halls of Montezuma 47
Hansen, Chester W. 15
Harding, Sen. Warren G. 10
Hardy, Maj. Herbert 37
Harris, Maj. Allen 130, 131
Harris, Rear Adm. Frederic R. 10
Harris, Sgt. William D. 113
Harrison, Maj. William H. 35
Henderson, USS 26, 27, 29
Hendricks, Maj. D.O. 153
Hermle, Lt. Gen. Leo D. 44, 54, 95, 140
Hill, Col. Charles S. 29
Hirt, Cpl. Margo 49
Historical Society 151, 154-156
Hochmuth, Maj. Gen. Bruno A. 60, 63, 84, 130, 131, 134, 142, 148
Hogan, Lt. Col. John J. III 162
Holcomb, Commandant, Maj. Gen. Thomas 43, 88, 109
Holladay, Col. J.M.D. 148
Hollywood, Calif. 31, 45, 99, 104, 109
Hooper, 1st Lt. Walter R. 117
Hope, Bob 45
Hotel Del Coronado 29
Houghton, Maj. Gen. Kenneth 65, 66, 120, 136, 144, 151, 154
Howard, Maj. Gen. Archie F. 140
Huerta, Gen. Victoriano 4
Huey, Lt. Col. James McE. 147
Hughes, Capt. William R. 108
Hunt, USS 48

Ibarra, Pvt. J.R. 84
Ike Puller 113
Indianapolis, USS 100
Intrepid, USS 145

Jackson, Col. Gilder 44, 54, 147
James, Col. William C. 147
James Jolly Plum Duff 124, 135
Jason, USS 34
Jessop, Dr. Alonzo D. 95
Jiggs 135
Johnson, 1st Sgt. Charles E. 112
Johnson, Thomas G. 156
Jones, GySgt. Mel 110, 112
Jones, GySgt. R.F. 64
Jones, John Paul 108
Jones, Lt. Gen. William K. 39, 40
Jones, MGy. Sgt. Thomas 85, 88, 89
Jones, Warren "Locker Box" 129
Jordan, Col. K.D. 148
Joslyn, Col. W.G. 148
Jupiter, USS 3, 4

Kaye, Louis 63
Kayser, Kay 45
Kearny Mesa 43
Kelley, Brig. Gen. Edwin C. Jr. 135, 146
Kennedy, President John F. 59, 60
Kerr, Brig. Gen. Hugh T. 145, 153
Kettner, Congressman William 5-7, 9-12, 15-17, 21, 24
King, Joe 133

Kingman, Brig. Gen. Matthew H. 45, 49, 53, 139
Kiter, Staff Sgt. Richard 63
Knerr, Jim 134
Kordela, George 153
Kraijeck, Capt. Karen 133
Krulak, Commandant, Gen. Charles C. 158
Krulak, Lt. Gen. Victor H. 38, 39, 55, 58, 61, 79, 97, 99, 100, 101, 131, 142, 154, 167

La Jolla Town Council 88, 92
Lachemann, Bill 134
Landing Force Training Command, Pacific 113
Lane, Col. Rufus H. 3
Langley, USS 3, 27
Laurenzi, Pvt. Anne 41
Lay, Col. Harry R. 33, 133, 147
Leatherneck Bowl 130
Leech, Lt. Col. Lloyd L. 35
Lefferts, George L. 156
Lejeune, Commandant, Maj. Gen. John A. 17, 20, 26, 27, 130, 132
Lindbergh Field 48, 55, 63, 67, 68, 116
Little, Maj. Gen. Louis M. 138
Liversedge, Col. Harry 54, 126, 147
Lloyd, Capt. Russell M. Jr. 59
Long, Brig. Gen. Charles H. 17, 18
Long, Maj. Gen. Earl 11, 54, 84, 140
Lott, Maj. Charles McL. 127
Lukeman, Lt. Gen. Anthony 145, 153, 154
Lyman, Maj. Gen. Charles H. 6, 35, 147

M-1 Rifle 90, 92
Madero, President Francisco 4
Mahler, Cmdr. Walter 47
Malcom, J.T. 118
Maloy, Patrick O. 156
Mare Island, Calif. 2, 4, 20, 99, 108, 124, 138
Marine Corps Air-Ground Combat Center 116
Marine Corps Air Station, New River, N.C. 63
Marine Corps Base, Naval Operating Base, San Diego 21
Marine Corps History and Museums Division 151, 152, 153
Marine Corps Human Relations Institute 64
Marine Corps League, Big D Chapter 135
"Marine Raiders" 30
Marine Security Force Btns. 113
Mark 4s (Sherman tanks) 55
Marsh, Lt. Ernie 64
Marston, Maj. John 8
Martin, Billy 130
Maryland, USS 3
Matthews, Brig. Gen. Calvin B. 84, 94, 96
Matthews, Chuck 134
Maxwell, Jeannette S. 156
McCawley, Brig. Gen. Charles 20
McCloskey, former Congressman Pete Jr. 100, 101

McClure, Pvt. Lynn E. 102
McCollum, Tom 134
McCormick, MSgt. Charles 66
McDonald, Jeanette 45
McDougal, Lt. Col. David S. 95
McDougal, Maj. Gen. Douglas C. 38, 39, 56, 95, 138
McGeehan, Capt. D.F. 115
McGill, John F. 24
McKelvey, Bruce 133
McKelvy, Maj. William 10
McLaughlin, Lt. Gen. John 62, 143
McMormick, GySgt. Chuck 72
McQueen, Lt. Gen. John C. 142
Meal Ready To Eat 159
Metcalf, Lt. Cmdr. Ralph J. 48, 50
Metro-Goldwyn-Mayer 109
Meyer, Henry 100
Mickelson, Col. Richard 151-154
Military Police School 122
Miller, Capt. Dorothy 49, 54
Miller, Capt. Ellis B. 7
Miller, John 134
Mission Beach 18
Mission Valley 18, 43
Mitchum, Robert 30
Montrief, Al 129
Moore, Maj. Gen. Marc 151-154
"Moran Of The Marines" 30
Morehead, Sgt. Robert A. 100
Morell, Col. Phil 55
Morley, Supt. of City Parks John 20
Moses, Col. Emil P. 20, 78, 108
Motor Transport School 122
Moulton, Sgt. Joe L. 47
Murray, Lt. Col. C.I. 38
Myers, 2nd Lt. Margaret E. 48
Myers, Col. John T. 147

Nat'l Athletic Health Institute 65
Nat'l Register of Historic Places 24
Navajo Indians 46
Naval Air Station, Miramar 117
Naval Air Station, North Island 34, 58, 124, 130
Naval Base, San Diego 17, 24, 124
Naval Station, San Diego 54
Naval Training Station, Great Lakes, Ill. 116
Naval Training Station, San Diego 18, 21, 36, 43, 44, 124
Navy Department 2, 7, 11, 15, 16, 23, 24, 36
Navy Pier, San Diego 58
Navy SEALS 158
Navy Yard, Puget Sound 2, 4, 20
Neil, MSgt. Jean 121, 126, 127
Newton, Col. George R. 80, 148
Nihart, Col. Brooke 153
North China Marine POW Memorial 154
North Island, Calif. 2-5, 33, 34, 58, 84, 130
Nubson, Maj. Troy A. 48

Oakland, USS 15
O'Brien, Hugh 99
O'Brien, Pat 30, 31
Observation Squadron One 34
Old Blue 155

Old Smokey 58, 67
Old Town San Diego 20
Orders and Medal Society of America 154
Osborne, Jack 134
"Outsider, The" 30
Oyler, Ray 133, 134

P-38, Army interceptor 47
Pacific Beach 110
Pacific Pocket Mouse 159
Packard, Maj. S.A. 104
Padgett, Congressman Lemuel 15
Palena, 1st Lt. R.A. 113
Panama-California Exposition 6, 8, 10, 16, 22, 130
Paramount Studios 109
Parks, Brig. Gen. Garry L. 104, 147, 162
Parks, Rear Adm. C.W. 17
Parris Island, S.C. 24, 101, 103, 118, 120, 128-134, 139, 147, 159
Paxton, Sgt. Maj. Bill 153
Pendleton, Maj. Gen. Joseph 1-12, 14-18, 20-26, 35, 44, 78, 95, 137
Pennsylvania, USS 3, 138
Perez, Victor 63
Petit, Paul T. 156
Pfister, Capt. Michael R. 162
Pickett, Lt. Col. H.K. 38
Picketts, Cpl. Laura 54
Pinney, Charles A. III 156
Po' Boy's Smokin' Joe 135
Poillon, Maj. Gen. Arthur J. 120
Point Loma 16
Point Loma Road Race 7
Poppleman: Raymond J.; Lyle H.; Clyde M. 125
Price, Maj. Derek W. 110
Pritchett, Lt. Col. William H. 147
Proctor, John 130
Puryear, Col. B. Jr. 38
Pyles, Jim 134

Quantico, Va. 27, 35, 65, 96, 115, 124-126, 130, 135, 137, 139, 140, 142, 144, 146, 155
Quinlan, Volney "Skeet" 128, 130
Quonset huts 23, 47, 50, 51, 55, 58, 61, 63, 65, 66, 72

Radar Technicians Course 116
Rappoport, Allan J. 156
Reagan administration 151
Reclassification and Distribution Center 50
Recruit Training Command 101, 102, 131
Recruit Training Regiment 62, 68, 69, 80, 94, 102, 122, 145, 148, 158, 160, 162, 167, 168
Recruiters School 68, 108, 117, 118, 120-122
Red Devil Squadron 34
Reimann, Capt. Thomas 113
Reineberg, Capt. Michael F. 113
Rhode Island, USS 96
Ribbon Creek 101, 102
Rice, Florence 31
Rice, Maj. Gen. W.H. 145, 152, 153

171

Richards, Thomas A. 156
Ridgely, Lt. Gen. Reginald H. 141
Rifle Range (Edson Range) 94, 96
Rifle Range (La Jolla; Camp Matthews) 33, 43, 46, 48, 54, 55, 78, 82-86, 88, 89, 92, 94, 96
Rifle Range (North Island; Camp Howard) 3, 4, 7, 84
Robb, Lt. Col. W.G. 58
Robinson, Floyd 133, 134
Rockey, Lt. Col. Keller 37
Rodney, Col. G.W. 148
Rodrique, Perry 130
Roll, Sgt. Roger 102
Rolwal Red Rival 135
Roosevelt, President Franklin D. 5, 23, 43-45
Roosevelt, President Theodore 6
Rose Bowl 124
Rowbottom, George V. 6
Rowell, Maj. Ross E. 34
Ruffin, Col. George R. Jr. 115
Rupertus, Col. William 38, 45, 147
Russell, Commandant, Maj. Gen. John H. Jr. 36, 37, 138
Ryan, Patrick 156

Salerno-Livingston and Partners of San Diego 153
"Salute To The Marines" 109
San Clemente Island, Calif. 35, 38
San Diego Bombers 129
San Diego Chargers 60, 127, 130
San Diego City Council 18, 88, 92
San Diego Council of the Navy League 154
San Diego Perpetual Trophy 95
San Diego Police 122
San Diego Railway Company 39
San Diego Securities Co. 11
San Diego State University 61, 80, 123, 124, 127, 129
San Diego, USS 6
San Diego Water Commission 18
San Diego Zoological Society 8
San Francisco, Calif. 2, 4, 6, 12, 14, 20, 21, 27, 29, 70, 138-140, 144
San Luis Obispo, Calif. 89
Savoy, Col. Ernest R. 62, 63, 148
Schubert, Maj. R.H. 38
Schulze, Maj. Gen. Richard C. 144

Scott, Randolph 30
Sea School 45, 55, 59, 78, 106-113, 154
Sellers, Adm. David F. 36
Separation Company 50, 53, 54
Serapis, H.M.S. 108
Sergeants Major 149
Sessions, Kate O. 20
Sessions, Milton P. 20
Seymour, Col. R.A. 148
Sgt. Sylvester Antolak, USS 58
Shapley, Brig. Gen. Alan 102, 123, 148
Shepherd, Commandant, Gen. Lemuel C. Jr. 154
Signal and Track Vehicle School Battalion 114, 115
Signal Battalion 114, 115
Simmons, Brig. Gen. Edward 151-154
Sirius, USS 20
Skinner, Bob 121, 132, 134
Skouras, Charles P. 45
Sledge, E.B. 100
Smith, Col. Nathan R. 154
Smith, Lt. Holland 3
Smith, Maj. J.T. 38
Smokey 135
Snead, Capt. Larry 113
Snow, Maj. J.E. 86
Soochow 135
South Dakota, USS 3, 4
Springfield Rifle, M-1903 2, 74, 83-85, 92
Stackpole, Col. H.C. III 148
Standard Operating Procedures 99, 102
Stephens, William 10
Stivers, Lt. Col. R.T. Jr. 58
Streeter, Maj. Ruth 48
Studds, Maj. Gen. J.A. 146
Swanson, Lt. Ernest 11
Symolon, Col. W.P. 148

Tabacchi, Ray 134
Tafoya, Max 129
Taft, President William Howard 2
Tent camp 44, 55, 61, 72, 79, 80, 89, 99
Teorey, WO Robert 122
Teson, Sgt. A.J. 94

Teverbaugh, Sgt. Jesse 59
Thacker, Col. Miles R. 54, 147
Third Marine Division Assn. 154
Thomas, Adm. Chauncey 3
Thompson, 1st Sgt. Robert 109
Thompson, Lt. W.O. 126
Tijuana, Mexico 46, 133
Titania, USS 58
Traveno, Herb 130
Trometter, CWO Robert "Bull" 124, 126, 129, 130, 131, 134
Trujillo, Sgt. Francisco 63
Twomey, Col. D.M. 148

Underhill, Lt. Gen. James L. 44, 46, 50, 140
University of California, San Diego 92, 93
Upshur, Maj. Gen. William 45, 139

V-J Day 53
Van Horn, Pvt. Gene 82
Van Riper, Lt. Gen. Paul K. 162
Vandegrift, Lt. Col. Alexander A. 27, 29
Vilbrandt, LCpl. Nancee 60
Vogel, Brig. Gen. Clayton B. 139
Vostry, Capt. Robert A. 112
Vouza, Jacob Charles 155

W.E. Kier Construction Co. 23
W6YDK, radio station 115
Waddell, Staff Sgt. Fred 133
Wade, Maj. Gen. Sidney 59, 143
"Wake Island" 109
Walker, Lt. Col. Emerson A. 63
Walker, Lt. Gen. John T. 141
Waller, Maj. Gen. Littleton W.T. 16, 74
Walski, Pete 134
Warfare Leadership Center 154
Warren, John Mitchell 63
Waterhouse, Reserve Col. Charles M. 150, 154
Watson, Lt. Col. T.E. 38
Weapons Training Btn. 55, 92, 95
Webb, Jack 30, 59
Webb, Lt. Col. J.W. 38
Weede, Brig. Gen. R.G. 148
Weiss, Maj. Arthur 153, 154, 155
Wells, Rear Adm. Roger 17, 18, 24

West Coast Expeditionary Force 34
West Coast Regional Championship 133
West Coast Service Championship 125
West Virginia, USS 3, 4
Western Mail Guard 26, 29
Western Platoon Leaders Class 37, 39
Western Recruiting Region 70, 117, 169
Whaling, Maj. Gen. William 132, 141
White, Capt. Robert P. 42
Whitworth, Bob 134
Wilkins, WO Ford E. 122
Williams, Brig. Gen. Dion 137
Williams, Brig. Gen. Richard 139
Williams, Capt. G.A. 38
Williams, Col. Alexander S. 26, 27, 29, 74, 147
Willis, Maj. V.T. 58
Wilson, Commandant, Gen. Louis H. 65, 102, 119, 120, 136
Wilson, Congressman Bob 92
Wilson, Donald E. 156
Wilson, Earl 133, 134
Wilson, President Woodrow 4
Wilson, Sen. Pete 153
Winans, Col. Roswell 147
Winslow, Carleton M. 15
Wolkovitz, Sgt. Peter Paul 39
Women Reserves (WR) 43, 48, 49, 54, 92, 133, 167
Wood, Cpl. Charles O. 100
Woodring, Col. W.J. Jr. 148
Woods, Albert "Red" 124
Woods, MSgt. Victor L. 92
Wornham, Lt. Gen. Thomas A. 134, 142
Wulbern, Capt. F.M. 37
Wyat, Capt. Jimmy 33

XB-32 (Experimental Bomber) 48

YMCA, Armed Services 40, 55

Zacker, Michael G. 156
Zangas, Charles L. 156
Zimmerman, LCpl. Fred 135
Zimmerman, Pvt James L. 63

Selected Bibliography

Asprey, Robert B., Once A Marine: The Memoirs Of General A.A. Vandegrift, 1964; Berry, Henry, Semper Fi, Mac: Living Memories Of The U.S. Marines In World War II,1982; Cotten, Lenly M. The Brig Rat, 1992; Condit, Kenneth W. And Turnbladh, Edwin T., Hold The Torch High: A History Of The 4th Marines,1960; Fahey, Col. John E., A History of the Marine Corps Recruit Depot, San Diego, California, 1974; Gunn, John Alan, The Old Core,1992; Gunn, John Alan, (Quite) A Few Good Men, 1992; Hooper, Walter R., Guide To Administration United States Marine Corps, 1943; Kettner, William, Why It Was Done And How, 1923; Krulak, Lt. Gen. Victor H., USMC (Ret.), First To Fight: An Inside View Of The U.S. Marine Corps, 1984; Master, Mike, Once A Marine: Always A Marine, 1988; Moskin, Robert J. The U.S. Marine Corps Story,1977; Sledge, E.B., With The Old Breed: At Peleliu And Okinawa,1981; Sudsbury, Elretta, Jackrabbits To Jets: The History of NAS North Island, San Diego, California, 1992; Witty, Robert M. and Morgan, Neil, Marines Of The Margarita: The Story Of Camp Pendleton And The Leathernecks Who Train On A Famous California Rancho, 1970.

Numerous articles were used from the following magazines and newspapers: *Leatherneck: Magazine Of The Marines*; *Traditions: San Diego's Military Heritage*; *Marine Corps Gazette*; *Marine Corps Chevron*; and *The San Diego Union*.

Some of the primary sources used in this book were: Maj. Gen. Joseph H. Pendleton papers; Lt. Gen. Edward A. Craig papers; Historic District Evaluation, MCRD, San Diego; Eleventh Naval District papers.

Lt Col Daniel B. Cooks USMCR
083846   516 32 5969   0302/2502

Private, USMC, 1274637
Platoon 464 (Honor Platoon)
MCRD, San Diego, California
July – October 1952
SSgt Ambrosio Guillen USMC
Senior Drill Instructor
MOH, Korea, July 1953